On the Road to Tribal Extinction

ON THE ROAD TO TRIBAL EXTINCTION

DEPOPULATION, DECULTURATION, AND ADAPTIVE WELL-BEING among the BATAK of the PHILIPPINES

JAMES F. EDER

UNIVERSITY OF CALIFORNIA PRESS
Berkeley   Los Angeles   London

University of California Press
Berkeley and Los Angeles, California

University of California Press, Ltd.
London, England

Library of Congress Cataloging-in-Publication Data

Eder, James F.
On the road to tribal extinction.
Bibliography: p.
Includes index.
1. Batak (Philippine people)—Social conditions.
2. Batak (Philippine people)—Population.
3. Acculturation—Philippines—Palawan—Case studies.
I. Title.
DS666.B34E34   1987   305.8′009599′4   87-1861
ISBN   0-520-06046-6 (alk. paper)

Printed in the United States of America

1 2 3   4   5   6   7   8   9

To Pia, Alan, and Jonathan

Contents

Preface

In the closing decades of the nineteenth century, the Batak of the Philippines were a physically and culturally distinct population of about six hundred individuals inhabiting the mountains and river valleys of central Palawan Island. Isolated by land from other indigenous tribal populations on Palawan and by the Sulu Sea from all but sporadic contact with Filipino and Muslim peoples elsewhere in the Philippine archipelago, the Batak had evolved an elaborate tropical forest foraging adaptation. Like their presumed distant relatives, the Andaman Islanders, the Semang of the Malay Peninsula, and the various Negrito groups on Luzon, they lived in small, mobile, family groups and hunted or gathered a variety of forest, riverine, and coastal foods. Whether or not they enjoyed a state of "primitive affluence," the Batak must have achieved at least a modicum of success in meeting their subsistence needs and in resisting whatever perturbations penetrated their realm from the outside world, for they had survived for centuries.

By the closing decades of the twentieth century, however, the Batak were in disarray. No longer were they isolated from surrounding populations; everywhere were the homesteads and villages of Filipino farmers who had come to

Palawan in search of land and a better way of life. And no longer did the Batak appear to be an economically, culturally, or evolutionarily successful people. They still survived, as did a part of their former hunting-gathering lifeway. But even as they had also adopted portions of the lifeways of surrounding peoples, they found themselves in much reduced circumstances. Undernourished as individuals, decimated as a population, and virtually moribund as a distinct ethnolinguistic group, the Batak appeared destined for extinction sometime early in the twenty-first century.

The story of the Batak is one that has been repeated throughout the contemporary tribal world: a society that has seemingly thrived for centuries suddenly falters and passes out of the human record. In some cases, the causes of tribal disappearance are tragically obvious. In the centuries following the era of European expansion, the ravages of epidemic disease and wholesale alienation of land and other tribal resources obliterated hundreds of tribal populations. Many escaped these catastrophes only to fall victim to less visible but equally powerful forces—the ecological changes, social stresses, and cultural disruptions set in motion by incorporation into wider socioeconomic systems. Such a people are the Batak.

This work is a detailed account of the Batak's encounter with, and apparent defeat by, the "outside world." To be sure, it is not the first book of its kind. Charles Wagley's *Welcome of Tears*, an eloquent account of the demographic and cultural demise of the Tapirapé Indians of Brazil, is probably closest in subject and intent. Colin Turnbull's controversial *The Mountain People*, a case study of the Ik of Uganda, centered needed attention on the potentially grim consequences of culture loss and social dysfunction (regardless of any ethical questions it may have raised). At a more regional level but of the same genre are Shelton Davis's *Victims of the Miracle* and Christoph von Fürer-Haimendorf's *Tribes of India: The Struggle to Survive*. And beyond these recent and most closely related works, there is a long and important tradition in

Western anthropology of documenting the impact of modernization and development on indigenous peoples.

This volume differs from previous work on the subject in two important respects. The first is the breadth and depth of my data, which span a period of fifteen years—from 1966, when I first encountered the Batak while a Peace Corps volunteer assigned to teach high school in Palawan, until 1980–81, when I studied them for sixteen months while supported by a sabbatical leave from Arizona State University and a Wenner-Gren Foundation Grant-in-Aid. In between, I made a series of shorter visits to the Batak. I visited them periodically during 1968, at which time I was still in the Peace Corps but teaching adult Tagalog literacy in a Tagbanua community close to the Batak's home. I lived with the Batak for four months during 1972, following twenty months of dissertation fieldwork in a Cuyonon farming community elsewhere on Palawan, while supported by a National Institutes of Mental Health Predoctoral Research Fellowship. I visited them again for two months during 1975, then supported by an Arizona State University Faculty Grant-in-Aid.

Repeated field visits to the Batak over an extended period allowed me to come to know the entire population rather than just a sample of it. By 1981, I had visited all local Batak groups numerous times, and there were almost no adults and few children whom I had not met personally. Moreover, return visits revealed to me, as a single visit could not, the rapid and profound changes that had overtaken the Batak, making it possible for me to adjust my methodological approach as my thinking on their plight evolved. During my earlier visits I employed Cuyonon, the local contact language, but I later learned to speak Batak and to employ it in my fieldwork. Eventually, I was able to complete two thorough censuses, eight years apart, of the entire population; assemble an extensive array of quantitative data on how Batak utilize their time and what they receive from their various subsistence pursuits; measure the height, weight, and skinfold thickness of a sample of adults and children; identify the principal cultural beliefs and institutions that have been lost since World War II; record a detailed, week-by-week account of the settlement pattern of one entire local group over the course of a year; and collect a variety of more qualitative information about traditional and present-day Batak economy, society, and culture. I obtained, in short, a uniquely comprehensive set of data to work with.

The second respect in which this book differs from others on the subject concerns my analytical orientation and theoretical intent. While this book is fundamentally a case study, I have made a systematic effort to use this case to address some wider issues having to do with human adaptation in general. I am concerned, in particular, with the vital but poorly understood role played by human motivation and with the importance of ethnic identity in fostering that motivation.

In overview, my argument is that something has gone wrong for the Batak, as evidenced by carefully collected data on demography and nutritional anthropometry. These data show that, as a population, they are failing to reproduce at a replacement level and, as individuals, they are in generally poor health. I attribute this circumstance to adaptive disorder in the following manner. The *proximate* cause of Batak adaptive difficulties, I argue, is a complex of dysfunctional economic and social behavior of the Batak themselves: disinterest in work, poor diet selection, inadequate infant care, and the like. Such behavior may not differ very much from how the Batak have always behaved, but it no longer measures up to the demands of physical and cultural survival. The *ultimate* cause, I argue, is growing articulation with the outside world—or, more particularly, the precise nature of that articulation.

Connecting my ultimate cause, articulation with wider Philippine society, and my proximate cause, dysfunctional individual behavior, which occupies much of my analysis, is the notion of *social stress*. I argue that the manner in which the Batak have been incorporated into lowland Philippine social and economic life has severely stressed many of their social roles and relationships. Simultaneously, many traditional cultural beliefs and institutions have been eroded or have even disappeared, thereby undermining individual and cultural capacity to cope with social stress. In consequence, in this admittedly functionalist view of culture, individual Batak are so debilitated as to be unable to adequately meet the physiological, psychological, and social stresses—that is, the adaptive demands—of everyday life.

A crucial point is that while the adaptive demands presently confronting the Batak may appear heavy, they are not impossibly so. I believe there are genuine and unexploited opportunities for the Batak to "do better"—yet they do not appear to strive to do better. Were the Batak fat and happy, this matter would be, at least for an anthropologist, a nonissue. But it becomes a critical issue in the present situation wherein individual and tribal well-being is at stake. I hasten to add that I do not attribute the Batak's failure to do better to any intrinsic shortcomings. While I am extremely interested in the interplay of economic behavior and the cognitive and noncognitive attributes of individuals, I see these attributes as largely derivative of a particular sociocultural system. The Batak's problem is that their own sociocultural system is malfunctioning. For fifteen years I was strategically placed to observe a massive failure in one society's capacity to equip and motivate men and women to cope adequately with the problems they face and to otherwise survive physically and culturally as a distinct ethnic group. This work represents my desire to describe and analyze that failure and learn from it.

The manuscript was completed in the Philippines during 1984–85, when I was a Visiting Research Associate at the Institute of Philippine Culture of Ateneo de Manila University and while I was supported by an ASEAN Fulbright Research Award to undertake some comparative research on the adaptive difficulties of other Philippine Negrito groups. I would like to thank these and the previously mentioned institutions and agencies for their generous support of my research. I also acknowledge permission from *Mankind* and *American Anthropologist* to use previously published material. In addition, many individuals helped make this book a reality. I owe special debts of gratitude to George Appell, Nelson Asebuque, Pons Bennagen, Sheila Berg, Apolinario Buñag, Eduardo Cacal, David Cleveland, Thomas Conelly, Carlos Fernandez, Rafaelita Fernandez, Raul Fernandez, Brian Foster, Robert Fox, Raymond Hames, Thomas Headland, Barry Hewlett, Connie Kloecker, Edward Liebow, Emilio Moran, Keiichi Omoto, Pedro Nalica, Roman Palay, Ben Pagayona, Steve Pruett, Andrew del Rosario, Marsha Schweitzer, Thayer Scudder, Rudy Tirador, Ernesto Torres, Pedro Vargas, John Vickery, Reed Wadley, Charles Warren, and Felix and Amelita Yara. Most of all, I want to express my deep gratitude to the Batak, a warm and gentle people who deserve far better than their present lot in life.

Tables and Figures

1

Introduction

One of the most pressing global social issues of the late twentieth century is the rapid disappearance of many of the world's remaining tribal populations. This disappearance, which entails an irreversible loss of cultural institutions and, in many cases, actual physical extinction, raises scientific and humanistic questions of the most urgent sort. On the one hand, there are clear scientific imperatives—to record for posterity as much as possible about vanishing and distinctive lifeways and to explain, in evolutionary terms, why these lifeways could be so summarily extinguished after surviving for generations. On the other hand, there is the more humanistic concern to *do* something about "detribalization"—a concern that reflects not only a moral imperative but a growing awareness of the practical contribution that the cultural knowledge of tribal societies might someday make to *our* survival. But what *can* be done, or even what *should* be done, is often unclear.

This careful, detailed analysis of the detribalization of the Batak, a Negrito group in the Philippines, provides important insights into these questions. Traditionally nomadic forest-food collectors, the Batak inhabit the interior of Palawan, where their hunting-gathering economy was once finely tuned to their tropical environment and relatively undisturbed by outside influences. But, as a result of contact with lowland Philippine society, the Batak long ago began to "settle down": while continuing to hunt and gather, they also plant crops and trade with and work for their neighbors. As the consequences of these changes have reverberated through the fabric of Batak society and culture, they have paid dearly; they are declining in number, and many elements of their traditional culture have been lost. Indeed, some local groups have already disappeared, and it seems to be unlikely that many others will survive long into the next century.

It is well documented, of course, that tribal people[1] in all parts of the world have for centuries suffered from the adverse effects of the expansion of "civilization" into their traditional territories. Tribal suffering, as the result of European colonial expansion and, later, incorporation into modern nation-states, has ranged from habitat despoliation to disease and malnutrition to the decline of traditional cultural practices to outright tribal extinction. The social science literature on these processes is voluminous and includes both case studies (e.g., Cipriani 1966; Turnbull 1972; Wagley 1977; von Fürer-Haimendorf 1982) and more general assessments (e.g., Davis 1977; Bodley 1982; Goodland 1982).

The title of John Bodley's book, *Victims of Progress*, effectively captures the implicit model underlying much of this work. On this view, it is held that prior to contact, tribal societies enjoy a state of harmonious equilibrium with their environment and, if not outright primitive affluence, relative contentment. Such societies are contrasted with tribal societies, or the remains of them, after exposure to industrial civilization and "modernization," when their traditional "adaptations" have been disrupted or even destroyed by outside forces that the tribal people themselves cannot control. Indeed, except as sufferers or innocent victims, these people scarcely participate in the processes in question. The victims-of-progress model has helped to draw needed attention to the often tragic human costs of colonial expansion

and development. But it must be refined if studies of detribalization are to advance our understanding of the more
general processes of cultural adaptation, change, and evolution or to serve as effective guides to policymaking. The
model is deficient in two respects: it incorrectly stereotypes
the nature of tribal societies and cultures, and, more fundamentally, it fails to come to terms with the complex nature of
human adaptation.

Incorrect stereotypes of tribal societies are scarcely a recent phenomenon in anthropology; those associated with the
victims-of-progress model reflect its characteristic preoccupation with the alleged contrast between tribal societies and
modern industrial societies. Thus, it is often said that tribal
cultures are antimaterialistic (e.g., Bodley 1982:10–11). This
is simply not true about all tribal societies. The traditional
cultures of the Tolai (Epstein 1968; Salisbury 1970) and the
Iban (Sutlive 1978), for example, are said to have fostered
such personal traits as individualism and achievement orientation. Such traits, predictably, powerfully influenced the respective responses of these peoples to the opportunities for
participation in wider socioeconomic systems. Similarly, in
the Highlands of Papua New Guinea, a traditional precontact
emphasis on wealth accumulation, status achievement, and
competition helped spur postcontact cash cropping (Finney
1973). Those who stereotype precontact and postcontact
tribal societies should take heed of Baker's observation that
"the present-day integration of traditional populations into
the modern urban industrial societies is not producing a
uniform set of stresses or responses in the various populations" (1984:11).

The incorrect stereotypes of tribal society and culture visible in some approaches to tribal social change reflect, in part,
broader shortcomings in anthropological theory. Thus, not
only observers of tribal social change but ecologically
oriented anthropologists in general have long characterized
uncontacted aboriginal societies as being in some sort of
natural equilibrium (Love 1983:4). According to Love, there

is in such models "very little sense of contradiction and conflict in human societies, especially small-scale ones, either internally or with neighbors. Aboriginals, lying on the other side of the Rousseauian great divide, apparently have no serious internal divisions and seem to make few ecological mistakes until pressed upon by outside forces, despite growing evidence to the contrary" (ibid.).

Although the equilibrium assumption has been abundantly criticized, it is still common among anthropologists, particularly when contrasts with the modern world are at stake. But if we are to make a more pragmatic assessment of the impact of change on tribal well-being, it is essential to recognize that at least some tribal societies had serious ecological and social problems of their own prior to contact. Van Arkadie, in critically examining the notion that indigenous peoples made effective and ecologically conservative adjustments to their environments, puts it thus:

> If there was in some sense a balance, this was in part because the human condition was often nasty and short (although not, we must add, brutish). Among the reasons why such communities survived over the long term and did not destroy their environments were high death rates, which kept the population in check, and extreme austerity of consumption for extended periods. Before we succumb to sentimental visions of paradise lost, it is worth noting that ecological balance may be maintained in some circumstances by the tight limits on both population size and choices open to humans—an equilibrium at a low level of human welfare. ... Moreover, it is not clear from the evidence available, how far an ecological balance was in fact maintained. (1978:163–164)

The victims-of-progress approach to tribal social change is also naive theoretically with respect to the nature of human adaptation: it fails to address a growing consensus that such adaptation must be understood in terms of the reproductive and other strivings of *individuals*. Indeed, it is often unclear who or what, precisely, is being "victimized" by progress. Many anthropological analyses of tribal sufferings are vague and overgeneralized, conflating questions of the welfare and survival of societies and cultures with questions of the welfare and survival of *people*. When tribal peoples are said to be in difficulty, the difficulties may be inadequately documented. The "evidence" of distress may consist of informants' invidious comparisons of life in the present with life in an idealized past, or it may consist only of the anthropologist's own ethnocentric assumption that a person ought to be distressed by those particular circumstances. Many anthropological analyses of the impact of development on tribal societies have the appearance of reasonableness, which, on closer scrutiny, is revealed to derive from functionalist assumptions rather than from hard evidence. Even when there is adequate documentation of particular and serious physiological, psychological, or social impairments, the analyses may fail to specify how particular exogenous or endogenous changes brought about the impairments.

Because this model does not deal adequately with human adaptation, it obfuscates the fact that change and adjustment—including demographic fluctuation and culture change and loss—are normal processes in human societies. Knowing where the "best interests" of tribal peoples lie—in change or in stability—is an extremely difficult problem for which the victims-of-progress model provides limited guidance. As humanistically inclined outside observers, we may lament *any* culture change or loss in tribal societies, but we must recognize that not all such change or loss merits our intervention.

Finally, treating contemporary tribal peoples as victims of the changes going on around them obscures their frequent complicity in the detribalization process. This is not to deny the numerous and well-documented cases of tribal destruction following establishment on tribal lands of homesteads, logging or mining operations, corporate agricultural plantations, or large water projects. Where such intrusions have brought land expropriation, habitat destruction, epidemic disease, or even genocide, tribal peoples literally are victims (for such a perspective on the difficulties of tribal Philippine peoples, see McDonagh 1983). But many contemporary cases of detribalization do not involve such dramatic or readily identified external factors. Rather, less visible forces associated with the political economics of modern nation-states—market incentives, cultural pressures, new religious ideologies—permeate the fabric and ethos of tribal societies and motivate their members to think and behave in new ways. These new ways of thinking and acting are often dysfunctional with respect to individual and tribal welfare; that is, by their own changing behaviors, values, and preferences, tribal peoples bring many of their difficulties on themselves.

It should be noted that this assertion does not establish blame but, again, points out a crucial shortcoming in the victims-of-progress model: it diverts attention from the very processes of individual choice and change that must be understood if we are genuinely to assist tribal peoples in distress. Many anthropologists would argue, of course, that tribal peoples are entitled to embrace change, if they want to, on their own terms. But the model provides little room for them to make free choices with respect to change and even less guidance for determining whether these choices are "well informed." To be sure, difficult questions are involved. How do we distinguish voluntary from coerced choices? At what point will we conclude that tribal peoples must bear the consequences of their behavior, even if those consequences include tribal disappearance? But if these are difficult questions, they are best met head on, unconstrained by a paternalistic, even ethnocentric model that celebrates tribal societies as essentially good and sees the rest of the world as essentially evil.

Central to my analysis and to the theoretical contribution I hope to make is a focus on the wellsprings of individual behavior. The failure to focus clearly on individuals in situations of change—on their wants and needs, on the demands placed on them—in part explains, I believe, why a large anthropological literature on the impact of modernization on tribal societies, however valuable it is for documentary purposes, has contributed relatively little toward the construction of a more adequate theory of human adaptation and culture change. Too many anthropologists pay lip service to anthropological truisms about the centrality of individual decisions in cultural evolution but in fact treat individuals as helpless (and hapless) bystanders in the change process. Hence, my concern here with the circumstances, abilities, and motivations that influence the individual's decision making in times of rapid culture change—with details of the what, how, and why of sociocultural function and malfunction.

But how, in practice, are "function" and "malfunction" in human societies to be distinguished? These notions are closely linked to a central anthropological concept, *adaptation*. Although definitions of this term are readily had, one of the thorniest conceptual and methodological problems facing anthropologists interested in cultural persistence and change is the construction of indexes that satisfactorily measure human adaptive function and malfunction, or, as I will have it, adaptive "success" and "failure." Following evolutionary biology, anthropologists of an ecological bent have interpreted human adaptability as referring to "ecological success as measured by demographic, energetic, or nutritional criteria" (Moran 1979:9). Examples of such criteria familiar to anthropologists are a group's balance between natality and mortality and the relative energetic efficiency of its food-getting activities. These are only indexes, however; they are not a firm measure of "fitness," which, on this view, is reproductive success, something that is difficult to ascertain directly (ibid.).

Many anthropologists (and others), of course, are uncomfortable with the use of such materialistic and biologically derived indexes as the energetic efficiency of food procurement to evaluate human adaptive success. But indexes that take into account the kinds of factors they would presumably like to emphasize—for example, quality of life—are even more difficult to develop. Bodley's (1982:150) discussion of how one might assess the "standard of living" of a society is helpful in this regard. He does not introduce the concept of adaptation at this point, but his list of possible indexes for assessing societal standards of living loosely suggests some additional criteria for evaluating adaptive success. This list includes not only such previously mentioned factors as nutritional status and demographic structure but also health status, crime, family stability, and relationship with the resource base.

Such "quality-of-life" criteria have the important advantage of being potentially measurable in field research. In practice, however (and in the case at hand), it may be difficult or impossible to assemble adequate longitudinal data on change in such social attributes as "crime" or "family stability." But these are precisely the kinds of data that are essential if we are to rest an allegation of societal malfunction or adaptive disorder on more than condemnation of the present and idealization of the past. (In what society today are crime rates and family instability not said to be increasing?) Later in this volume, I attempt to build an inferential argument that factors not unlike increasing crime and family discord are in fact part of the general deterioration of the Batak lifeway. But I do not want the burden of proof that the Batak are in serious adaptive difficulty to rest on such allegations.

With the intent of keeping my own criteria for determining the presence or absence of adaptive disorder as broadly based as possible, I was initially attracted to Jochim's (1981:19) definition of human adaptation as "the possession of a valid set of solutions to a variety of problems." His approach, which owes much to Dobzhansky (1974), calls attention to the strategizing or decision-making aspects of human adaptation and to the fact that diverse goals, only one of which is reproductive success, underlie that decision making. I find both emphases congenial. But like many anthropological usages of *adaptation*, it is not clear in Jochim's definition how to distinguish, in practice, adaptation-related behavior from all behavior. Thus, while adaptive failure would presumably occur when a people's solutions for dealing with life's problems were no longer "valid," it is not readily apparent how to assess validity or how to distinguish *problem solving* from *living*.

I return in the conclusion to an emphasis on adaptation as successful coping with life's problems. For purposes of developing my empirical argument for the Batak case, considerations such as the foregoing led me to settle on a recent, narrower definition of adaptation articulated by Baker:

> An adaptation is simply any biological or cultural trait which aids the biological functioning of a population in a given environment. Thus, it includes such aspects as a population's health, ability to feed itself adequately, functional capability in its physical environment and reproductive performance. This definition encompasses the more precisely defined forms of adaptation used in genetics and the adaptability responses which are denoted by such terms as acclimatisation. However, it stops short of encompassing sociocultural adjustments which do not have demonstrable effects on human biological functions. (1984:2)

In my view, this definition has the advantage of implicitly specifying what will be taken as *evidence* of adaptive failure: presumably, it occurs when a population's biological and cultural traits are inadequate to support its "biological functioning," that is, to maintain its health, its subsistence, and its reproductive performance. These are the criteria by which I assess how well the Batak population is functioning (chaps. 4 and 5). Baker, furthermore, specifically juxtaposes against the concept *adaptation* the important concept *stress*. According to him "stresses are defined as those natural or cultural environmental forces which potentially reduce the population's ability to function in a given situation" (ibid.:2). This concept (developed in chap. 6) provides the crucial causal link, in my analysis, between biological malfunction (my proximate evidence of adaptive difficulty) and wider patterns of cultural disruption. The significance of such disruption is visible, in turn, in a final important attribute of Baker's relatively strict definition of adaptation: it specifies that certain particular cultural traits are involved with adaptation, namely, those that demonstrably affect biological functioning. This precision orients my analysis of how the disappearance of certain traditional cultural institutions and beliefs that once functioned to contain stress has undermined individual coping abilities and Batak adaptive well-being (chap. 7).

Despite my attempt to be precise, some may find my definition of adaptation—and thus my criteria for assessing adaptive well-being—too broad. Those of sociobiological inclination might want to argue that my approach diverts attention from the central issue of reproductive success. Durham (1979:47), for example, believes that successful human adaptation would be measured simply by the long-term representation of an individual's genes in a population. I have sought to make my approach consistent with evolutionary biology by using the concept of human adaptation in a way that rejects "adaptationism" (Gould and Lewontin 1979) and allows for imperfect adaptations and even for extinction (Greenwood 1984:66–69). However, in my view, which I believe is shared by many of my anthropologist colleagues, there is more at issue in human adaptation than reproductive striving.

Indeed, some might argue that my approach to human adaptation is too narrow. My criteria for assessing adaptive well-being, it could be said, take no account of such uniquely human attributes as highly developed cognition and emotion and thus do not allow for a response, for example, to the question of how tribal peoples themselves may feel, regardless of their physiological or demographic circumstances, about their changing lives. Certainly, the presence or absence of subjective or *psychological* distress is another possible index of societal ill-health or malfunction, one that has, in fact, also been employed by anthropologists. Savishinsky's (1974) study of the Hare Indians focused on the manner in which contact-related experiences have exacerbated endogenous social and psychological stress loads, with a heightened incidence of mental illness or psychopathology (as defined by the people themselves) being indicative of severe adaptive difficulty (pp. 217–219). Similarly, Bruner (1976:242), examining the kinds of adaptations that the Toba Batak have worked out with the modern world, takes their apparent "lack of internal stress" (i.e., psychological stress) as prima facie evidence that they are "successfully adjusting." The use of the absence of psychological distress as a criterion for adaptive success offers the advantage of being relatively nonpaternalistic. According to this, in effect, if people are satisfied with their new lives, who are we to question their well-being?

But this reasoning conflates broader issues of *adjustment* (admittedly important in its own right) with narrower issues of *adaptation*, which, after all, has to do with persistence over time. If methodological problems could be overcome, however, increasing psychological distress would in my view be a legitimate, even desirable addition to the more biologically oriented criteria I employ here to establish the presence of adaptive malfunction. Further, I see it standing in the same relationship to my variables as the criteria I have employed, that is, like nutritional and demographic difficulties, psychological difficulties (were they present) would likely have antecedents in ecological disruption, social stress, and cultural change. As it happens, I believe that the Batak suffer from a certain psychosocial malaise, but I did not attempt to systematically document this belief in the field. Later chapters will, however, provide some inferential evidence to support it.

Some may find the evidence of adaptive breakdown I do present to be equivocal. The Batak may seem to be disappearing, it could be argued, but it has seemed so for years. Similarly, some Batak may be ill or undernourished, but others are healthy and robust. That is precisely the point. The "disappearance" of the Batak has been protracted. In any one year, therefore, the circumstances of the Batak do not look so bad; to some, they might appear to be surviving or even adapting. I should perhaps point out that there is a timelessness to many studies of tribal societies which obscures the trajectories of change that such societies travel (and thus the historical and political economic factors that underlie these trajectories; see Love 1983:4). In my view, the emphasis in this work on the history of the Batak (or one hundred years of their history) is one of its great strengths. In any case, I hope that anyone doubtful of the evidence presented in chapters 4 and 5 supporting my argument that the Batak are in serious adaptive difficulty will withhold skepticism about the imminence of Batak disappearance until after consideration of the entire analysis.

Organization

Chapter 2 concerns the Batak as they were around 1880, on the eve of greatly intensified contact with outside peoples and with wider socioeconomic systems. While the Batak may have long practiced agriculture to a small extent and been in contact with trading populations in the Sulu archipelago for centuries, in 1880 they were still quite isolated in their traditional territory and firmly committed to a hunting-gathering way of life. The closing decades of the nineteenth century initiated a period of sustained migrations to Palawan by land-seeking migrant farmers from throughout the Philippines. Migration of lowland Filipino farmers, which greatly increased after World War II and continues to the present, would ultimately precipitate irreversible changes in Batak adaptation. But when these migrations began, the Batak, although not untouched, were still relatively undisturbed.

My reconstruction of Batak life one hundred years ago is only that. It is based on the earliest historical accounts of the

Batak, on comparative data from other, more isolated Southeast Asian Negrito populations, and on the oldest Bataks'
personal accounts of "life in the old days." These accounts
are stereotypical at best and of uncertain date, but with
caution, they can reasonably be projected back to the turn
of the century. If these sources seem an unsatisfactory basis
for an ethnographic account of a vanished lifeway, my approach is far more satisfactory than the commonly practiced
alternative—taking the surviving hunting-gathering component of a foraging people's present lifeway, blowing it up
to full size, and projecting it back into a timeless past as
allegedly exemplifying a once-universal hunting-gathering
way of life in some part of the world.

My particular concern in chapter 2 is to describe Batak
demography, subsistence economy, and settlement pattern at
the turn of the century. Whether my account applies equally
well (or with equal error) to the Batak economy and settlement pattern at some other time in the past is a moot point.
It is not my intention to present my account as some sort of
timeless, "aboriginal" baseline from which the Batak departed
only after millennia of stasis and isolation. Indeed, a second
concern in chapter 2 is to explore the forces of change that
had already shaped and altered Batak adaptation prior to
1880.

This provides the backdrop for chapter 3, which is a detailed account of how the Batak live today. I begin by
examining the striking changes in Batak settlement pattern
after 1880, as lowland colonization of Palawan progressed
and as they added new subsistence activities or changed their
emphasis on others. This is followed by an examination of
the annual subsistence round today, using an array of quantitative data on contemporary patterns of mobility between
various residential locations—settlement houses, agricultural
field houses, forest camps—to establish the rhythm of
economic life. Finally, I consider separately and in detail the
various components of contemporary subsistence economy:
shifting cultivation, collection and sale of forest products,

and wage labor. For each activity, I examine the characteristic patterns of time utilization involved and the typical caloric, protein, or cash returns.

The Batak's present-day subsistence stance exemplifies a type widespread among surviving Southeast Asian hunting-gathering populations, and in that sense, my account in chapter 3 is intended as a contribution to the ethnographic literature on the subsistence economies of such peoples. In my analytical emphasis, however, I depart from what I see as a common, but facile, assumption that the present-day "subsistence multidimensionality" of people like the Batak is evidence of their flexibility or adaptability. This is true of the Batak in the trivial sense that they have changed their use of time and resources in the face of changing circumstances, but such a characterization would divert attention from the *distortions* in Batak time allocation and resource use which are engendered by the political and economic pressures of a wider social system. This reasoning leads me to reject, for example, the view that Batak failure to farm more effectively stems from some covert cultural agenda, such as an alleged Negrito distaste for sedentary living or agricultural labor routines. Rather, I argue, continuing insecurity about land tenure and the threat of incremental alienation by lowlanders of any Batak agricultural improvements better explain the current state of Batak agriculture.

More broadly, however flexible or ingenious present Batak subsistence adaptation may appear, it is not oriented toward meeting some timetable or resource use optimal for the Batak alone but toward meeting the pressures and re-quirements of lowland Philippine society. The Batak do what they do because it is what they are *allowed* to do. Their subsistence system may seem flexible as a result, but, in fact, it is inadequate to their own subsistence needs. And while the Batak still survive, they are on the brink of physical and cultural extinction.

The evidence supporting this argument is presented in

chapters 4 and 5. Chapter 4 is concerned with adaptive difficulties at the population level. Based on a series of population estimates made since 1900, my own complete censuses of the Batak population in 1972 and 1980, and an analysis of fertility and mortality patterns, I argue that the core Batak population experienced a sustained decline from about 600 individuals at the turn of the century to less than 300 individuals in 1980. During this period, mortality was high at all age levels, and fertility was strikingly low. Women averaged only about four live births each on completion of their reproductive careers, not because they spaced their births but because many ceased childbearing altogether by their late twenties or early thirties.

Compounding (and in part concealing) the decline in the number of ethnic Batak was a dramatic increase, after about 1960, in the proportion of Batak who married outsiders. Indeed, by 1980, it appeared there would be few additional marriages between ethnic Batak. "Out-group" marriage, itself largely a consequence of prior depopulation and cultural disruption, has helped to stabilize the remaining population. But it has also accelerated the disappearance of characteristic Batak physical and cultural attributes; those who do remain are of increasingly ambiguous ethnicity.

Chapter 5 deals with the adaptive difficulties of individuals. The Batak have escaped the kinds of massive depopulating epidemics that have ravaged tribal populations in other parts of the world. But over time, small, localized epidemics of measles and influenza and a variety of chronic respiratory and gastrointestinal infections have taken their toll. I argue, however, that chronic undernourishment, rather than any unique genetic or physiological susceptibility, primarily underlies Batak problems with infectious diseases. A series of anthropometric measurements made over the course of a year show that many Batak are only at 70 to 80 percent of weight-for-height standards and, furthermore, that they undergo a famine season weight loss on the order of 3 percent. My interpretation of these data concurs with the appraisals of doctors and other trained medical personnel who have seen the Batak.

Taken together, chapters 2 through 5 document one hundred years of change in Batak demography and subsistence economy and, I believe, convincingly demonstrate that the Batak are in severe adaptive difficulty. Crucial causal links with respect to the behavior of individuals remain undeveloped, however. While such "involuntary" factors as high infant mortality rate and poor maternal nutrition help limit family size, some Batak deliberately restrict their own fertility and—the exigencies of poverty aside—are dilatory in caring for their living children. Again, even poor people are not helpless in the face of infectious disease, and the Batak's failure to mobilize the kinds of health and social support systems that are present among other tribal peoples must be accounted for. Similarly, although resource depletion and competition with neighboring peoples have certainly made the food quest more difficult (if the apparent ethnocentrism may be allowed here), the Batak could do better with their available resources.

These matters are taken up in chapters 6 and 7, wherein I relate the demographic and physiological evidence of adaptive difficulty (presented in chaps. 4 and 5) to wider patterns of social stress and cultural disruption attending the political, economic, and ideological intrusion of lowland Philippine society into Batak society. Sociologists and psychologists have placed more explanatory emphasis on the concept of social stress, and I begin chapter 6 by reviewing briefly the significance of this concept in these sister disciplines. In particular, I examine how the origins, mediators, and manifestations of social stress have traditionally been conceived, suggesting some modifications in these conceptual domains which make them more useful for anthropological purposes. I then describe how increasing stress levels have affected many traditional Batak social roles and relationships: those within domestic families, those between settlement neighbors, and those between the Batak and outsiders. I support my claim of growing social stress among the Batak with comparative observations of stress in other tribal groups undergoing similar changes.

Chapter 7 is concerned with how stress adversely affects the Batak. I show how culture change and culture loss attending the partial incorporation of the Batak into lowland Philippine society have undermined Batak ability to cope with the (growing) stresses of everyday life. Distinguishing between social networks and ego resources for coping with life's everyday stresses, I argue that many traditional cultural beliefs and practices functioned to sustain such resources. As these beliefs and practices have declined, stress-coping resources and individual well-being have deteriorated apace. Thus, the demise of shamanistic curing ceremonies during the 1960s and 1970s reduced Batak ability to mobilize vital supernatural and social support in times of sickness. Similarly, cultural disintegration and an associated erosion of ethnic identity have undermined an important ego resource, self-esteem. I cite comparative data relating disruption of psychological coping resources such as self-esteem to low fertility, impaired recovery from illness, inadequate care of the young and sick, and disinterest in work and suggest that similar relationships may obtain in the Batak case. Batak, meanwhile, emulate the life-styles of neighboring lowland Filipinos, but they so lack the wherewithal that the major outcome, I show, is further erosion of their own social identities and the creation of still other patterns of stress.

Chapters 6 and 7 thus detail the ultimate consequence, for one people's adaptive well-being, of rising stress loads and, at the same time, decreased stress-coping capacity, namely, a perilous decline in individual and collective ability and motivation to cope with the exigencies of survival. These chapters support and flesh out, in effect, the popular notion that indigenous peoples can be so overwhelmed by contact with (and incorporation into) the outside world that they lose the will to live.[2]

Chapter 8 places my findings on a broader stage—anthropological concern with the circumstances promoting the survival of tribal populations as distinct cultural entities. Briefly examining a series of apparently successful cases of adaptation and survival of tribal peoples, I explore the role that ethnicity and culturally constituted patterns of motivation play in helping such peoples resist marginalization to wider social systems. This exploration leads me to the notion of a "healthy society," one whose members possess sufficient resources to cope, individually and collectively, with the variety of threatening environmental situations posed by everyday life. A tribal people's resources for this endeavor may range from ancestral lands to curing ceremonies, but an underlying sense of ethnic identity everywhere imbues these resources with an overall coherence and thus helps to provide tribal peoples with a purpose in life. The familiar observation that contemporary tribal peoples somehow (like the Batak) lack motivation stems in part, I argue, from the vulnerability of tribal peoples' ethnic identities—and hence the vulnerability of their sense of purpose in life—to deculturating change.

2

The Batak as They Were

Palawan Island lies west and south of the main body of the Philippine archipelago, along a line running northeast from Sabah in the island of Borneo (see fig. 1). The fifth largest island in the Philippines, Palawan is home to three indigenous tribal peoples: the Palawan or Palawano, a shifting cultivation folk inhabiting the mountains in the south; the Tagbanua, another group of shifting cultivators inhabiting the riverbanks and valleys of the central mountains; and the Batak, a Negrito people inhabiting the north central part of the island.

The Spanish encountered Palawan in 1521, when the survivors of Magellan's expedition stopped there to seek provisions during their search for the Spice Islands. Based on his reading of Pigafetta's chronicle, Fox (1982:19) believes that the people they met may have been Tagbanua. In any event, their reception was friendly, and the Spanish apparently found food in abundance (Blair and Robertson 1903–1909, vol. 33, pp. 210–211). Spain, however, showed little interest in Palawan during its 350-year rule of the Philippines. Not until 1622, when five Recollect fathers reached the island of Cuyo, well east of Palawan in the Sulu Sea, did she attempt to garrison or establish missions in the region. There fol-

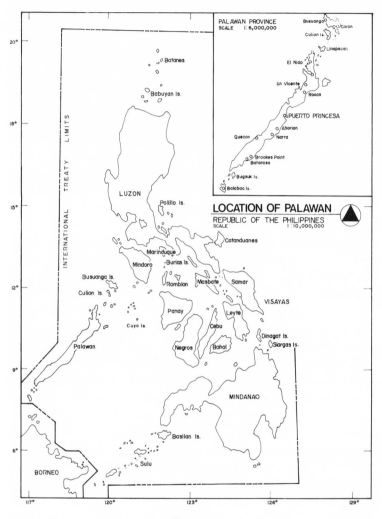

Figure 1

lowed sporadic efforts to extend Catholicism and political control of the island, particularly in the north. For the most part, these efforts came to nothing. Spain did construct a church and a fort at Taytay, a considerable distance north of the Batak. But until late in the nineteenth century, Cuyo Island, which had become the capital of Palawan Province, remained her only important outpost in the region.

More than lack of interest accounted for Spain's limited impact on Palawan proper: throughout most of her rule in the Philippines, Spain was locked in futile and costly combat with seagoing Muslims, who emanated from the sultanates of Sulu and Brunei, for political control of the more southerly portions of the archipelago, including Palawan. Despite numerous attempts, the Muslims never succeeded in capturing the fort at Taytay, but no Spanish outposts farther south on Palawan were secure from attack. The Spanish gained the upper hand in combat against the swift Muslim sailing craft only after 1848, when they acquired steam vessels (Saleeby 1908:221–223; Fox 1982:22). Even then, Muslims continued to raid Palawan's indigenous population for goods and slaves until the American occupation of the Philippines. Islam, too, retained its cultural presence in southern Palawan: the Palawano there show Muslim influence, and large numbers of Muslim migrants from Sulu and Cagayan de Sulu have settled in the region since the late eighteenth century (Conelly 1983:40).

By the midnineteenth century, some migrant lowland Filipinos were apparently already present in limited areas on Palawan's southern coast, on parts of the west coast, and in the extreme north. But only after 1872, when the town of Puerto Princesa was founded on a small, east coast bay on the middle part of the island, did Palawan become a destination for significant numbers of migrant lowlanders, first from Cuyo Island and later from throughout the Philippines. Even then, Palawan remained a little-known area on the periphery of Philippine economic and political life until well into the twentieth century (ibid.:39). In 1903, the total population of Palawan Island was estimated to be only 10,900 persons (National Economic and Development Authority [NEDA] 1980); most of these were probably Tagbanua or Palawano. Today, Palawan remains extensively forested and sparsely populated, and it is commonly regarded as the Philippines' last frontier. But, like all frontiers, it is rapidly becoming settled. In 1980, the island's population was approximately 270,000.

Of Palawan's three tribal populations, the Batak were always the fewest in number and the most localized in distribution. At the turn of the century, about 600 to 700 Batak inhabited a series of river valleys along a 50-kilometer stretch of coastline northeast of what is today Puerto Princesa City. As now, they closely resembled other "Philippine Negritos," both in their mobile hunting and gathering lifeway and in the physical attributes—short stature, dark skin, and curly hair—that earned these distinctive-looking people their name.[1] Approximately two dozen ethnolinguistically distinct groups of such peoples are found in the Philippines, including the Mamanwa of Mindanao and a series of groups known variously as Agta, Ayta, Aeta, Ata, or Ati scattered widely in northern, eastern, and west central Luzon, the Bicol Peninsula, and the islands of Panay and Negros. Philippine Negritos, in turn, resemble other small, dark, hunting and gathering folk of Southeast Asia, in particular, the Andaman Islanders and the Semang of the Malay Peninsula. Collectively, "Southeast Asian Negritos" have long been presumed to represent the surviving remnants of what was once a more widespread and more racially and culturally homogeneous population (e.g., Cooper 1940; Fox 1952). Such claims remain speculative. A more recent, and probably sounder, view is that each group of Southeast Asian Negritos represents the outcome of long-term, local evolutionary development under similar ecological conditions (Solheim 1981:25; Rambo 1984).

Philippine Negritos have been unevenly studied. The best known ethnographically are those of Zambales in west central Luzon (Reed 1904; Fox 1952) and the various Agta or Dumagat groups in northeastern Luzon (Vanoverbergh 1937–38; Peterson 1978; Griffin 1981). The Batak did not receive significant scholarly attention until after World War II. Charles Warren's fieldwork among them during 1950–51 led to a master's thesis (1961) and a series of publications (notably, Warren 1959, 1964, 1975). More recently, the Batak have been the subject of a doctoral dissertation by Rowe Cadeliña (1982).

I describe here the Batak lifeway as it probably was during the closing decades of the nineteenth century. The basis for my reconstruction is Batak oral history, comparative data on other, less disturbed Southeast Asian foraging populations, and the only two significant historical accounts of the Batak: a manuscript written in Spanish in 1896 by Manuel Venturello (1907), a member of the Puerto Princesa municipal council and a report by E. Y. Miller (1905), an American army lieutenant. I also make use of Warren's (1964) ethnography, which was based in part on these same sources. My purpose is not to determine whether in 1880 the Batak were "pure hunter-gatherers" (they were probably not). Rather, I want to establish two points: first, at that time, the Batak were still firmly committed to a hunting-gathering way of life in which other subsistence activities were recent or peripheral, and second, in 1880, they were still demographically, socially, and culturally intact.

My emphasis is on settlement pattern, subsistence economy, and those aspects of culture most closely tied to the business of making a living. Given the nature of my sources, my account must be largely qualitative, although I will hazard some quantitative estimates of those aspects of Batak adaptation of greatest comparative interest: local group size, frequency of mobility, length of workday. I have eschewed the temptation to report here any of the quantitative data (which instead appear in chap. 3) on such facets of the present-day Batak hunting-gathering economy as time allocation patterns or returns to labor at forest camps. For reasons explained below, however "aboriginal" life at contemporary forest foraging camps may appear, data obtained at them are of doubtful value for purposes of reconstructing the past.

A Tropical Forest Foraging Adaptation

TRADITIONAL TERRITORY

Palawan Island occupies a unique geological position in the Philippines. It lies at the northern edge of the Sunda shelf, separated from the main part of the archipelago by deep ocean waters but from Borneo by only 50 kilometers of shallow sea. When ocean water levels dropped dramatically during the Pleistocene glaciations, portions of the Sunda shelf were exposed as land bridges that connected Palawan to Borneo and thence to the Southeast Asian mainland. This circumstance explains the close present-day affinities between Palawan and Bornean fauna and the failure of a number of animal species (including some hunted by the Batak) to reach the remainder of the Philippine archipelago.

A chain of mountains runs the length of Palawan and is responsible for some marked climatic differences between the east and west coasts. Although the entire island generally has a June to December rainy season and a relatively severe January to May dry season, the western and northern parts of the island receive considerably more rainfall than the east coast, much of which is sheltered from the southwest monsoon. Indeed, the east coast of Palawan receives only about 1,600 millimeters of rain a year, making it one of the driest areas in the Philippines (Wernstedt and Spencer 1967:438). With regard to vegetation, such seasonally dry tropical environments contrast in important ways with humid tropical environments. In the humid tropics—roughly, where temperatures are consistently high and where average monthly rainfall is not less than 100 millimeters for any month of the year—are found the tall, lush, and species-rich evergreen rain forests often associated with this region (Hutterer 1983:178). In those tropical areas affected by marked and prolonged seasonal droughts, however, as in that part of Palawan where the Batak live, forests are consistently reduced in height, density, and species richness. Paradoxically, seasonally dry forests generally provide more plant food for human consumption than do rain forests. The latter have little vegetation at ground level, most potential plant food being in the canopy. But seasonally dry forests typically have a variety of more accessible trees, shrubs, and vines producing carbohydrate-rich seeds, fruits, and tubers. Such forests also tend to have more clustering of individuals of the same species than is found in forests of the humid tropics (ibid.:180–181).

Because of the rainfall regime and the soil and topography, Palawan has only limited agricultural potential. Rivers are characteristically short and steep, and the coastal plains are generally narrow. The kinds of fertile, alluvial soils most favorable to irrigated rice cultivation are found in only a few coastal areas. In the hills and mountains, thin and relatively infertile sandy clays and clay loams prevail (Wernstedt and Spencer 1967:437–438). Cashew and other tree crops prosper in Palawan, however, and recent years have seen considerable government interest in developing the uplands through various sorts of agroforestry projects.

Figure 2 illustrates that part of the island inhabited by the Batak. The area is rugged and mountainous. In some places, the mountains fall directly into the sea; elsewhere, there is a narrow coastal plain up to a few kilometers in width. Nine successive valleys whose rivers empty into the east side of the island compose the principal homeland of the Batak. From south to north, these are the Babuyan, Maoyon, Tanabag, Tarabanan, Langogan, Tinitian, Caramay, Quinaratan (Rizal on some maps), and Buayan River valleys. Today, most of these provide the names for a series of lowland communities strung along the highway that winds

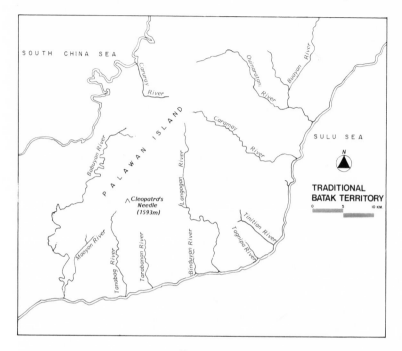

Figure 2

up the east coast of the island from Puerto Princesa City to Roxas. In terms of distance along the coast, Batak territory lies adjacent to a 60-kilometer section of coastline from the mouth of the Babuyan (58 km north of Puerto Princesa) to north of the Quinaratan. The coastline of Palawan makes a sharp turn between Langogan and Caramay, however, and the headwaters of the first five of these east coast river valleys are, in fact, all found on the various slopes of Cleopatra's Needle (1,593 m), a prominent cone-shaped mountain lying in the center of the island.

Some early sources report that Batak also traditionally inhabited a small area of the west coast of Palawan, on the Caruray River (see fig. 2). Indeed, much of Venturello's account derives from firsthand observations made during "the six years that [he] lived in Caruray at a place near the Batacs" (1907:549). Miller's oldest informants even claimed that the Batak of the Caruray area "are the ones from whom the [Batak] tribes of both coasts sprung" (1905:186). In contrast, Conklin's (1949:272) map of the distribution of the Batak shows them limited to the east coast, and I could find no contemporary Batak residents in the Caruray area. My own informants, however, agreed that Batak did once inhabit the Caruray area and that the present-day "tribos" there, an unusually dark-skinned folk known as "Caruraynen" and today regarded as a kind of Tagbanua, are of Batak descent. My own interpretation (in chap. 4) is that the Caruray River valley was once an alternative residence for the group of Batak who traditionally inhabited the Buayan River valley (fig. 2), from which it is easily accessible. The "Buayan" Batak, now extensively intermarried with Tagbanua, share some physical and linguistic features with the Carurayan "Tagbanua," with whom they in fact claim some affinity.

Excluding the Caruray region as anomalous, a crude estimate of the total area of aboriginal Batak territory may be obtained by totaling the separate areas of the nine successive east coast river valleys, following all drainages back to the spine of the island or to where they abut the watersheds of adjacent river valleys. The area thus obtained (shaded on fig. 2) is approximately 1,200 square kilometers, and it appears that despite its considerable size, the Batak were thoroughly familiar with it. Present-day Batak preserve remarkable inventories of place-names to identify various points on the streams and watersheds of their respective river valley. For example, along the meandering, 36-kilometer main course of the Langogan River, between its mouth and its headwaters at the spine of the island, Batak identify 90 distinct locations. More than 300 other features—mostly tributary streams, forest zones, and ridge tops—are identified elsewhere in the valley. Thus, a total of about 400 features are identified across the entire river basin, an area of approximately 240 square kilometers, for an average of about 1.7 named features for every square kilometer.

SETTLEMENT PATTERN AND SOCIAL ORGANIZATION

At any one time (or even in any one year), of course, the Batak occupied or visited only a fraction of their territory. They were a highly mobile people, however, broadly dispersed across the landscape in a series of transitory forest and riverine camps of constantly shifting size and membership but always consisting of a cluster of related, nuclear families (Warren 1964:89). As with other bilaterally organized peoples in this part of the world, nuclear families are the basic Batak production and consumption units. Such families make their own decisions concerning residence, activities, and relations with other people, and each is potentially self-sufficient economically, for a man and woman working together can obtain all the necessities of life (Estioko-Griffin and Griffin 1981:98; Endicott and Endicott 1983:5).

At the close of the nineteenth century, approximately twenty to fifty Batak families were associated with each of the river valleys that composed their traditional territory. The inhabitants of each apparently saw themselves as somewhat different from the Batak of neighboring river valleys. How extensive such differences may have been is difficult to reconstruct, but a suggestive comparison may be drawn with the socioterritorial organization of the Agta of northeastern Luzon and the Batek of the Malay Peninsula. Both are foraging peoples resembling the Batak, but their aboriginal settlement patterns are still relatively intact. The Batek reside within a nesting series of socioterritorial units, each more inclusive than the preceding one. The everyday residential units of family and camp fall within wider "river valley groups" and "dialect groups." When a dialect group spans several river valleys, differentials in social interaction are such that subtle cultural differences arise between valleys, as with respect to particular religious beliefs (Endicott and Endicott 1983:9–11). Agta settlement pattern is much the same (Rai 1982:61–83).

It appears that a greatly atrophied version of what was once a comparable form of socioterritorial organization still persists among the Batak today. Residents of the six southernmost river valleys, for example, share a single dialect, while two other dialects (one now moribund) are indigenous to the remaining three river valleys. It is also said that only in two river valleys did Batak ever practice their distinctive honey-season ritual.

A headmanshiplike institution may have given some political expression to the feelings of social and cultural solidarity shared by residents of the valley. Certain older men, by virtue of personality, emerge as natural leaders and become the focus of a residential aggregate. The opinions of such individuals are respected but are not binding; the others are free to argue or to leave (Estioko-Griffin and Griffin 1981:98). The degree to which such leaders traditionally influenced the affairs of Batak in an entire river valley (rather than day-to-day residential clusters; see below) is unknown. Warren does speak of a Batak "kapitan" for each river valley, but Batak political organization has been changed greatly by extensive borrowings from the Tagbanua and incorporation into the modern Philippine political system (Warren 1964:93–95).

Beyond any more structured social or cultural differences among Batak inhabiting different locales, each individual Batak has a powerful emotional attachment to the particular river valley in which he or she grew up. Similar attachments have been reported for the Agta (Griffin 1981:32) and the Batek (Endicott and Endicott 1983:5), and they are rooted at least in part in the practicalities of everyday life. Typically, one's closest kin are found there, and there, too, one gains an intimate knowledge of the terrain and the location of important subsistence resources. Not surprisingly, in these circumstances, most nuclear families ordinarily confined their movements to their river valley. Most marriages, furthermore, were between inhabitants of the same locale—a practice that, in turn, helped to maintain subcultural differences among river valleys. To be sure, marriage between Batak inhabiting different river valleys also occurred regularly and ensured that most Batak had kin in many locales. But the Batak were isolated enough and their numbers (both overall and within river valleys) were robust enough so that they had little opportunity, inclination, or need for marriage with members of other ethnic groups. They were, in short, still self-recruiting. As recently as 1950, when demographic disruption was already extensive, Warren observed that the Batak "seldom married Tagbanua" and that out-group marriage in general was only "occasional" (1964:65).

Whatever similarities or communities of interest all of the Batak inhabiting a single river valley may have shared, they did not ordinarily reside together. From the standpoint of the everyday business of making a living, the most important aspect of settlement pattern was the smaller living group in which the Batak went about their day-to-day affairs. Nuclear families may have been independent production and consumption units, but cooperation in production and sharing in consumption are central characteristics of hunting-gathering societies. Among the Batak, the principal social organizational context for economic cooperation and food sharing was the camp, a temporary residential aggregate sometimes consisting of only two or three nuclear families, sometimes many more.

A Batak camp consists of series of leaf shelters, each with a hearth in front. The shelters are cone-shaped dwellings constructed by placing palm fronds or wild banana leaves over a triangular framework of three or four poles that are positioned on the ground in a semicircular fashion and tied together near the apex with bark or rattan. Each nuclear family has its own shelter and hearth, as do any widows, widowers, or (at times) adolescents living in camp. The shelters are at varying distances and randomly located with respect to one another. Fairly steep slopes are sometimes favored, in which case simple floors are constructed. Camps can be located almost anywhere but are always near a water source, whether a riverbank, stream, or seep. They may also be located under rock overhangs (leaf shelters are not entirely waterproof) or on tops of boulders or rock outcroppings above streams (to escape mosquitoes and other pests).

Camp size and duration varied with resource availability, season, and inclination. At times, it was said, the entire population of a river valley—as many as forty families— would camp together. But more common, apparently, were extended family clusters of two to five households. Unfortunately, none of our turn-of-the-century observers of the Batak had much to say about settlement pattern. But the Cummings expedition of 1911–12 did report that the Batak lived in groups of two to three households (Field Museum 1983). Also, Warren believes that the Batak lived in small bands until the end of the Spanish era. He reports that even in 1950, and when the Batak were not at their (recently organized) settlements, they were dispersed in "highly transitory" groups of ten to twenty individuals (Warren 1964:89, 1975:68).

After two or three weeks, it is said, a group of Batak

camped at a particular location would deplete local resources
or tire of the area. They would then move elsewhere in the
forest and establish a new camp. This memory estimate of
past forest camp mobility, equivalent to about 17 to 26
residential moves per year, is consistent with ethnographic
observations of other, more isolated Southeast Asian hunting-
gathering populations. Rai observed local groups of Agta to
change residence 20 times per year (1982:105–107), and
Kelly, using data obtained during the 1920s, estimates that
Aeta bands shift residence 22 times annually and Semang
bands, 26 times annually (1983:280–281).

The Batak deployed from such camps to search for food.
A few subsistence activities—fish stunning, communal pig
hunts—involved all camp members in a common effort.
Most subsistence activities, however, were conducted by
smaller task groups, formed according to inclination and the
activity at hand. Thus, a group of three women might go off
to fish or to dig tubers or two men might go in search of
honey. In this fashion, men and women came and went
throughout the day. Any adults remaining in camp would
look after any children who had been left behind (Endicott
and Endicott 1983:7–8).

As food was brought into camp, it was shared with others.
While food sharing was a central aspect of camp life, it was
not done indiscriminately. Just how much food sharing
occurred one hundred years ago is, of course, a moot point.
The following description of food sharing in contemporary
Batek camps is strongly reminiscent of the way Batak talk
about food sharing in the past.

> Meat and vegetable foods are shared according to the same
> principles: that food is shared first with one's own children
> and spouse, then with parents-in-law and parents, and then
> with all others in camp equally. The result is that small
> amounts of meat, such as a small bird, and vegetables may
> not extend further than the immediate family. Usually, how-
> ever, meat comes into camp in the form of monkeys or other

animals large enough to ensure that all families in camp receive a share. Each household can normally procure enough tubers in a working day to last it a day or two, depending on the size of the family. Despite each family's having an independent supply of tubers, plates of cooked tubers are shared with each family in a small camp or with an equivalent number of families in a large camp. In times of need a family without food thus receives a share of vegetable foods, and in times of plenty the sharing takes on the appearance of a ritual exchange. (Endicott and Endicott 1983:8)

RESOURCE UTILIZATION

The Batak traditionally exploited food resources in three major resource zones: the forest, freshwater rivers and streams, and along the seashore. The first two zones were the most important. Tropical forests contain numerous useful plants and animals, and rivers provide a variety of protein foods. Ecozones in themselves, the latter also break the closure of the forest, which results in a distinctive growth of herbaceous vegetation at river's edge (Rambo 1982:264). The Batak were cut off early from effective access to the ocean (see chap. 3), and none of the historical sources mentions any Batak use of coastal resources. Many of the adults still living today did periodically visit the seashore during their youth to fish in the surf, collect clams, or make salt. But based on the Batak's own version of their past, foods obtained from the ocean, tidal flats, coral reefs, or strand were never of more than secondary importance. Indeed, Warren (1964:46) was told that in the distant past, the Batak did not fish in the ocean at all. The possibility that the Batak once extensively utilized coastal resources cannot be ruled out entirely, however; reef shellfish, for example, are important to Agta along the Pacific coast who often camp at river mouths (Griffin 1981:32, 35).

Tables 1 and 2 show the principal animal and plant foods the Batak say they once utilized. Much could be said about

TABLE 1
Batak Animal Foods

	Batak name	Other local name	Scientific name
Mammals			
Wild pig	baboy	baboy damo	Sus barbatus palawensis (Nehring)
Porcupine	dugian	durian	Thecurus pumilus (Gunther)
Palawan stink badger	tuldo	pantot	Sullotaxus marchei (Huet)
Scaly anteater (Palawan pangolin)	bay'i	balintong	Paramansis culionensis (Elera)
Palawan bear cat	amantoron		Arctictis whitei (Allen)
Little leopard cat	mire'	singarong	Felis minuta (Temminck)
Dwarf small clawed otter	dengen		Amblonyx cinerea cinerea (Illiger)
Macaque	bakes		Maceca philippinensis (Geoffrey)
Flying squirrel	biya'tat	tapilac	Hylopetes nigripes nigripes (Thomas)
Palawan tree shrew	ka'may	vilic	Tupaia palawanensis
Squirrel (small)	bising		Callosciurus (Gray)
Squirrel (large)	soysoy		Callosciurus (Gray)
Fruit bat	paniki	kabeg	suborder Megachiroptera (Dobson)
Insectivorous bat	kalagbeng	paniki	suborder Microchiroptera (Dobson)
Birds/jungle fowl			
Palawan peacock pheasant	tandikan		Polyplectron emphanum (Temminck)
Wild chicken	katian		Gallus gallus allus L.
"Birds"	manmanok		class Aves

Reptiles		
Box pond turtle	bayo'o'	*Cuora amboinensis*
Python	maraniyog	*Python reticulatus*
Water snake (?)	balinaynay	suborder Ophidia
Fish		
River eel	katsili	order Anquilliformes
"Fish"	seda'	class Osteichthyes
	(16 named varieties)	
Mollusks/crustaceans		
Shrimp	carundang	class Crustacea
Crab	kaye'ke	class Crustacea
Univalves	be'gay	class Gastropoda
	(17 named varieties)	
Insects		
Honey bee larvae	aniran	order Hymenoptera
	(5 named varieties)	

TABLE 2
BATAK PLANT FOODS

Batak name	Description	Scientific name
Tubers		
Kudot	wild yam	*Dioscorea hispida* Dennst.
Abagan	wild yam	*Dioscorea luzonensis* Schauer (?)
Ayabe'		
Banag		
Su'dan		
Suga'ok		
Wanday		
Carindang		
Greens		
Dar	escape taro	*Colocasia esculentum* (Linn.)
Katumbal	escape pepper	*Capsicum frutescens* Linn.
Sugi-sugi		
Katebek		
Bago		*Gnetum gnomom* L.
Biasaian		
Sandaen		
Paco-paco	fern	*Athyrium esculentum* (Retz.) Copel.
Baradong		
Bayakbakaw		
Anopol		*Poikilospermum suaveolens* (Bl.)
Fruits		
Popoan	breadfruitlike	*Artocarpis attilis*
Balisangkad	wild rambutan	*Nephelium lappaceum* Linn.

Bonog		
Paraminlolon		Koordersiodendron pinnatum
Malinapog		Durio graveolens Becc. (?)
Amogis		
Magarugian		Garcinia lateriflora
Candis		
Pangi		
Daga'a		
Lipsu'	applelike	Aglaia sp.
Alandeg	santollike	
Pega-pega	limelike	Citrus aurantifolia Swg.
Pa'o	mangolike	Mangifera altissima Blco.
Pali	mangolike	Mangifera sp.
Arupiran	carambola	Averrhoa carambola L.
Lakyaw		
Kindi-kindi		
Bul		
Lupok-lupok		
Wayway		
Bago		Gnetum snonom L.
Keliat		Gnetum indicum (Lour.) Merr.
Akaray		
Wild bananas (2 named varieties)		Musa errans (Blco.) Teodoro
Palms (5 named varieties)		Arenga sp.
Rattans (7 named varieties)		
Fungi (14 named varieties)		
Bamboos (3 named varieties)		Bambusa sp.

NOTE: Only those plants used for *pagka'nen*, or food, are shown; plants used solely for *pagagseum*, or seasoning, are excluded.

these, but here I will only discuss the more important ones and describe the ways they were obtained, loosely distinguishing among gathering, fishing, and hunting. For stylistic convenience, I write partly in the present tense, but it should be noted that I am attempting to describe the subsistence economy that may have prevailed one hundred years ago.

GATHERING. Wild yams and wild honey once provided most of the carbohydrates in the Batak diet. Approximately eight species of yams or other tubers were consumed. Each is seasonal and favors a particular environmental zone, where there is considerable clustering by species. The seasons of each species do not coincide, however; nor do their characteristic microenvironments. Thus, some yams were always available somewhere, although it was necessary to search for them. When and in what numbers harvestable wild yams will be found is somewhat unpredictable, but the Batak return annually to some areas known to have good stands. In general, though, yams were like other subsistence resources: they were sought and obtained by forest camp task groups going out in different directions over a period of time until the readily collected supply was exhausted. Small groups of women, together with their children, normally gathered yams, although men dug for them as well and helped carry loads back to camp (Endicott and Endicott 1983:12–13).

Kudot and *abagan* were the two most important wild yams (see table 2). Kudot is available from July through May. Its shallow, large tubers are easily dug, but they contain a poisonous alkaloid, dioscoreine, and must be peeled, thinly sliced, soaked in water, and rinsed before cooking and eating. This leaching process takes approximately three days, although it can be shortened by using seawater instead of fresh water. Abagan is available from September to July. While it may be roasted or boiled immediately, without processing, and is in fact quite tasty, its long, slender tubers grow deep in the ground and can be difficult to dig up.

The Batak collected the honey of five species of bees

during a honey season lasting from March to September. Seasonality in the availability of honey reflects seasonality in the food supply. The Batak identify about fifteen species of trees that flower between March and August and are thus important to bees. Honey collecting is a male activity, normally done in two steps. Suitable hives first had to be located, and to this end, men usually went out alone, walking transects in the forest while looking and listening for bees. (Of course, they also discovered hives in the course of other subsistence pursuits.) Those who were merely searching for hives often left their collection equipment behind, on the grounds they would not find a hive anyway or the hive they discovered would be so large that assistance would be needed or so small that collection would have to be postponed. If the finder of a hive did not plan to collect its contents immediately, he left a marker nearby to inform other would-be collectors that this particular hive was claimed.

Collection of honey from a previously located hive was normally done by a task group of two or three men assembled by the finder. A large and relatively aggressive bee (*Apis dorsata?*) provided the bulk of the Batak's honey supply. This bee characteristically builds a large comb on the underside of a seemingly inaccessible tree branch high in the forest canopy. The Batak, however, are skillful and daring tree climbers. If the main trunk is sufficiently gnarled or covered with vines, a man simply climbs it, cutting steps as necessary. Younger or lighter men may dispense with climbing the main trunk altogether, instead climbing the latticelike lianas that hang from the canopy to the forest floor. Once in the treetops, the Batak easily move from branch to branch and even from tree to tree. The necessary collection equipment is prepared in advance. A small, smoking torch of bark or bark cloth is used to drive the bees off the comb. Pieces of comb are then broken off, wrapped with the paperlike covering of a palm trunk, placed inside a container woven from rattan, and lowered to a companion waiting on the ground. The collectors first relax and eat their fill. Comb rich in larvae is

wrapped in tree leaves to take back to camp. The honey from
the remaining comb is squeezed into basins of palm or tree
bark, which are, in turn, emptied into bamboo storage con-
tainers. Up to 15 liters could be extracted in this fashion from
a single large hive.

Other important gathered foods included palm shoots and
rattan pith and various kinds of greens. Like wild yams, many
of these supplementary vegetable foods are seasonal and
irregularly distributed. Some of these foods could always be
obtained in the vicinity of a forest camp, however. Finally,
although the Batak recognize a large number of edible fruits,
only a few, such as the wild rambutan, apparently were of
more than secondary or incidental importance in the diet.

FISHING. Rivers and streams provided much of the animal
protein that Batak consumed on a daily basis. "Fishing" is a
broad term used here to include a variety of techniques used
to exploit aquatic food resources, such as hook and line,
stunning, damming, jigging, and simple collection by hand.
Both men and women, singly or in pairs, fish with hook and
line. A favorite time is the afternoon, partly because a Batak
can assess then what protein food might be available for
dinner, and if there is none, he can go fishing. Before trade
goods were available, Batak fashioned their hooks from
wood or bamboo and their lines from tree bark.

A more ambitious fishing technique entailed mobilization
of all the members of a camp to stun the fish in a section of
river or stream. Large quantities of a particular kind of bark
were obtained, twisted and pounded, and then soaked in the
stream to release the stunning agent, which temporarily in-
terferes with gill function. As the stunned fish floated to the
surface, they were collected by waiting men, women, and
children. As many as forty or fifty persons, it is said, would
participate in this activity. In another communal fishing technique, practiced when the rivers ran low at the height of the
dry season, a section of stream or river was dammed off,
rechanneling the flow into a flat area where any fish could be

caught by hand. River eels are a prized food, and a variety of ingenious methods were employed to obtain the elusive creatures. In one, a sort of underwater snare was set at dusk, using a small fish as bait and an overhead tree branch to set the hook. If the attempt was successful, an eel would be found dangling from the tree the next morning. In another method used at night, an injured frog was tied to the end of a stick and dangled in shallow water at river's edge. When an eel came to investigate the smell, it was killed with a club.

Finally, several important aquatic resources, for example, turtles and small crabs, were simply collected by hand. Most important, however, were the univalves, which are small black mollusks inhabiting the undersides of stones in rivers. Univalves are abundant and, unless the rivers are flooding, always available. A basketful can be obtained on short notice if nothing more appealing is available for dinner. Collection is easiest during the night, when they lie on the tops of rocks and, with the aid of a torch, are easily seen from above the water.

HUNTING. "Hunting" embraces a variety of methods for obtaining forest animals. Culturally and perhaps also economically, wild pig was the most important. It is the only wild animal that is the focus of any ritual activity (e.g., hunting charms), and Batak hunters consider themselves, first and foremost, to be pig hunters. Both the bow and arrow and the spear (the latter in conjunction with hunting dogs) are employed today to take pigs. Batak now say they have "always" hunted with spears. But use of spears was not reported by Miller (1905) or Venturello (1907), which suggests that the spear/hunting dog complex may have been acquired in more recent times from the Tagbanua (see Conelly 1983:366–368).

Bow and arrow hunting is unquestionably "Batak." The bow is of palm; the arrow is of rattan, with a bamboo point. Ambush hunting by solitary archers was the most common technique. Fallen fruits are a major food source for wild pigs,

and the Batak identify about fifteen species of trees whose
seasonal fruits are of sufficient interest to wild pigs to justify
an ambush attempt near one of them. During any month
(although not necessarily every day), an ambush hunter
could locate a tree with its fruit rotting on the forest floor. A
pig arriving to feed was shot from a distance of 3 or 4
meters, either after a soundless stalk or from a blind previously constructed high in a nearby tree.

A communal pig hunt was more distinctive. A line of
women would ascend a mountainside shouting and beating
the bush and thus driving any pig in the area toward a line of
waiting archers at the top. A group of at least 15 to 20 men
and women was required, with 50 to 60 said to be optimal.
Venturello apparently observed such a hunt firsthand. He
provided the following colorful narrative:

> The most interesting and peculiar way among [the Batak] in
> hunting the wild boar and perhaps the most certain and
> complete method is the following: All of the people of the
> settlement, including women and children, will go to a place
> known by them to be the trail of the boar. The place is
> usually some point of the mountainous land lying along the
> sea. Certain men who are skilled in shooting the arrow take a
> position well selected, where in all probability the animals
> will pass. The women and children and unoccupied men will
> spread about in the woods, breaking forth into terrible
> shrieks, some howling and others barking like dogs. These
> shouts and noises bewilder the boars, which hasten toward
> the positions taken by the shooters who await them with
> bow and arrow. Very often they escape the darts and jump
> into the sea. But two bancas having previously been pre-
> pared and manned, the poor animals cannot escape that way.
> This hunt usually continues for a day and even longer. After-
> wards they return to their houses with the spoil. (1907:554)

Several ingenious hunting techniques were used to obtain
a variety of other forest animals. Some, like the Palawan
peacock or the scaly anteater, were exceptionally tasty and

only a relatively infrequent part of the Batak's diet; others, like the gliding squirrel, may have contributed to the Batak's meat supply to an extent comparable to wild pig. Gliding squirrels are primarily nocturnal and are taken during daytime hours by surprising them in their nests, which are typically located well above the ground in holes in tree trunks. As any untoward noise on a nest-bearing tree may cause the nest's inhabitants to depart before they can be captured, the hunter often climbs an adjacent tree and works from there. He uses a long pole to maneuver a pluglike tube made of bark and filled with dry leaves into the nest opening. With the squirrels thus prevented from escaping, the hunter then climbs to the nest and ignites the contents of the tube, drawing out the air from the nest and asphyxiating the occupants. A lucky hunter might catch an entire family of four or five in this fashion. Gliding squirrels might be the primary object of the hunt or they might be taken in the course of searching for pigs or honey.

Some animals, such as anteaters and porcupines, were captured with the hands or killed with a pointed stick or club when encountered. Snares were used to take jungle fowl. Monkeys and other small mammals were taken with the blowgun—also once used, it is said, to repel would-be Muslim slave raiders. How important the blowgun may have been for subsistence purposes, in comparison to the bow and arrow, is impossible to know, for the weapon fell into disuse after World War II. At the time of Warren's postwar fieldwork, the Batak apparently still had blowguns but used them "infrequently for hunting" (Warren 1964:44). Today, the blowgun has disappeared entirely, and only the oldest Batak men report that they hunted with them during their youth. Turn-of-the-century observers, however, all reported that the Batak used blowguns (e.g., Miller 1905:183–184), and Cole, based on his 1907 visit, even described it as their "chief weapon" (1945:82). It may be that changing dietary preferences and growing market involvement led the Batak to abandon the blowgun about the time they began using

spears and hunting dogs and, perhaps, became more preoc-
cupied with hunting wild pigs.

I do not want to offer any argument concerning whether
one of these subsistence activities was in some way traditionally "more important" than another or whether one sex traditionally contributed more than the other to the food supply. These are not unimportant questions, but they simply
cannot be answered in any reliable way for the Batak based
on what they do or say today. The salient point, in my
opinion, is that all the evidence suggests the Batak found
wild plant and animal food resources sufficiently varied and
abundant that they could indeed have subsisted by hunting
and gathering alone, did they ever need or choose to do so.

Just how reliable this food supply was and how much
work normally was necessary to obtain it are questions that
are similarly unknowable, but the urge to speculate is irre-
sistible. While the Batak generally view the past as a time of
plenty, they do say that their forebears knew hunger. But
such hunger, it is said, was only experienced from "time to
time" and, even then, only for a day or two. It seems to me a
reasonable enough, perhaps likely, proposition that even
under the old subsistence regime, food periodically ran short.
A single, late season rainstorm can make trails difficult, rivers
impassable, and people cold, wet, and miserable. Further,
people do, after all, procrastinate or grow lazy now and
again, and food is not always found where it is sought.
Hence, any arcadian notions that one never went hungry in
the tropical forest should be laid aside. There may even be
some truth to the Batak's claim that when food was scarce,
the rattan waistbands traditionally worn by women for deco-
ration also helped to minimize hunger pangs.

As for how much "work" the Batak did to obtain the food
they ate, four hours a day per adult seems an appropriate
estimate. I arrived at this by deflating the current work load
(chap. 3) to take account of the resource depletion and market involvement that today affect Batak subsistence behavior

and also to take account of similar work load estimates for other, more isolated Southeast Asian hunting and gathering populations (e.g., Fernandez and Lynch 1972:45). For example, Endicott has attempted to reconstruct how much work the Batek would have to do if they dug tubers to obtain the calories they now get by collecting and exchanging rattan and thus obtained all of their food by hunting and gathering. He estimates that men would work about 34-1/2 hours per week, yielding the same average per adult—about 28 hours per week—as my own estimate (Endicott 1984:40). I return to the question of length of the Batak workday below (chap. 3).

Trade, Agriculture, and the Aboriginal Southeast Asian "Hunting and Gathering" Adaptation

The account of Batak subsistence activity at the close of the nineteenth century is idealized in several obvious ways, one of which is the absence of any mention of possible Batak involvement with other subsistence pursuits—trade, agriculture—besides hunting-gathering. To be sure, the Batak themselves are emphatic in their claim that in the distant past their ancestors survived *only* by hunting and gathering. Projected far enough into the past, this proposition is indisputable. But the fact is that at the close of the nineteenth century, the Batak were already engaged in some trade and some agriculture. Unfortunately, however, there is little evidence that can be brought to bear on the intriguing question of precisely when the Batak (or any other Philippine Negritos) first became involved with these activities.

Agriculture is likely the newer of the two pursuits. Venturello apparently thought that agriculture was then a recent acquisition. "Twenty-five or thirty years ago," he wrote, "the Batak were nomads. They formed no rancherias and slept

wherever night overtook them" (1907:547). His account is
self-contradictory, however, and the reader is unsure of what
to conclude from passages such as the following.

> The Batacs of the mountain engage neither in agriculture nor
> in commerce. They show no kind of interest or love for
> planting palay which is their principal food; neither do they
> care to plant the tubers which are a substitute for rice in
> times of scarcity. For this reason there is much misery when
> there is no harvest. Scarcely one family among them will
> plant in their badly prepared soil 6 gantas of palay, and
> seed fields are very rare that contain 25 gantas of seed.
> (Ibid.:553)

Miller (1905:183) had even less to say about Batak
agriculture, commenting only that "they do not cultivate the
soil, except to set out a few plants which yield edible roots,
and in a few places plant small fields of rice." Of course, a
casual or ethnocentric observer could make similar observations about Batak agriculture today, and so we are scarcely
able to conclude that agriculture was a recent acquisition
at the time the Batak were observed by Venturello and
Miller.

Actually, a case can be made that *rice* may have been
acquired by the Batak only in the latter part of the nineteenth
century. The Batak themselves still make statements like "Rice
is new here" and "I don't know where that rice came from."
Perhaps it was introduced by migrant Cuyonon swidden
farmers, pushed outward from their home island of Cuyo
by population growth and declining soil fertility to search for
frontier lands for rice cultivation. By the nineteenth century,
many Cuyonon traveled by sailboat to Palawan each January
to make their swiddens on rich, virgin forest soils, returning
home in September with their newly harvested rice. Many of
these farmers eventually settled permanently in Palawan and
founded scattered communities along the coastal plain. In
that part of Palawan inhabited by the Batak, Cuyonon came
to employ them to assist in the chores of field clearance; it

may be that the Batak learned the techniques of rice cultivation from these early lowland arrivals. The Batak do speak
of a prerice agricultural complex, in which millet, yams, taros,
and sweet potatoes were the principal crops planted. But
there is no evidence on the possible antiquity of such a
complex in Palawan.[2]

Contemporary observers of other Philippine "hunting-
gathering" peoples now stress the antiquity of agriculture
among them. Rai (1982:165–166) estimates that the Agta
have practiced some horticulture for at least two hundred
years, and he points to some sketchy evidence that other
Negrito groups have practiced it even longer. Estioko-Griffin
and Griffin (1981:97) say that rumors of remote present-day
Agta who neither trade nor cultivate "seem to be without
substance." They believe that "all but the most remote Agta"
were involved with horticulture after about 1900, noting that
the group had been in regular contact with farming peoples
since the earliest Spanish attempts to conquer the Cagayan
Valley (ibid.:102). Qualifying statements, however, often
call attention to the limited *dependence* of Negrito groups on
farming. Thus, Agta families in the Casiguran area make
swiddens, but even today, "few do it every year" (Headland
1975:249).

A large part of deciding when particular groups of people
began to practice agriculture lies, of course, in identifying
what "agriculture" in fact is. Reviewing current knowledge of
the history of Southeast Asian agriculture generally, Hutterer
(1983) has correctly criticized a long-standing tendency to
regard hunting and gathering and agriculture as fundamentally different kinds of subsistence pursuits. While it is true
that farmers manipulate their environment to increase food
production, hunter-gatherers do so as well, deliberately or
inadvertently. Thus, hunter-gatherers are known to disperse
the seeds of valued wild fruit trees, to use fire for clearance,
and to replant wild yams after collection or to otherwise look
after wild plants of interest to them. Such activities are not
far from the characteristic agricultural activities of domesti-

cation and cultivation, and they have probably gone on for a
very long time indeed (ibid.: 171–177).

Trade relationships involving Negritos and centering on
the exchange of commercially valuable forest products for
foodstuffs and manufactured goods are probably of still
greater antiquity. All turn-of-the-century observers of the
Batak commented on their involvement with trade. Alfred
Marche, an early European visitor to Palawan, wrote a colorful narrative. Although it is of limited utility with regard to
the Batak, he does report that he visited Babuyan in 1883 in
the hope of seeing the Batak, "who came sometime to bring
almaciga (copal), which they exchanged for rice, but the
strong rain of the preceding day made them stay in the
mountains" (Marche 1970:224). Miller (1907:547) noted
that the Batak brought copal to the coast to exchange for
"rice, beads, and bolos." And, according to Venturello:

> Now they have commercial relations with strangers and
> admit them with hospitality and confidence. Among this
> number they choose one who inspired them with confidence
> and gave them protection. The Batacs give to him the title of
> agalen, which means friend. He it is who provides all they
> need, such as bolos, cooking utensils, etc., including rice in
> times of scarcity; in exchange for these articles bringing to
> him almaciga, bejuco, and wax. (1907:547)

Venturello apparently believed that Batak trade relations
were relatively new. In the passage cited earlier, he reported
on Batak located more remotely who still engaged "neither
in agriculture nor in commerce" (ibid.:553).

Other kinds of evidence suggest, however, that the Batak
may have engaged in trade for centuries. According to Hutterer (1977), based on ceramic evidence, foreign trade con-
tacts with the Philippines, in general, began sometime during
the period from the tenth to the twelfth century, and foreign
trade may be of even greater antiquity than a preoccupation
with Chinese ceramics suggests. South China is known from
documentary evidence to have carried on a vigorous trade

with the Philippines at least since the early thirteenth century (Fox 1967; Conelly 1985). Although there is no unambiguous reference to Palawan in early Chinese documents, Kress (1977:46) believes that the island was involved in the Chinese trade from the beginning, that is, for about one thousand years. The first documentary evidence of such involvement comes from the early seventeenth century: in a letter to the king of Spain, Recollect missionaries who had settled on Palawan commented favorably on the productivity of its forests and noted that rattan, beeswax, and edible bird nests were common trade items (Blair and Robertson 1903–1909, vol. 21, pp. 309–310). By the latter part of the eighteenth century, and as the sultanate of Sulu grew in influence, trade in rattan and copal flourished between British merchants in northern Borneo and Muslim traders in southern Palawan (Warren 1981:138).

Unfortunately, nothing is known about when the Batak first became involved in Palawan's external trade. But other Philippine Negrito groups are known to have engaged in trade for hundreds of years. In the 1600s, for example, trade (subsequently stopped by the Spanish colonial government) was reported between Pampanga Negritos and Chinese (Larkin 1972:48). The Spanish themselves bartered with some Negrito groups, exchanging tobacco for beeswax, which was needed to strengthen Spanish looms (Rahman 1963:144). Rai (1982:154) surmises that Agta-lowlander trade must be at least three hundred years old. While the evidence is circumstantial, an assumption of Batak involvement in trade for at least a comparable period seems justified.

In practice, collection and exchange of commercially valuable forest products and hunting and gathering of wild foods for subsistence purposes fit so closely together in this region—and have fitted so closely for so long—that there may be little point in speculating about what a "pretrade" Southeast Asian hunting-gathering adaptation might have been like. Indeed, the view that any of the world's remaining hunting-gathering peoples were isolated until recently from regular social interaction with their more settled neighbors is now widely questioned. It has long been assumed, for example, that Pygmy populations inhabited the tropical rain forest in the Congo Basin long before the advent of agriculture in the region (e.g., Turnbull 1965; Cavalli-Sforza 1977). But based on their research among the Efe Pygmy, who obtain much of their subsistence from the Walese, their horticultural neighbors, Bailey and Peacock (n.d.) have questioned whether the Efe or any other human population ever inhabited the African rain forest independent of contact with agricultural peoples.

Similarly, Fox (1969) has criticized the view that such South Indian hunter-gatherers as the Birhor and Chenchu are some sort of isolated and independent cultural "leftovers" from the past. He argues that their entire economic regimen is geared to trade and exchange with the more complex agricultural and caste communities within whose orbits they live (ibid.: 141). While they are not residentially enclaved, Indian hunter-gatherers otherwise resemble the occupationally specialized, hereditary caste groups that evolved with wider Indian civilization. They may dwell in the forest, but they are not self-sufficient there, for they regularly obtain essential subsistence and ceremonial goods from an outside society that they, in turn, supply with "desirable, but otherwise unobtainable, forest items such as honey, wax, rope and twine, baskets, and monkey and deer meat" (ibid.). Furthermore, such vital aspects of tribal social structure as settlement pattern and family and kin organization all reflect a distinctive lifeway as forest-dwelling traders or "professional primitives" (Fox 1969; see also Morris 1982).

The cases of the Birhor and the Chenchu may be extreme, if only because these peoples evolved within the orbit of India—a civilization both economically and socially complex. But recently, two more isolated and seemingly classic cases of "surviving hunter-gatherers," the San of the Kalahari and the Punan of Borneo, have been reinterpreted along similar lines by Schrire (1980) and Hoffman (1984), respectively. Both critically reassess the available evidence and argue that these allegedly "pristine" hunting and gathering peoples, or peoples very much like them, have actually been in regular outside contact with surrounding populations for centuries. Both also criticize as too facile the tendency of earlier anthropologists and observers to dismiss any observed "effects of contact" as if they were a recent "overlay" on an otherwise pure hunting and gathering base (Schrire 1980:12).

In summary, in 1880, the Batak were already engaged in some trade and some agriculture. Although the available data are inadequate to determine how recently these activities might have begun, it seems reasonable to conclude that the Batak then were still an endogamous and largely self-sufficient population, demographically and culturally intact and still firmly committed to a hunting-gathering economy.

3

The Batak as They Are Today

Even today, the Batak can be characterized as hunter-gatherers. They still hunt and gather, and unlike those numerous farming folk who hunt and gather to supplement their agricultural activities, the Batak can do it on an exclusive basis for weeks or even months at a time. But the Batak today could just as well be characterized as shifting cultivators who also hunt and gather or as traders of forest products and wage laborers who also happen to forage and farm. We must set aside the legacy of a now-distant past and recognize that today it is difficult to give priority to any one activity in characterizing contemporary Batak subsistence economy. One hundred years of change have left the Batak with a genuinely multidimensional subsistence adaptation, each component of which is interwined with (and in part constrained by) the others.

I would not claim that the Batak's present subsistence adaptation represents an end or steady state; further change is certain. I do not believe, however, that the Batak are traveling an evolutionary trajectory from full-time hunting and gathering to full-time agriculture. Such assumptions are common with respect to Philippine Negrito groups and are apparent in the title of Warren's (1964) monograph on the Batak ("A Culture in Transition") and Rai's (1982) dissertation on the Agta ("From Forest to Field"). My opinion is that the "forager to farmer" assumption is naive, for it fails to recognize either the possible antiquity of part-time Negrito farming (chap. 2) or the possibility of other outcomes besides full-time farming for Negrito groups undergoing subsistence change. A tendency to see Philippine Negritos as being "in transition," or at least as being more in transition than other kinds of people, is probably more an artifact of anthropological reliance on "pure" models (pure hunter-gatherers, pure agriculturalists) than reflective of any actual tendency for mixed adaptations to be likelier to change over time than pure ones.

   This chapter begins with an examination of the evolution of Batak subsistence economy during the last one hundred years. I show how, as new subsistence activities were added or old ones grew in importance after 1880, the complexity of settlement pattern increased rapidly. To develop the rhythm of contemporary economic life, I explore how the kinds and frequency of mobility between various residential locations over the course of a year reflects the characteristic scheduling of the principal Batak subsistence activities. I also relate the evolution of Batak settlement pattern and subsistence activities to wider patterns of sociopolitical change affecting this part of Palawan after 1880.

   I do not break new ground in emphasizing the opportunistic, multidimensional nature of contemporary Batak subsistence economy; similar interpretations have been offered by Endicott (1974:32–36) for the Semang and by Griffin (1981:32) for the Agta. But I do depart from what I see as a common but simplistic assumption that a people's subsistence multidimensionality is prima facie evidence of their "adaptability" or "flexibility." While the Batak engage in a variety of subsistence pursuits, they do not perform any of them very well.

   In the second part of the chapter, I support this seemingly ethnocentric assertion by examining separately and in turn Batak hunting-gathering, agriculture, and trade/labor relationships with lowlanders, as these activities are practiced today. I use data on time allocation and returns to labor to argue that Batak pursuit of each activity is at a comparatively low level of efficiency and remuneration. My wider point is that we have every reason to expect less than optimal economic performance from the Batak. Depopulation and deculturation (taken up in later chapters), together with ecological displacement and partial sedentarization, have helped make Batak subsistence decisions—and even Batak settlement pattern itself—uniquely responsive to the insistent pressures of an outside economic system rather than to the needs and interests of the Batak themselves. While one can argue that the Batak are somehow making the best of a bad situation, it is essential to recognize that the situation is such that the Batak's economic performance may not be adequate to the exigencies of physical and cultural survival.

A Settlement Pattern Approach to Batak Subsistence Economy

It has been shown (chap. 2) that shifting cultivation, trade in forest products, and perhaps even wage labor for lowlanders were all part of Batak subsistence economy by the end of the nineteenth century. But the importance of these activities was sufficiently peripheral that it seemed reasonable to believe that the Batak then still *lived* as hunters and gatherers, in lean-tos at temporary forest camps inhabited by small numbers of closely related families. As the present economy evolved, however, Batak settlement pattern changed accordingly, with consequent rearrangement of spatial and social relationships among the Batak themselves and between the Batak and lowlanders.

THE EVOLUTION OF BATAK SETTLEMENT PATTERN, 1880–1980

Two major changes in Batak settlement pattern occurred after contact with lowland peoples and social systems intensified. The first, dating to the closing decades of the nineteenth century, was the emergence of a pattern of seasonal residence in upland rice fields. The second, dating to the early decades of the twentieth century, was the emergence of a pattern of seasonal residence in lowland-style "settlements." Each change fundamentally reoriented Batak economic affairs and social relationships toward greater participation in lowland Philippine society, even as each change reflected, in part, incremental land alienation and other threats to Batak resources by Filipino settlers.

Only after the arrival of lowland settlers in Palawan, it is said, did Batak involvement with agriculture intensify to the extent that they actually lived in their fields. Before this time, particularly when root crops still dominated Batak agriculture, fields were visited periodically but were not occupied for any extended period. When the Batak first began to live in their agricultural fields, it is said, all the households in the same swidden cluster lived together in the same large dwelling. As many as fifteen households could share a dwelling, which consisted of a large central room surrounded by a series of small apartmentlike rooms. In these smaller rooms, individual households had their own hearths and lived with their infant children; in the central room, older children slept together and were fed jointly by the adult residents. Similar dwellings are found today among some of the remoter groups of Palawano. Only the oldest Batak still remember such dwellings, which soon gave way to smaller swidden field houses more like those of the Batak's Cuyonon and Tagbanua neighbors. In this fashion, a pattern of seasonal residence in agricultural fields was established. During the off-season, however, the Batak presumably continued to live much as they had before, in temporary forest camps.

This settlement pattern had undergone further change by the 1920s. Under a variety of local auspices, lowland settlers and officials began to encourage the Batak to establish permanent settlements. In about 1910, for example, the governor of Palawan asked the Batak inhabiting the Tanabag River region to make way for lowland colonization there by es-

tablishing a settlement of their own on the coastal plain at
nearby Sumurod (Warren 1964:30–33). In 1930, five of the
"rancherias" thus established were declared by the Bureau of
Non-Christian Tribes to be reserved for the Batak's exclusive
use. Figure 3 shows the historical locations of these five
reservations and their relationships with present-day lowland
communities and Batak settlements. Despite government en-
couragement, the Batak never occupied their reservations
full-time, although they did build houses and plant some tree
crops on them, which was consistent with the government's
intent in setting aside the land for their use.

Actually, the government's purpose in establishing the
reservations is unclear. The "civilizing" of tribal populations
was, of course, everywhere a motive in the American-
administered Philippines. One entailment of reservation life
still unhappily recalled by the oldest Batak was the official
dictum that cooking fires should be outside the house or at
least in a separate room, as among lowlanders, rather than
inside, adjacent to sleeping areas, as was customary among
the Batak. For people unable to afford blankets and long
accustomed to keeping warm by the heat of a fire, this bit
of "civilization" was a definite hardship. More practically,
settling the Batak on the coastal plain would facilitate the
provision of education and medical services.

Securing at least some aboriginal Batak territory against
encroachment by lowland settlers was also a motive for
establishing the reservations. But lands ostensibly set aside
were of uncertain legal status and, in any case, would have
been inadequate for Batak subsistence under all but the most
intensive agricultural regimes. During the 1930s, as many as
forty to fifty Batak households were associated with some
reservations, but reservation areas were only on the order of
8 to 40 hectares. In these circumstances, foraging trips to the
interior remained essential, and a Batak's reservation house
became a sort of base for operations during the off-season,
much as his field house had already become such a base
during the agricultural season.

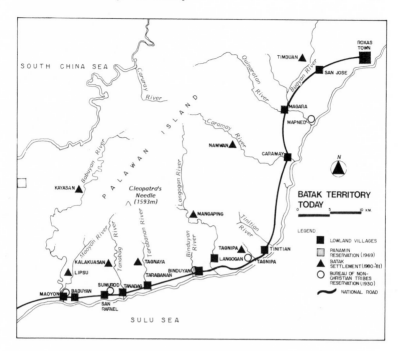

Figure 3

TABLE 3
POPULATION GROWTH IN PALAWAN

	1903	1918	1939	1948	1960	1970	1980
Palawan Province[a]	35,696	69,053	93,673	106,269	162,669	236,635	371,782
Palawan Island	10,900	31,868	42,959	56,380	102,540	162,042	269,081
Puerto Princesa District	1,208	6,427	10,887	15,177	23,125	37,774	60,234
Roxas District	NA	NA	NA	NA	9,329	16,341	24,890
Villages established in aboriginal Batak territory[b]:							
Tagabenit (Babuyan)							258
Maoyon (Maoyon)							577
Babuyan (Maoyon)							837
San Rafael (Tanabag)							497
Tanabag (Tanabag)							245
Concepcion (Tarabanan)							375
Binduyan (Langogan)							382
Langogan (Langogan)							797
Tinitian (Tagnipa)							903
Jolo (Tagnipa)							560
Caramay (Caramay)							2,749

Rizal (Quinaratan)   432
New Cuyo (Quinaratan)   874
Malcampo (Quinaratan)   1,969
Magara (Buayan)   926
San Jose (Buayan)   601
Abaraoan (Buayan)   1,197

Sources: National Census and Statistics Office (1970, 1980).

[a] Palawan Province was divided into twenty census districts or municipalities in 1980. Ten of these districts, including Puerto Princesa and Roxas, are located on Palawan Island.

[b] By 1980, approximately 17 lowland villages, or *barangays*, located in northern Puerto Princesa and southern Roxas, had been established in aboriginal Batak territory (see fig. 3). Most of these villages did not grow large enough to gain recognition as independent political units (and hence as separate census units) until after 1950. (Names in parentheses refer to river valleys traditionally inhabited by the Batak.)

In any event, lowland colonization proved overwhelming. Table 3 shows the striking population growth that occurred between 1900 and 1980 in Palawan Province. Most of this growth took place on Palawan Island, where the number of inhabitants has increased twenty-five-fold since the turn of the century. Particularly apparent is the large surge in immigration to Palawan Island following World War II. This resulted in the establishment of a string of settler villages along the island's coastal plain (see, e.g., Eder 1982). As these villages were established and the coastal plain filled up in aboriginal Batak territory, other changes inevitably followed. Copal, honey, and rattan concessions were granted to politically influential lowlanders, and collection and exchange of these commodities by the Batak grew in economic importance. Everywhere wage labor grew in importance also, as lowland farmers employed Batak to help clear and plant their homesteads. No road entered Batak territory until after World War II; for years, the highway leading north from Puerto Princesa stopped at the Babuyan River (see fig. 3). But in 1956, the Babuyan River bridge was constructed, and the road was extended to Tarabanan. In 1970, the road was extended to Binduyan and soon after, to Langogan. By 1975, the highway was open all the way to Roxas.

Even before the highway came, however, the Batak reservations were overrun by settlers. In some cases, Batak were actively intimidated into leaving their land by aggressive Filipinos. Elsewhere, there appears to have been considerable truth to the claim of early settlers that the Batak simply "left," not wanting, it is said, to mingle with outsiders. Indeed, some lowlanders even paid particular Batak for improvements they had made on reservation land before vacating it. A number of Batak at the Lipsu and Calacuasan settlements can still point to downstream stands of coconuts that they "sold" to lowlanders. The reservation at Mapned (fig. 3) was abandoned by Batak before World War II; the other four were abandoned soon after. During the 1950s, the government acknowledged political reality and revoked all the reservation decrees, enabling those lowland settlers then occupying the land to file homestead applications. More recent, but similarly unsuccessful, government efforts to reserve land for the Batak are discussed in chapter 6.

However ineffectual the reservations ultimately proved in terms of their intended purpose, their creation and dissolution exerted a lasting influence on Batak settlement pattern. Batak evidently found settlement living congenial, for even before their official reservations had been fully overrun by lowlanders, the Batak had begun to live part-time in more isolated reservationlike settlements of their own. Each local group has, on several occasions, relocated its settlement site farther up its respective river valley, moving just ahead of advancing lowland populations. Thus, the Batak did not embark on a wholesale retreat to the interior after the arrival of lowlanders. Instead, in a stepwise series of movements of only a few kilometers each, they have maintained some degree of isolation while keeping a convenient spatial relationship with both forest resources and the lowlanders.

Figure 4 illustrates the settlement site history of five contemporary Batak local groups, dating the series of movements that occurred as each group moved toward the interior following the postwar abandonment of the three reservations involved. This history is somewhat simplified, for there were some years when certain local groups failed to aggregate in any permanent settlement at all but simply alternated between forest and swidden field residence, as in years past. Also, no account is taken of the complete disruption of Batak settlement pattern caused by the abortive 1969 PANAMIN resettlement attempt (chap. 6). But the overall pattern of Batak retreating to smaller and more fragmented interior settlements is clear.

It is difficult to identify formally the geographic boundaries of Batak territory today. In some senses, it remains the same as their aboriginal territory (described in chap. 2 and shown in fig. 2). The Batak still reside within this territory and retain an extensive knowledge of its features and re-

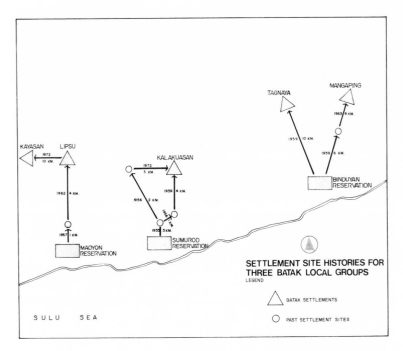

Figure 4

sources. Two important differences with the past arise, however, because now outsiders also reside in this territory. First, the coastal plain—and, increasingly, portions of foothill and upriver areas—is extensively occupied by lowland Filipinos. Batak now rarely visit these areas. Second, while most of the traditional Batak territory still seems to be open to them, there is a pervasive insecurity about their tenurial status. Legally, the Batak are "indigenous inhabitants" on public forest land not yet officially released for settlement by the Bureau of Forest Development. If this land is released, the Batak face an unequal competition with lowland settlers for private ownership. Batak land has been alienated in the past, and, with considerable justification, they fear that more will be alienated in the future. The most likely outcome over the near term is a continuation of the pattern of the past several decades: each local group is periodically pushed still farther into the interior, losing existing dwellings and agricultural improvements.

THE RHYTHM OF CONTEMPORARY ECONOMIC LIFE

To disclose the nature of contemporary Batak economy, it is useful to continue to focus on Batak settlement pattern but with a shift in that focus from long-term evolutionary changes in patterns of residence and mobility to short-term cyclical changes. Foraging trips upriver, visits downstream to lowland patrons and employers, and an annual dispersal to swidden fields are still regular elements of Batak subsistence economy despite the advent of settlement living. These activities take individual Batak households away from their settlements for days or weeks at a time.

Figure 5 shows the residential locations associated with these subsistence activities as well as the intersite distances, population sizes, and durations of occupation for these locations, which are based on observations I made at the Langogan settlement during 1980–81. The settlement site of the Langogan Batak has been fixed in its current location since

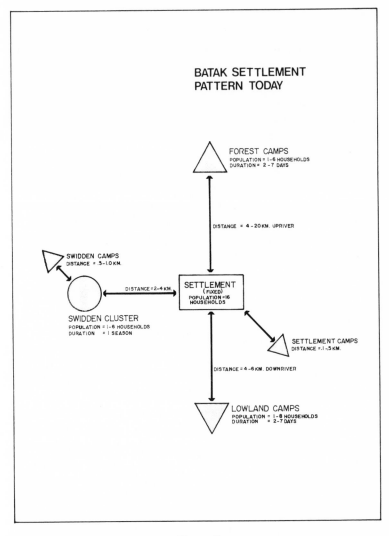

Figure 5

1963. The site and its immediate environs consist of scrubby regrowth and a few tree crops, the legacy of nearby swiddening in years past, but the settlement is otherwise surrounded by primary forest. It is a 12-kilometer walk downriver to the coast. By 1981, when more than one hundred lowland families lived along the first 10 kilometers of the river, one encountered isolated lowland homesteads soon after leaving the settlement in the downstream direction. A number of the settler families living more upriver periodically employ Batak to make swiddens, clear undergrowth from trees, pick coffee berries, and so forth. When such work opportunities are more than a few kilometers walk from the settlement, Batak work groups typically travel to them the day before they are scheduled to work and camp in lean-tos along the river, on or near the homestead where work is available. These are the lowland camps shown in figure 5. They may be occupied for up to seven days, or until work opportunities in the area are exhausted. Usually, entire households travel together to such camps. If only the men hire out, the women may fish or gather, much as they would at camps in the forest.

On the upstream side of the Langogan settlement, it is about 24 kilometers, following the main river course, to the river's headwaters, from which point one could descend to the west coast of the island. Since many tributaries flow into the main river, each with headwaters of its own, the Batak have access to extensive forest and riverine resources. Despite the presence of the settler families at the downstream end, the Batak still consider the entire river basin to be their territory. This basin encompasses an area of approximately 240 square kilometers. In any given year, the Batak forage in only a fraction of this territory, occupying the forest camps shown in figure 5. These camps, called *daes* by the Batak, are also occupied for up to seven days, before the households involved return to their swiddens or the settlement.

Figure 5 identifies two other kinds of more specialized camps: "settlement camps" appear during the height of the dry season, particularly in April, when warm nights and mosquitoes drive the Batak out of their settlement houses and into cooler, open sleeping areas at the river's edge or short distances inside the forest; "swidden camps" appear during the same period and provide a temporary residence during the slash-and-burn phase of the swidden cycle, until swidden field houses are constructed in May. Altogether, the sixteen Batak households at Langogan probably occupied between them about sixty to seventy different named camps, of all kinds, during 1981. The swiddens were distributed in three clusters. Two clusters were about 3 kilometers apart; the third was about 6 kilometers from the other two. The degree to which the members of any particular local group coalesce or disperse in their swidden-making activities in any one year is highly variable, depending on ecology and on personal preference.

Table 4 shows the percentage of time the sixteen households at Langogan allocated to these various residential locations during 1981, classified by month. The table is constructed from data obtained from nine seven-day periods, during which times I recorded the whereabouts each night of every individual in the group. Data for May, November, and January are estimated. Because these are composite data, they do not tell us how any *particular* household spent its time during 1981. Thus, a few households spent a lot of time in the settlement, others rarely visited it, and so forth. Nevertheless, much of the rhythm of Batak subsistence life is visible. During the six months from May to October, from rice planting to rice harvesting, the swidden field house is the primary residential location. During the leisurely, postharvest months of November, December, and January, the settlement is the focus of activity. During February, March, and April, the Batak are primarily on the move between encampments of various kinds. Overall, table 4 shows that the Batak spend about 60 percent of their time in settlement or swidden houses and about 40 percent in encampments.

Not immediately apparent in figure 5 or table 4 are some important seasonalities in abundance and scarcity, in labor

TABLE 4
Batak Settlement Pattern: Time Allocated to Various Residential Locations (Percentage of Nights, Classified by Month)

	Houses		Camps				Visiting other local groups
	Settlement	Swidden	Settlement	Swidden	Forest	Lowland	
January*	50.0				30.0	20.0	
February	6.3		13.4	31.3	48.2		
March	10.7		9.8	50.0	19.2	10.7	
April	3.6	5.4	58.9	26.8	4.0	1.3	
May*	5.0	45.0		5.0	45.0		
June	9.8	45.5			34.8	5.4	4.5
July	10.7	62.5			25.9		1.8
August	14.3	82.1			2.7		
September	6.7	92.4			0.9	0.9	
October	20.5	63.4			4.5		11.6
November*	79.5	11.6			8.9		
December	79.5	11.6			8.9		
	24.7	35.0	6.8	9.4	19.4	3.2	1.5

*Estimated.

and leisure, and in sociality and isolation entailed by the annual Batak subsistence round. A closer look at this annual round helps to reveal these seasonalities as well as the market incentives, social pressures, and scheduling concerns that influence Batak economic behavior.

Let us begin in early February, with the start of a new agricultural season. The December to April dry season that characterizes this part of Palawan is well established, and households that were living in the settlement since the conclusion of the previous agricultural season now gradually drift away to begin work in their new rice fields. From now until swiddens are burned in April, solitary families or groups of families that have chosen to work together reside primarily in swidden camps or *langsan*, clusters of temporary hillside dwellings near the sites of their future rice fields. Depending on how a particular local group has dispersed for purposes of swidden making, what looked like only one group in January may seem to be several quite independent groups in March. Batak sharing a common langsan (and later, a common swidden cluster) generally have more economic and social interaction with one another for the duration of the agricultural season than they do with Batak in other swidden clusters.

While slashing, felling, and burning orient Batak economic life during langsan residence, these agricultural chores must be coordinated with the labor demands of lowland farmers wanting to employ Batak in *their* swiddens. Many Batak exhaust their own previous season's rice harvest as early as December, and by January they begin to obtain advances of rice from lowland farmers against the promise of providing such labor when it is needed. Thus, the labor demands of lowland farmers often cannot be ignored. Further, langsan locations are selected with agriculture, not hunting and gathering, in mind. Nearby forest food resources may be limited or soon exhausted, and langsan camp members generally come to alternate periods of langsan residence with foraging trips to the interior to look for food at daes. Wild yams may be dug at such camps, which would limit the need to purchase or borrow rice in the lowlands. Therefore, while a Batak's home base is at a langsan during February and March, there is considerable residential mobility back and forth between langsan, daes, and lowland work locations.

Sometime in March, when the dry season is at its peak, swidden fields are burned. Some Batak may then return to their settlements to await the arrival of the rainy season. Most can be found in forest camps, enjoying a brief respite from agricultural labor and the heat of the dry season. April brings the rains and rice planting time. First, however, field houses are constructed; here the Batak will primarily reside until the harvest is threshed and stored in late October. April also brings the start of the honey season, and until the first rice is ready for harvest in mid-August, collection and sale of honey will compete with management of maturing rice fields for Batak attention. The pattern of field residence during this period thus is punctuated with forays into the forest to search for honey.

Rice planting begins in late April and continues well into May. Staggered planting along with varietal differences in maturation time extend the Batak harvest over several months. Swiddens are weeded in June. July is dominated by the urgency of the food search. The price of honey falls as the season progresses, and Batak begin to experience difficulty obtaining loans of rice from settlers, many of whom suffer a famine season as well. While women remain behind at field houses, making the baskets, sacks, and mats needed for the upcoming harvest, men frequent the lowlands attempting to *remedio begas*, "get some rice". Their attempts are often unsuccessful, and all Batak suffer from hunger at this time of year.

All of this ends abruptly in mid-August with the *tarakabot*, the ritual first harvest of the earliest maturing varieties of rice. Soon after, the real harvest is in full swing, and until the end of October, Batak eschew further collection of honey and most foraging trips of any kind, remaining in their rice fields to harvest, thresh, and store the grain. Particularly in September, there are weeks at a time when all Batak are at work harvesting in *somebody's* rice field—probably the only time of the year they so systematically pursue a single economic activity for such a lengthy period.

Finally, November, December, and January constitute an interlude between the agricultural season just completed and the new season yet to begin. November brings the last heavy rains of the year, and with the watershed unable to absorb additional runoff, rivers are often swollen and impassable. By late October, therefore, most Batak intend to have threshed and secured their rice and to have returned from their fields to their settlements. Here, residentially aggregated until February, the Batak come closest to "sedentary" living, and here, too, they engage in what lowlanders consider some of their most stereotypical behaviors. Newly harvested rice disappears at an alarming rate as, in the lowlander view, the Batak consume excessive quantities themselves and too readily exchange more for dried fish and alcoholic beverages. Extended visits to relatives in other local groups, drinking to excess, and relaxation appear to be the order of the day, confirming the lowlander opinion that the Batak are a people with "no thought of the future."

There is work to be done, of course. Settlement houses, long unoccupied, are in disrepair, and Batak divide their working time between constructing or repairing houses and earning money. For if the Batak now have adequate rice, they have little else. Their preoccupation with obtaining adequate carbohydrate supplies during the famine season left them without time or resources to obtain other foods, clothing, or drink, and they are now anxious to obtain and enjoy these items as well. The Langogan and Caramay River valleys are suitable for coffee, and at this time of the year, Batak men and women there pick coffee berries on lowland farms. Elsewhere, Batak men earn needed cash by collecting rattan or copal. Nevertheless, the emphasis during this period is on sociability and relaxation—in effect, the Batak's version of the postharvest life-style of their agricultural neighbors.

TABLE 5

PROPORTIONAL CONTRIBUTIONS OF DIFFERENT SUBSISTENCE
ACTIVITIES TO TOTAL ANNUAL FOOD SUPPLY AND CASH INCOME
OF LANGOGAN BATAK (1981)

Activity	Food supply[a]	Cash income[b]
Hunting and gathering		
Subsistence consumption	25	—
Sales/exchange	25	50
Agriculture		
Subsistence consumption	25	—
Sales/exchange	5	10
Wage labor	20	40
Total	100	100

[a] Valued in calories.
[b] Includes cash spent for food.

I have estimated the proportional contribution that hunting and gathering, agriculture, trade, and wage labor made to the total annual subsistence and cash income of Langogan Batak during 1981 (see table 5). The Batak obtained approximately half of their food supply from foraging and farming and purchased the other half with the proceeds of wage labor and the collection and sale of commercially valuable forest products. Variation in local patterns of economic opportunity leads to considerable group-to-group variation in the proportional importance of these various activities. During 1980, for example, farming alone contributed 60 percent of the Tanabag Batak food supply, with foraging and wage labor contributing far less there than at Langogan (Cadeliña 1982:245).

Jack-of-All-Trades, Master of None?

With some overlap, then, each of the Batak's different residential locations provides the base for a characteristic economic activity: hunting and gathering at forest camps, rice cultivation at swidden field houses, and trade and wage labor near settlement houses. Examination of the actual patterns of time utilization and returns to labor associated with these economic activities, as pursued at their characteristic residential locations, provides further insight into the nature and causes of contemporary Batak economic difficulties. I studied time allocation using a sort of "all-day follow" of the precise subsistence, domestic, and leisure activities pursued by a group of Batak residing at a forest foraging camp or a swidden field house. At the core of this procedure lay a series of coded observations, made at 15-minute intervals for a 24- to 72-hour period, of what each group member was doing at the instant of observation. I employed a series of forty-four basic codes divided into six basic activity categories: subsistence (e.g., hunting, wage labor), domestic (e.g., firewood collection, food processing), tool manufacture and maintenance (e.g., basket weaving, bolo sharpening), leisure (e.g., visiting, sleeping), illness, and child care. Many of my basic codes were further subdivided. Thus, the subsistence code "horticulture" was further divided into codes for planting, weeding, harvesting, and so on.

This procedure, modified from Johnson (1975), was designed to obtain a large amount of information about Batak time allocation patterns during relatively short and purposively chosen study periods at typical work settings. In each work setting, I limited my study to those adult individuals I could normally scan within my field of view, that is, those individuals with whom I was actually living and with whom I thus shared a common lack of privacy. Even then, observation was not complete. At forest camps, for example, where the proximity and openness of leaf shelters normally revealed all but sexual activities, some subsistence activities, such as pig hunting or honey collecting, took individuals outside my field of view for various lengths of time. In such cases, I had to rely on others' statements about where an individual had gone or what he or she was doing; insofar as it was possible, I cross-checked the information when the individual returned. Observations were also problematic because the

Batak may pursue two activities (e.g., conversation and coffee drinking) at once. This was particularly true of child care, which so often occurred in conjunction with other activities that I was more interested in studying (or was shared among several adults simultaneously) that I rarely coded it as a primary activity, and I ultimately completely eliminated child care time from my tabulations.

I recorded observations for all 24 hours of a day (rather than for only daytime hours) since Batak may rise during the night and eat, work, or converse by moonlight or firelight. In tabulating and interpreting the data, I assumed that whatever an individual was observed to be doing at the instant of observation was what he or she had been doing for the previous 15 minutes, and sufficient numbers of observations were assumed to even out sampling errors within study periods. I chose the particular study periods purposively; the time-consuming nature of the procedure and the complexity of Batak subsistence economy made meaningful random sampling impossible.

HUNTING AND GATHERING

At least to the Western eye, the temporarily inhabited foraging camps (described in chap. 2) still found on streams or riverbanks in isolated parts of the forest are the most endearing, or at least the most authentic-looking, aspect of contemporary Batak economic life. Leaf shelters are still the most common form of forest dwelling, although at the height of the dry season, the Batak may dispense with these and sleep along the water in an area cleared of stones and debris. While any nearby resources are fair game for those camped together, such encampments often have a characteristic focus—to stun fish, dig wild yams, collect honey, or gather palm leaves for basket making. Thus, forest destinations are usually selected in advance, in accordance with seasonal subsistence needs and current Batak knowledge about resource availability and distribution.

I visited numerous forest encampments during my year at Langogan, staying for periods ranging from minutes to days. Inevitably, each camp was different, but I found living conditions at them to be uniformly delightful. Heat, mosquitoes, and social tensions can make Batak settlements oppressive, and in the cool, quiet, and beauty of the forest, the Batak seemed to realize a measure of happiness and relaxation that I never knew them to attain in other settings.

Table 6 presents pooled time allocation data for three forest camps. Men and women devoted an average of 4.8 hours per day to "subsistence"—in my coding, activities such as fishing, honey collecting, jigging for eels, and looking for turtles which generally took a Batak away from camp (travel times are therefore included). Men and women devoted an additional 3.6 hours per day to such domestic activities as processing food, cooking and eating, bathing, and collecting firewood. Finally, they devoted one hour per day to manufacturing or repairing various weapons and implements. While these conclusions are based on a total of only seven days of observations, I visited and observed informally numerous other forest camps in the course of my fieldwork, and life at the three camps described here appears to be fairly representative of camp life in general. In any event—and depending, of course, on one's notions about what constitutes "work"—the Batak appear to keep busy while at their forest camps.

It is tempting to assume that Batak forest camps provide some sort of window to the past, a window to a pre-Neolithic lifeway. That the settings are so pristine and camp life so primitive contributes to an aura of authenticity. Indeed, only a few superfluous manufactured goods hauled to camp—a radio, a gun, or some purchased clothing—may seem to separate the observer from a once-universal way of life. This last leap of faith is readily abetted by the Batak themselves, who often assured me that "this is how we used to live all the time." But this window to the past is, if not opaque, considerably more refractory than it might ap-

TABLE 6
TIME ALLOCATION AT BATAK FOREST CAMPS (1981)

| Camp location | Dates | Number of observations[a] | | Activity, percentage of time (24-hour day) allocated[b] | | | | |
		Adults	Hours	Subsistence	Domestic activities	Tool manufacture and repair	Leisure	Illness
Papandayan	3/15–3/17	7	48	21.6	15.4	2.0	58.1	2.9
Kaybacong	4/7–4/9	13	48	15.0	13.1	7.1	62.0	0.8
Ganed	5/23–5/26	2	77	23.7	15.9	3.1	57.3	—
Mean[c]				20.1	14.8	4.1	59.1	1.2
Mean expressed as hours in a 24-hour day				4.8	3.6	1.0	14.2	0.3

[a] Coded observations made at 15-minute intervals.
[b] Adults only; combining data for men and women.
[c] Weighting data for each case equally.

pear. There are substantial differences between the hunting-gathering life observable at contemporary forest camps and the hunting-gathering way of life the Batak apparently enjoyed as recently as one hundred years ago (see chap. 2). Occupation periods at a given location are considerably shorter today than in the past, being a matter of days rather than weeks (up to three or four weeks, in the memories of older informants). The reason for this is that the Batak have many other important demands in their lives besides hunting and gathering. In particular, individuals must reconcile the demands of foraging with the demands of shifting cultivation and the market economy. A Batak is only in camp a few days before he remembers the fresh batteries he ordered from a lowland settler, the chickens he left behind at his settlement house, or his unguarded swidden. Even more pressing may be the need to deliver some newly found wild honey to an impatient creditor or to locate lowland buyers for some highly marketable (but perishable) wild pig meat. Not only are contemporary forest encampments of limited duration but Batak (with occasional exceptions) leave them to return to their settlements or swidden houses rather than to establish other forest camps.

Similarly, encampments are now much smaller. Today, only 2 to 7 households typically camp together at a particular location. In the past, even as recently as the 1930s, up to 30 or 40 households would camp together. This change has occurred, in part, because of secular demographic processes (i.e., population decline, local group retreat to the interior). Encampments were larger in the past, however, not simply because there were more Batak but because entire local groups often camped together. Indeed, on occasion, two local groups might occupy a single encampment. Today, the two largest local groups still total 24 and 16 households, respectively, but never in recent memory have the members of either one all encamped as a group. Underlying the shift to smaller encampments are some of the same scheduling considerations affecting camp duration. Just as contemporary encampments are of relatively short duration, because those camped together have other subsistence activities that require attention, relatively few people camp together, because the scheduling considerations in question are somewhat different for each Batak household; for example, each household's swidden field is in a different location, the timing of each household's agricultural cycle is somewhat different, and each household has a different set of ties and obligations to lowlanders. Not everyone, in effect, can "get away to the forest" at the same time.

The Batak today also utilize a narrower range of forest plant and animal resources. Tables 1 and 2 enumerated the animal and plant resources said to have been utilized traditionally. The number of these resources actually consumed during 1980–81 is considerably less. Indeed, at all residential locations where I observed or obtained reports of diet patterns during my stay (see chap. 5), the Batak only consumed 3 of the 14 mammals, 1 of the 8 tubers, 2 of the 7 rattans, less than one-half of the greens, and only a few of the fruits listed. This apparent narrowing of the Batak diet may be spurious. It may be, for example, that some of these resources have always been uncommon or even rare and were simply not encountered by Langogan Batak during 1980–81. Some, too, while edible, have never been preferred foods; the tuber *carindang* causes diarrhea, and the otter and wild cats have oily or gamy flesh. If the Batak eschewed such foods during 1980–81, they may have eschewed them in earlier years as well.

At the same time, however, it is likely that wild resource utilization has in fact narrowed, for two reasons. First, wild resources, which are seasonally available, may no longer be utilized if their seasons of availability coincide with a period when hunting and gathering has become of little importance to the Batak. The tuber abagan, for example, once a major carbohydrate source during September, October, and November, is now virtually ignored at Langogan because its period of greatest availability coincides with the rice harvest

(Flannery 1968). Second, and probably more important, a variety of latter-day cultural circumstances and values influence Batak decisions concerning wild resource utilization. The Batak are acutely aware that continued use of many forest foods helps to mark them as "primitives" in the eyes of lowland Filipinos (although a few such foods, like wild pig, honey, and mushrooms, are highly valued by lowlanders). At the same time, the Batak now routinely obtain a variety of lowland foods—coffee, sugar, baked goods—and it is reasonable to assume that access to them has altered Batak preferences for some traditional foods (e.g., wild fruits).

Another difference between present and past forest camps concerns the organization of labor. The traditional group foraging activities (chap. 2) are now difficult or impossible to organize as the necessary numbers of people can rarely be mobilized. I never witnessed, for example, a group pig hunt, although Cadeliña (1982:262) reports that he witnessed three such hunts at Tanabag during 1980, said to be the first to have occurred there in ten years. Similarly, group fish stunning, once practiced on entire rivers when fifty or more individuals could be mobilized at once, is today limited to smaller groups and tributary streams.

There have also been subtle changes in the sexual division of labor. During the swidden-harvest months of August, September, and October, for example, any forest camps tend to be occupied by men only; women stay behind in the rice fields to harvest. Over the entire year, largely because of such divisions of labor among different economic activities, husbands and wives reside separately almost 10 percent of the time—a phenomenon with no apparent aboriginal counterpart.

A case can also be made that today the Batak work longer hours—that is, they devote a greater proportion of their time to productive activities—at forest camps than did the Batak in the past. First, at least some of the foraging effort of men is directed today at the market as well as at subsistence; all households would like to return from a forest camp to the settlement not only with the night's meal but also with some honey or pig meat to sell. Second, some of the work activities of women at contemporary camps involve weaving such agriculture-related articles as harvesting baskets and rice-drying mats (classified under "tool manufacture and maintenance" in table 6). (By the same token, of course, there may have been certain work activities traditional to the hunting-gathering economy which are no longer pursued at camps today.)

A final and intriguing question is whether, in the face of all these changes, the "returns to labor" for hunting and gathering have increased or decreased in comparison to one hundred years ago. At first glance, it seems that such returns (whether measured in calories or protein) ought to be *higher* today: fewer people forage at a given location, and they do not stay as long. And yet, the returns may well be lower. The shorter duration of camp occupation makes round-trip travel more costly (i.e., the energetic costs of getting there and back from the settlement must be amortized over several days rather than several weeks). It may be, of course, that the Batak do not locate their camps as far away from the settlement and from one another as they once did, but any energetic advantage here is most likely offset by lower returns as a result of resource depletion in frequently visited areas.

Certainly, in the immediate vicinity of settlements, foraging returns can be very low indeed. Table 7 shows that the per-hour protein returns to selected foraging activities are considerably lower in the vicinity of the Langogan settlement—where much foraging in fact occurs—than are the returns to the same activities at remoter locations. The likelihood that a particular foraging attempt will fail completely is also greater near settlements. I observed numerous efforts to snare eels during my stay at Langogan; most efforts at forest camps were successful, whereas most efforts near the settlement were not. The same was true of efforts to stun fish. The situation was even worse at other settlements. At Lipsu, for example, it was said that there were no univalves

TABLE 7
Protein Returns for Selected Riverine Foraging Activities

Activity	No. of hours (episodes) observed	Protein (in live wt.) obtained per adult	
		Within 15-minute walk from settlement	More than 1-hour walk from settlement
Hook-and-line fishing	26.2 (19)	109 g/hr	204 g/hr
Univalve collecting	87.3 (54)	341 g/hr	755 g/hr

worth collecting left in the river and that the only time eels could be obtained was following a storm, when some might be washed downstream. Declining returns to traditional hunting-gathering activities are both a cause and an effect of subsistence change, for even as the new economic regime encourages settlement living and hence local resource depletion (below), such depletion itself encourages the Batak to seek new ways of making a living.

Moreover, regardless of location, the energetic costs of travel to and from forest camps are high because the Batak bring along more baggage than they used to: pots and pans, flashlights, radios, and even radiophonographs are among the items Batak take to camp today. The relatively small number of individuals foraging in the vicinity of contemporary forest camps may in fact be too small for optimal resource exploitation. The more men who are off hunting pigs, for example, the more likely it is that at least one will encounter and kill a pig large enough, perhaps, to feed the entire camp. At contemporary camps, however, only a few adult men are available to hunt pigs. Furthermore, that certain kinds of group foraging strategies are now no longer practiced may well have influenced overall labor productivity—although we cannot say in what direction in the absence of data on the productivity of these now-abandoned strategies.

Finally, the narrowed diet at Batak camps is not necessarily indicative of greater energetic efficiency in foraging. Cultural factors, themselves sensitive to outside influences, help to determine diet choice and thus foraging strategies. The large amount of time that Batak men continue to devote to wild pig hunting, for example, may have less to do with any relative abundance of pigs or any Batak success in obtaining them than with the fact that pig meat is a very tasty and marketable food. Such behavior, furthermore, could conceivably be abetted by the circumstance that the Batak can afford to be less risk aversive in their foraging activities than they may have needed to be in the past, given that a Batak today can draw on lowland traders and his own agricultural stores for part of his food supply. In the absence of data on encounter rates and search and pursuit times for the animals listed in table 1, we can only speculate on these points.

TRADE, CLIENTAGE, AND WAGE LABOR

That the Batak today are more likely to return to their settlements from a forest camp than to move on to another such camp is a measure, as we have seen, of the fact that some of the wild pig or honey obtained in the forest is often intended for delivery to the lowlands to pay a debt or exchange for some needed goods. More than at other Batak residential locations, the settlement is a locus for interaction with lowlanders who have dealings with them. Here, many time and resource allocation decisions are made and scheduling conflicts in the demands of foraging, agriculture, trade, and wage labor are resolved.

We have already seen how trade and wage labor fit generally with the wider rhythm of the annual economic round and in what proportions these activities contribute to total income (table 5). Table 8 presents the actual incomes received during 1981 by a sample of Langogan Batak households from their four major cash income sources: sale of coffee berry shares, sale of honey, sale of rice, and wage labor. I have valued all market-derived income for these households in money terms, although only some of this income was actually received in cash; most of the rest was characteristically received as rice, the Batak's single greatest market want. Other trade goods, such as radios, also figure in Batak income accounting, as when an individual agrees to provide a certain amount of honey or to work a certain number of days in the lowlands in exchange for the desired item. Moreover, considerable income of all kinds is received in advance, on credit, against honey, rice, or labor days to be provided later.

Even by the standards of the rural Philippines, the amounts

TABLE 8
Market Income in Six Batak Households (1981)

Household	Sale of honey[a] (gallons)	Sale of rice[b] (cavans)	Sale of coffee[c] (pesos)	Wage labor[d] (man-days)
Buyung'og	19	20	680	72
Tomas	20	5.5	230	31
Boxer	47	5	70	9
Valentin	13	3	140	15
Agapito	21	4	240	26
Gabriel	10.5	2	100	14
Mean	21.75	6.6[e]	243	27.8
Estimated cash equivalent	554 pesos	396 pesos		222 pesos

Estimated total annual
cash income per household = 1,405 pesos[f]

[a] Honey is worth an average of 25 pesos per gallon over the course of the season.

[b] Rice is worth 60 pesos per cavan at harvest, but most was sold in advance at deflated prices (see text).

[c] Batak pick coffee berries on a share basis and sell most of their shares back to the owner after drying and processing.

[d] Principally field clearance, harvesting, and tree crop maintenance. Payments received in cash or to reduce outstanding debts are valued at 8 pesos per day; those received in goods are valued at their prevailing market prices.

[e] The average 1981 harvest for these six households was 16.4 cavans; a cavan weighs approximately 50 kilograms.

[f] In 1981, one peso was worth U.S. $0.12.

of income shown are small; the Batak are perennially short of cash. This shortage arises not because their market wants are excessive but because their opportunities to earn cash are relatively few, seasonal, and unremunerative. This places the Batak at an immediate disadvantage in their rice- and cash-earning efforts: (1) like poor people everywhere, the Batak have virtually no withholding power and are thus the victims of a certain amount of exploitation in their economic dealings with outsiders; (2) some important hidden costs in Batak income-earning activities keep hourly or daily returns to labor even lower than they would appear to be in any simple input-output calculus, even as the opportunity costs of pursuing these activities limit Batak ability to develop a more independent (and potentially more remunerative) subsistence stance; and (3) the sedentarization necessitated by successful maintenance of trade and labor relations has contributed to resource depletion in the vicinity of Batak settlements, depressing foraging returns for many everyday subsistence foods.

My emphasis on the costs to the Batak of their economic interdependence with their lowland neighbors stands in marked contrast to the interpretation offered by Peterson (1978), another observer of a similar case of Negrito-lowlander economic interdependence involving the Agta of northeastern Luzon and their sedentary agricultural neighbors, the Palanan. She places food exchanges between these two populations in an analytical framework that emphasizes the mutually beneficial nature of that exchange as well as its interdependent nature. In particular, exchanges of Agta non-domestic protein foods (wild pig, deer) for Palanan domestic carbohydrate foods (corn, yams, manioc) allow each population to, in effect, specialize in what it does best. The Agta find it relatively easy to produce a surfeit of protein foods but suffer chronic shortfalls in carbohydrate foods because they plant few crops and, apparently, obtain little in the way of wild starchy foods (ibid.:339). Palanan farmers, in contrast, produce an abundance of carbohydrate foods but either do not or cannot raise enough livestock to supply their animal protein needs (ibid.:338–339). Because it is energetically efficient and therefore makes "good sense" for the parties involved to match their complementary shortfalls and surfeits, the Agta-Palanan exchange relationship is portrayed as voluntary and based on a simple cost-benefit calculus by each party rather than on coercion or any obsessive Agta preference for agricultural foodstuffs (ibid.:337).[1]

Peterson is ambiguous about the extent to which she is generalizing, but it is at least implicit that her analysis might apply as well to other cases of Negrito-lowlander exchange in the Philippines. My opinion is that a more realistic view of such exchange—and certainly of Batak-lowlander exchange—is achieved if we realize that a range of exchanges characteristically occur between the members of these populations, not just exchanges of wild meat for domestic carbohydrates, and that there is a basic asymmetry in all such exchanges which is obscured by any analytical emphasis on voluntarism or complementarity. The asymmetry arises because Negrito populations are usually small, isolated, and unsophisticated, while the lowland populations they trade with carry behind them all the "structural weight" of the legal apparatus and superior cultural capital of lowland Filipino society.

While I may overstate the situation somewhat, I do so to raise the question of whether the exchanges in the case at hand might routinely occur to the advantage of lowlanders and to the disadvantage of the Batak. Exploitation is a thorny issue, and I do not want to imply that the present reduced socioeconomic circumstances of the Batak necessarily arose because they have been exploited—although many observers have commented on the poor economic treatment Philippine Negritos generally have received from outsiders. Indeed, Rai (1982), another observer of the Agta, has aptly described this treatment in the course of specifically addressing and refuting Peterson's (1976:329) claim that Agta/non-Agta exchange is symmetrical and, if anything, biased in favor of the Agta:

> I suggest that the symbiosis is biased in favor of the outsiders. This bias arises because the external dependence of the Agta today is crucial to their economic survival. If the neighboring agricultural populations were called upon to make minor adjustments in their animal protein acquisition (and their seasonal labor requirement), they could maintain an independent economic system without their trade relation with the Agta. The Agta, on the other hand, have become virtually dependent on the outside system. Given their shift away from the traditional mode of life, the Agta cannot remain economically self-sufficient.... It is thus an impera-

tive for the Agta to maintain the trade or other economic relationship with outsiders even at the cost of their own economic exploitation and subordination.... The economic exploitation of the Agta by outsiders takes many forms. In Agta trade of forest items to outsiders, the latter control the market.... For example, ... three to nine wild pigs (approximate value 600 to 2,000 pesos) must be paid for one second-hand transistor radio (approximate value 200 pesos).... Most Agta are unfamiliar with the units of exchange and get further cheated. In wage labor, Agta are often paid less than their agricultural counterparts. Whereas an Agta is hired for only thirty pesos for four days of portering, an outside plowman summoned to work in the Agta field may demand as much as half of the production of the field. (Pp. 191–192)

Similar observations may be made about exchange between lowland traders and the Batak. These traders do provide a number of vital services to the Batak: they make available rice and other desired goods, extend credit, and accept payment in a variety of forms (in honey, rice, or labor days). But the cost of these services is high. For example, as their own previous season's rice runs out and as the new agricultural season gets under way, most Batak periodically obtain advances of milled rice from lowland creditors which are to be paid back threefold at harvest time. Thus, in February 1981, a Batak obtained four gantas of polished rice from a trader, agreeing to eventually pay him one cavan of un-husked rice (equivalent to twelve gantas of milled rice). As late as August, another Batak obtained one cavan of milled rice, to be paid for with six cavans of unhusked rice. (The trader bears the cost of milling in these transactions.)

Once the new harvest has begun, some of the new rice not already promised to lowlanders is exchanged for food and other goods. The Batak fare badly in such exchanges. In 1981, a measure of unhusked rice worth 10 pesos in the lowlands could purchase a measure of sugar worth 3 pesos, a measure of rice worth 15 pesos could purchase some dried fish or a bottle of gin worth 4 pesos, and so on. (The trader bears the cost of transport.) Having done without for so long, the Batak find such "purchases" difficult to resist, and the knowledge that the goods are overpriced does not seem to bother them. "So what if the goods are expensive, as long as we can buy them" was a commonly expressed sentiment. A similar attitude underlies a Batak's willingness to contract with a lowlander to complete a certain project—for example, clearing and burning a half-hectare upland rice field—in return for a highly desired consumer durable, such as a radio or kerosene pressure lantern. In such cases, the Batak are not oblivious to whether the value of the item preferred is appropriate to the amount of labor required to complete the project in question. But they also realize that a way has been found to obtain a desired good they would otherwise probably be unable to obtain at all. (The Mbuti Pygmy similarly rationalize their participation in commercial meat trading, despite the exploitative tactics of traders; see Hart 1978:345. Like Philippine Negritos, African Pygmies in general are far more dependent on their settled, agricultural neighbors than the latter peoples are on them; see Bailey and Peacock n.d.)

There is a sense in which the issue of "exploitation" should not be overemphasized. For example, it can be argued that if an item bought for 15 pesos from a Negrito forager brings 50 pesos someplace else, that is merely characteristic of a capitalist society such as the Philippines. Further, that Negritos are often exploited does not itself necessarily undermine Peterson's (1978) analysis. But what has more serious consequences for the Batak is the fact that the exchanges they engage in with outsiders entail a variety of hidden costs and opportunity costs that simply make them less remunerative and less "efficient" than they appear at first glance. For analyses that only compare production times for the goods to be exchanged (e.g., search, pursuit, and kill times for wild game; in-field agricultural labor costs) ignore a variety of ancillary activities and scheduling considerations necessary to the *maintenance* of exchange relationships.

A striking aspect of Batak behavior is the pervasive in-

fluence that exchange relationships—and concern about
maintaining those relationships—have on all aspects of
Batak economic life. Thus, Batak take time out from whatever
they are doing to talk with or entertain their trading partners
whenever they visit a Batak settlement. Scheduling of other
Batak subsistence activities is often subordinated to meeting
the needs and demands of traders, who are also, not inciden-
tally, often creditors. I often heard a Batak say that he was
unable to forage for food because he had "too much work to
do," that is, work to be done for a lowlander. Travel alone is
a significant element in the successful maintenance of trade
and labor relationships. Batak frequently travel to the
lowlands to deliver goods previously promised, to collect
payment for goods previously delivered, to obtain an advance against goods yet to be delivered, to inquire about
future work or exchange possibilities, and so on. Such travel
may take from several hours to a full day, since Batak, once in
the lowlands, are often dilatory about returning. While the
actual "returns" to particular episodes of travel may be difficult to identify, such travel is "all part of a day's work," and
any accounting of the comparative cost-effectiveness of
meeting subsistence needs through exchange relationships
must take account of it.

Indeed, after some episodes of travel, the Batak had nothing to show—the lowlander was not at home, or he had not
yet been to town, or he had forgotten to buy the radio
batteries as he had previously promised. A considerable
amount of Batak time is thus spent simply finding out about
trade and labor matters. In May, a Batak neighbor of mine
spent most of a day traveling round trip to the lowland
community of Langogan to borrow rice. A settler, he said,
had previously promised him such a loan against a future
payment of wild honey. He returned empty-handed, however, because the settler was unwilling to loan rice after all. In
July, another Batak carried three gallons of honey to his
lowlander trading partner to exchange for rice, as previously
agreed. But the trader's order of rice had not yet arrived from

town, and the Batak returned empty-handed to the settlement after a laborious eight-hour trip. An additional, six-hour trip was necessary two days later to collect the rice. In March, a Batak husband and wife left the settlement on a Sunday at 4:30 P.M., bound for a lowland farm that was a distance of about one and one-half hours' walk where they had been promised a day of work on Monday. But it turned out that the farmer did not want to employ them until Tuesday, so the couple stayed there for another day, engaging in some minor subsistence pursuits. They did work on Tuesday but were too tired, they said, to return immediately to the settlement. They remained there to rest Wednesday morning and finally returned home Wednesday noon. Thus, they completed their day's work in the lowlands but tied up almost three days in the process.

The opportunity costs associated with trade relationships are particularly visible in July, just before the harvest, when Batak efforts to secure loans of rice intensify as larger and larger amounts of time become necessary to locate smaller and smaller quantities of borrowable rice. This effort often comes at the expense of forest foraging or such vital agricultural chores as guarding maturing rice fields against the depredations of monkeys and wild pigs. In August, a Batak went to a lowland patron's house and secured one ganta of unhusked rice against his promise to deliver a load of split bamboo several weeks hence. After pounding, the rice thus obtained was scarcely sufficient for two meals for this man and his wife. Meanwhile, the loan had taken a full half-day just to arrange, and the promised work, which would effectively occupy a whole day, was yet to be done.

Travel and opportunity costs aside, there are intrinsic energetic inefficiencies in some of the exchanges that Batak work out with lowlanders. In some areas, Batak are accustomed to collecting and selling Manila copal and using the proceeds to purchase milled rice. At least during some months of the year, such Batak would obtain about 50 percent more food calories per hour of work expended if they instead simply dug and processed the most common species of wild yam (see Eder 1978). Similarly, as the honey season progresses and the amount of trade rice and a gallon of honey can command falls, a Batak exchanging honey for rice gets back fewer food calories than he parts with. (To be sure, the Batak wish to eat rice in lieu of wild yams or honey, which is an issue I return to in chap. 6.)

Finally, Batak involvement with exchange and labor relationships with outsiders has been a major cause of the depletion in local food resources (discussed above). Batak desire to obtain lowland foods and other goods and thus to have access to the lowland traders who can provide these goods leads them to locate their settlements within reasonable walking distance of lowland communities. Not surprisingly, such traditionally important riverine foods as fish and mollusks are badly depleted in the vicinity of Batak settlements (see table 7), and such important game as wild pig, jungle fowl, and gliding squirrels can scarcely be found there. Batak speak nostalgically about the relative abundance of fish and game in the interior, away from their fields and settlements, but their involvement with exchange relationships prevents them from foraging in the remoter parts of their territory to the extent they otherwise might. Because food purchases or added foraging effort during periods of settlement residence do not compensate for the reduced availability of forest and riverine foods, diet is visibly poorer at such times than at interior forest camps (see chap. 5).

AGRICULTURE

Batak affinities with the forest may be stronger, but one of my most enduring images of the Batak concerns their life as guardians of rice fields, high on isolated mountainsides with commanding views of the jungle and the ocean. There is some intercropping in such fields; corn and sweet potatoes are usually planted, and yams, taros, and bananas may occasionally be found as well. In years past, Batak have also planted coconuts and other fruit trees in their fallow swiddens. More recently, some have begun to plant coffee. But tree crops are few in number and inadequately cared for, and nowhere are they a significant source of cash income. Finally, Batak own virtually no pigs and few chickens. Thus, rice cultivation is by far the most important agricultural enterprise, and it provides an alternative both to hunting-gathering and to trade and wage labor as a source of subsistence as well as cash income.

Rice fields may be near or far from settlements, in isolated clearings or in large clusters, in low or high fallow second growth, or, if the Batak are so inclined and think they can escape detection by the government, in virgin forest. While comparatively simple in technology and ritual, Batak shifting cultivation otherwise resembles a type widespread in the Philippines and elsewhere in Southeast Asia. Local variants of this type have already been abundantly described (e.g., Freeman 1955; Conklin 1957; and numerous studies inspired by these early works), and I will devote little additional attention here to technological matters.

My most detailed picture of Batak time allocation patterns under agricultural conditions comes, again, from a series of time allocation studies. This time my subjects were the adult members of the household or group of households domiciled together in a single swidden field house. As in the case of forest camps, I visited numerous such field houses during the course of my stay with the Batak. On occasion, I remained for 24 to 48 hours of detailed observation. Table 9 presents pooled time allocation data for four such observation periods at field houses, each period during a different stage in the cycle of rice cultivation. These data, while limited, suggest that in the field, agricultural workdays are on the order of 3.5 to 4.0 hours per working adult—approximately one hour less per day than Batak dwelling in forest camps devote to hunting and gathering (table 6). Other observations support this estimate. In July, I observed a group of women to spend 2.5 hours in the morning and 1.5 hours in the afternoon

TABLE 9

TIME ALLOCATION AT BATAK SWIDDEN FIELD HOUSES (1981)

| Cultivation stage | Dates | Number of observations[a] | | Activity, percentage of time (24-hour day) allocated[b] | | | | |
		Adults	Hours	Subsistence	Domestic activities	Tool manufacture and maintenance	Leisure	Illness
Field clearance	2/23–2/24	4	48	18.8	10.0	6.3	65.0	—
Planting	5/13–5/14	5	24	13.0	21.5	2.7	59.3	—
Weeding	7/21–7/23	4	48	5.8	17.8	5.9	70.1	—
Harvest	9/3–9/5	5	48	18.0	17.5	1.5	64.8	—
Mean[c]				13.9	16.7	4.1	65.6	—
Mean expressed as hours in a 24-hour day				3.4	4.0	1.0	15.6	—

[a] Coded observations made at 15-minute intervals.
[b] Adults only; combining data for men and women.
[c] Weighting data for each case equally.

weeding a rice field. In October, I observed the members of several households to work together at late harvest labor for approximately 2.5 hours in the morning and 2.0 hours in the afternoon.

On the surface, given that the Batak must also devote some effort each day to domestic activities, this seems like a reasonable amount of effort to devote to agricultural labor. But what do Batak get in return? A complete answer to this question should address the cost of mobilizing field labor, the productivity of that labor once mobilized, and actual farm yields—topics about which I have only fragmentary data. I am convinced, nevertheless, that the returns to land and labor in Batak swiddens are much lower than local lowland swidden farmers realize in the same environment—perhaps as much as 50 percent lower. In the Batak fields I observed at Tanabag during 1971 and 1975, for example, returns to land were on the order of 750 to 1,250 kilograms per hectare. Headland (1986:352), who similarly believes that the Agta are ineffective agriculturalists, reports that yields in the 43 Agta fields he studied in the Casiguran area in 1983 averaged only about 900 kilograms per hectare. Rice yields of this magnitude are low by the standards of most farming peoples in upland Southeast Asia. Spencer (1966:21–22) estimates that upland rice yields in the region as a whole, for "first year cropping of mature forest lands in good years," range from 1,100 to 2,800 kilograms per hectare. Similar estimates have been made by Freeman (850–2,100 kilograms per hectare [1955:96–99]) and by Conelly (1,600 kilograms per hectare [1983:175]). The returns to labor in Batak rice fields are also comparatively low. Taking account of all labor inputs from field preparation to threshing and storing (but excluding milling), the Batak receive only 2 to 3 kilograms of husked rice per day of labor. By contrast, Cuyonon settlers in the same area receive 4 to 5 kilograms per labor day.

The proximate causes of the desultory state of Batak agriculture are found in an array of poor management practices, scheduling conflicts, social pressures, and cultural values that not only depress swidden yields and labor productivity but result in a surprising number of cases of out-and-out farming failure. With respect to yields, for example, the Batak tend to make small fields to begin with. Their technological knowledge of upland agriculture is relatively unsophisticated. They plant few rice varieties and engage in little or no intercropping. Such discretionary activities as secondary burning, weeding, and guarding may be ignored or haphazardly pursued; every year monkeys and wild pigs take a heavy toll in Batak rice fields. Even basic activities such as planting and harvesting may be ill-timed or postponed to the extent that the rice crop suffers in consequence.

Inadequate or poorly scheduled labor inputs in Batak agriculture in part simply reflect the exigencies of poverty and the competing demands of a multidimensional subsistence economy. A hungry Batak family may have to leave its maturing rice field untended in July to seek food in the forest, and they may have to leave it unharvested in September while they help a lowland creditor harvest *his* field. Following a storm at harvest time, when the mature grain is vulnerable to lodging, I have known Batak thus summoned to the lowlands to return to find much of the rice in their own fields blown over or soaking wet.

Other difficulties with labor mobilization extend beyond the economic circumstances of individual households and involve some distinctively Batak customary practices. Consider the reciprocal agricultural labor work parties that many Batak mobilize at planting time. These arrangements are ubiquitous in Southeast Asia; the Batak probably acquired the custom from the Cuyonon at the same time they acquired upland rice farming. Undoubtedly, such work parties are never models of efficiency; people turn to them, in part, precisely because they often are unhurried, socially pleasurable occasions. But according to my observation and in comparison with reciprocal labor groups on neighboring Cuyonon farms, Batak labor groups are particularly unproductive even as the Batak find them quite costly to mobilize.

The cost stems from the fact that Batak reciprocal labor groups are also reciprocal eating groups; both husband and wife typically appear for the noon meal, even though only one may actually be exchanging a labor day. Nonworking spouses help with gathering firewood or cooking, but their numbers are often excessive for these chores. Further, any lowland passersby may also invite themselves to the noon meal. It is not uncommon to learn of a Batak who postponed a previously scheduled field planting because he was unable to borrow the rice necessary to feed those who would attend.

A reciprocal labor party I observed in late February was fairly typical. Seven men, including the man whose field was being planted that day, were involved in the actual exchange of labor days. They departed from the field owner's settlement house at 8:30 A.M. and returned at 11:15 A.M. for the noon meal; they left again at 3:00 P.M., returning at 5:45 P.M. Since it took them about 15 minutes on foot to reach the field, the labor group spent a total of approximately 4.5 hours actually working, which is consistent with the data reported in table 9. Thirteen adults and two children attended the noon meal, which consisted of rice and boiled greens. In addition, the field owner provided some puffed rice candy and three bottles of gin. Two bottles were consumed after lunch, and the third was taken to the field in the afternoon "so that the work would go faster." (A lowland settler with a comparably distant field would have his noon meal brought there, both to minimize travel time and to reduce the temptation of his exchange laborers to dally during the midday break.)

Other customary practices that dampen yields and labor productivity become visible at harvest time. For a lowland settler, the crucial measure of farming success is how much rice ends up in his own granary for his family's future use. This is the effective return to his season of agricultural labor, and a good farmer makes every effort to minimize the amount of newly harvested rice that is used to buy goods,

pay debts or laborers, and so on. Among the Batak, such
demands dissipate an alarming amount of rice, and what
appears to be an abundant harvest in September can result in
surprisingly few sacks of stored rice in November. First, as
we saw above, there are famine season debts to be paid and
goods to be purchased. Second, during the tarakabot, or
ritual first harvest, as many as ten individuals may enter a
Batak's rice field and harvest for a day, keeping all of the
proceeds for themselves. Even after the tarakabot, when any
harvesting in another's field is nominally done on a share
basis, neighbors and kin expect concessions from the more
successful farmers. In ten Batak fields I monitored at Tanabag
in 1971, these various harvest time rice allocations accounted
for 35 percent of the total harvest and on a number of fields,
exceeded 50 percent.

Ironically, even as Batak rice production suffers from
inadequate labor inputs during some phases of cultivation, at
other times, excessive labor is invested in farming with only
limited marginal returns. An illustration of how the exigencies of poverty may lead a farmer to expend extra effort
without adding to total output is seen in the Batak practice
of *tianek* making. Tianek is made in July and August, when
near-ripe grain not yet ready for harvesting, threshing, and
pounding in the normal manner is nevertheless harvested,
laboriously threshed using a shell scraper, and then roasted
and dried over a fire before it can be pounded and consumed.
Rice thus prepared has a delightful nutty flavor and is much
favored. But Batak make tianek not because it is tasty but
because they are hungry and cannot wait until their grain has
fully ripened. One episode of tianek making I observed in
early August ultimately yielded about 2 kilograms of husked,
ready-to-cook rice. The episode began in the late morning,
when two women harvested some near-ripe grain, and continued as other women assisted with the tasks of threshing,
roasting, drying, pounding, and winnowing. Excluding mat
drying, which took four hours but needed only occasional
attention, seven hours of adult labor were necessary for these

tasks. It was almost 8:00 P.M. when the rice was ready to be eaten.

On occasion, the kinds of attitudes, practices, and circumstances that keep rice field returns to land and labor relatively low also result in outright farming failure. Of the twenty-five Batak households who made rice fields at Tanabag during 1975, for example, four ultimately harvested little or no rice. One cleared and planted a field but essentially abandoned it after the husband was summoned to another local group by his mother, whose chronic illness was said to have worsened. She was actually in reasonably good health but prevailed on her son to stay. In a second case, an old man living alone prevailed on his nephew to clear, and on his niece to plant, an isolated field for him. He was to guard the field himself, but most of his time was spent visiting kin in another local group. Very little rice survived to be harvested. Another couple made a field, but, after planting, the wife decided to return to the local group of her birth to be near her brothers. Forced to choose between his field and his wife, the husband chose the latter. A final case of field abandonment occurred as a result of sheer laziness. A man burned and planted his field a month late because, it was said, "he went fishing when others were working [in their fields]." He and his wife planted the field together, but she subsequently refused to cooperate in weeding or guarding, instead spending most of her time at an uncle's house. She was still lonely, it was said, from the death of her father two years before.

What more general explanation can be offered for why the Batak do not farm more successfully? Forest resource depletion and the Batak's own evolving life-style lend some urgency to understanding this failure, for it would seem that even modest improvements in Batak agricultural yields or labor productivity would considerably improve their lives. A frequent explanation is that Negrito peoples such as the Batak do not *like* to farm. According to this reasoning, Negritos simply prefer to obtain most of the goods they need from the outside world through trade and wage labor rather

than through resorting to such sedentary occupations as
farming, and they behave accordingly.

Writing of the Batek, K. M. Endicott (1979*a*) has argued
persuasively along these lines. His argument has considerable
intuitive appeal, and versions of it have been applied to Philippine Negrito groups as well (e.g., Headland 1985). Most
(Malaysian) Negritos, he says,

> intensely dislike agricultural work and will do it only when it
> is impossible to earn a living any other way. They much
> prefer collecting and selling rattan to agriculture because it
> permits them to live in the cool forest, to move around
> whenever they like, to hunt and fish, and to collect their
> reward in cash, which they vastly prefer to a yield of food
> alone.... This preference is widespread among Negritos and
> is a serious impediment everywhere to attempts to settle
> them. (P. 184)

According to Endicott, not only do Negritos dislike agricultural *work*—because of "their preference for the coolness of
the forest to the heat of the clearings," their "intense dislike
of ... living in one place for an extended period," and their
"avoidance rules between kin which severely limit who may
live with whom"—but they also find the house layout and
domestic arrangements of Malay-style agricultural villages
"almost the exact opposite" of what "they look for in a living
place" (ibid.: 184–187). (Similar cultural preferences have
been attributed to African Pygmies; see, e.g., Turnbull 1965.)

Applied to the failure of Batak farming, this would be the
charitable explanation of the anthropologist. Lowland Filipinos have a less charitable explanation: Batak are lazy. Indeed, Batak are widely portrayed as lazy by lowland Filipinos
precisely because of their failure to farm more effectively—
that is, they are perceived first and foremost as lazy *farmers*.
My view is that both explanations miss the point. By looking, relativistically or ethnocentrically, at factors presumed
intrinsic to the Batak themselves (or Negritos in general),
such explanations divert attention from a vital, broader pat-

tern of social and economic relationships. I do not deny that
Negritos in general (or the Batak) talk and behave as if they
do not like farming work and the farming life-style. But I do
question whether these facts are adequately accounted for
by the claim that agriculture, as a subsistence adaptation, is
simply a "poor fit" with traditional Negrito social organization, culture, or personality. To fully appreciate the motivational patterns in question, we must again look at the wider
social and economic context in which the failure to farm
effectively occurs. If we are to invoke that context to explain
why the Batak and other Negritos have become such inveter-
ate collectors of commercially valuable forest products, surely we must consider it as well in accounting for their failure
to move into full-time farming. I believe that the "terms of
incorporation" of Batak society into lowland Filipino society
do not simply select *for* trade; they also select *against*
farming.

First, it is important to recognize that specialization and
success in one activity precludes, to some degree, success
and specialization in another activity. I argued earlier that
Peterson (1978) ignored some significant opportunity costs
associated with developing and maintaining exchange relationships. Some of these same opportunity costs also figure
in Batak farming failure. In particular, the ongoing concern of
an individual Batak to stay in the good graces of his lowland
patron/creditor/exchange partner leads him, among other
things, to accept offers of employment in his patron's swidden field, performing such tasks as clearing or weeding—the
same tasks that are extremely important in his own swidden.
The fact that during the swidden season Batak may be seen
busily laboring in the fields of others while their own fields
(or would-be fields) lie unattended is commonly cited by
lowlanders as indicative of the kinds of personality shortcomings that explain why the Batak have been unable to
improve economically. In fact, however, many Batak are ob-
liged to work in this fashion because they had previously
obtained food or another item from their employers which

was to be paid for either in forest products or in agricultural labor. In short, involvement in exchange and labor relationships seriously inhibits the Batak's *ability* to become more successful farmers, whatever their *inclinations* may be. Writing of the Tagbanua, Conelly (1985) similarly emphasizes how some of the time spent collecting and selling forest products might alternatively be devoted to clearing larger fields and to more careful maintenance.

More than the opportunity costs of exchange relationships with lowlanders keep Batak from moving into full-time farming, however. I do not think it is unreasonable to argue that lowlanders do not want Batak to move into full-time farming. Conscious motivations along these lines may not exist, but it is important to recognize that particular lowland Filipinos—and the wider socioeconomic system—benefit economically from the present subsistence orientation of many Philippine Negrito groups. Consider that any significant movement by Negritos into full-time farming would (1) increase competition for agricultural land in certain Philippine frontier areas already filled with land-hungry settlers and (2) decrease the number of marginalized individuals available to hire out as agricultural wage laborers or to collect and sell forest products.

Two aspects of the Batak case are relevant here. First, on numerous occasions I have observed lowland settlers, usually those with exchange relationships with Batak, attempt to intimidate the Batak about their allegedly illegal swidden making on forested mountainsides. For example, stories may be told about how a certain government forester, having spotted illegal Batak swiddens from his helicopter, is on his way to make arrests. I have known such efforts to be successful, with the Batak abandoning their swiddens and retreating to the forest for a time. Such behavior, which may occur during any phase of the swidden cycle, obviously undermines agricultural productivity as much as any aversion to working in the heat of the sun. (Ironically, the Bureau of Forest Development is more concerned with the illegal swiddens of lowlanders than with those of the Batak.) A similar kind of intimidation was reported by change agents working with the Batak. Employees of World Vision, for example, found that their efforts to assist Batak at Tanabag and Buayan to become more self-sufficient were resented or even actively opposed by local lowlanders who had commercial dealings with them.

Second, from a historical perspective, arriving Filipino settlers did not simply displace the Batak from part of their aboriginal territory and then use that land for agriculture; they preempted land on which the Batak had already made agricultural improvements. The five Batak reservations established in 1930 were all partially planted in bananas and coconuts by the time they were overrun by lowlanders. Batak remember this experience bitterly. A similar pattern continues today. At Caramay, for example, Batak complain that forestland they clear for agriculture purposes is subsequently encroached on by lowlanders, who plant tree crops, declare the land their own, and pay the necessary taxes to the Bureau of Lands. In my opinion, the fear that unimproved or improved land could similarly be taken in the future together with continued uncertainty about their land tenure status generally are major factors explaining why the Batak have made only tentative efforts to develop their agricultural economy by planting such high value and easily transportable tree crops as coffee and cashews.

In short, there is more to the story of desultory Batak farming than "Batak don't like to farm." The pressures and opportunities of an external social system have a powerful influence on all aspects of Batak behavior. Just as Batak *do* collect and sell certain forest resources because an external economy needs them to do so, they *do not* become full-time farmers because that same economy does not need them to—indeed, it does not want them to. Success in trade and failure in farming are two sides of the same coin—not that of the likes and dislikes of Negritos but that of the pressures and requirements of a wider social system. In such circumstances, it should not be surprising that people like the Batak might attempt to make the best of their difficult situation by surrounding their inability to farm effectively with talk of how they do not like farming anyway.

I have argued here that the Batak's seemingly "flexible" subsistence system is uniquely responsive to the pressures and demands of outside peoples and social systems rather than to their own needs. In particular, the constraints posed by land insecurity and a considerable degree of clientage lead to significant inefficiencies in the practice of hunting-gathering, trade, and agriculture, making the typical Batak the peripatetic jack of all trades, master of none.

I fear that a new romanticism has come to influence analyses of hunting-gathering populations: the old romanticism about "pure hunter-gatherers" has given way to a new but equally naive glorification of "generalized foraging," "exchange," and "multidimensional subsistence strategies" as those activities which comprise the life of the sensible and well-adjusted modern hunter-gatherer. It certainly seems odd that anthropologists who work with agricultural peoples continually emphasize the importance of greater attention to subsistence production and the nutritional, socioeconomic, and other dangers of cash cropping (i.e., specialized production for exchange), yet anthropologists who work with hunting-gathering populations, at least in Southeast Asia, have not voiced a similar concern. We should be more attuned to the possibility that what a particular foraging people may be doing at the moment may not in fact be in their own best interests, however difficult it may be to define those interests. In the next two chapters, I attempt such a definition for the Batak.

4

Demographic Evidence of Adaptive Difficulty

Here, I investigate, in effect, how far the demographic data go toward supporting my contention at the outset that the Batak are a "disappearing people." My underlying premise is the conventional wisdom of population ecology that a central measure of adaptation is the ability of a population to *persist*, that is, to reproduce itself in numbers equal to or exceeding the rate of mortality. While either growth or stability might be taken as evidence of successful population persistence, decline is problematic. Just as it would be wrong to imply that any population decline is necessarily pathological, it is erroneous to assume that all demographic changes are necessarily adaptive or contributory to successful persistence. Territorial abandonment, instability (as opposed to flexibility), and sustained decline, in addition to outright extinction, are all accepted indicators of a population's failure to persist—and hence to adapt—successfully (Swedlund 1978:144–145).

In human populations, of course, "persistence" (like "disappearance") has cultural as well as biological dimensions. Hence, in the case at hand, we will have to examine more precisely just who is included in the Batak population and what its alleged disappearance in fact consists of. I begin by describing my field methods and defining the total study population and then lay out the principal demographic features of this population and examine the apparent direction of the change in its size over the past one hundred years. I examine fertility and mortality separately for a dwindling population of pure or "core" Batak and for a growing population of intermarried Batak. In doing this, I distinguish between "physical extinction" and "cultural extinction" in human populations and explain how the disappearance of the Batak entails elements of both.

In particular, I argue that a sustained decline in physical numbers antedated—and even helped precipitate—a latter-day trend among those Batak who remained toward out-group marriage and consequent "assimilation" into a wider population. To those who might observe that out-group marriage is not necessarily pathological and may even be considered adaptive to the degree that it has contributed to the persistence of Batak genetic material, I acknowledge that the physical disappearance of the Batak is incomplete and, indeed, in the genetic sense, might never occur. But I also argue that the remaining, still-evolving population is of *increasingly ambiguous ethnicity* and thus that a good deal more is at stake than simple "culture change" among a group of people who otherwise continue to be identified by themselves and by others as "Batak."

Principal Demographic Characteristics of the Total Population

Definition of the Population

The total Batak population whose characteristics will be examined here is the summation of the members of the eight local groups of "Batak" identified in figure 3. Each such local group typically includes a number of "pure" Batak individuals (i.e., individuals descended from other Batak who can identify no non-Batak ancestors), a number of Tagbanua or

TABLE 10
TOTAL BATAK POPULATION CLASSIFIED BY GEOGRAPHIC LOCATION
AND ETHNICITY (NOVEMBER 15, 1980)

River valley	Batak	Part-Batak[a]	Non-Batak[b]	Total Persons	Households[c]
A1 Babuyan	21	14	8	43	9
A2 Maoyon	36	15	6	57	15
B1 Tanabag	80	3	1	84	24
B2 Tarabanan	5	5	1	11	3
C Langogan	58	2	2	62	19
D1 Tagnipa	14	6	5	25	7
D2 Caramay	26	42	4	72	15
E Buayan	14	45	11	70	17
Total	254	132	38	424	109

[a] Most of these individuals are the unmarried offspring of out-group marriages.
[b] Tagbanua and lowland Filipino spouses of Batak, plus one adopted child.
[c] Most are simple nuclear families.

lowland Filipinos who are married to (and living like) Batak, and a number of ethnically mixed individuals, the offspring of such out-group marriages. Table 10 shows how the total 1980 Batak population of 424 individuals, classified according to these several ethnic categories, was distributed among the eight river valleys.

Whatever other difficulties the Batak may have posed for demographic study, finding them was not a significant problem. While out-group marriage has led increasing numbers of outsiders to permeate the inclusive, territorially defined population boundary just described, few Batak have as yet escaped across this boundary to disappear into the wider population of rural Palawan. In other words, out-migration is not a significant factor, and where out-group marriage has occurred, the non-Batak spouse has gone to live among the Batak rather than the Batak going to live elsewhere. While there have been exceptions, I believe that my focus on local groups led me to miss (because they might have been living elsewhere) no more than five living persons said by themselves or by others to be Batak or part-Batak.

The Batak are, however, spread over a considerable geographic area, and each local group is characteristically located closer to a neighboring lowland community than to any other Batak community. Table 10 shows that two centrally located river valleys, Tanabag and Langogan, contain more than half of the total pure Batak population, while the numbers of in-marrying Tagbanua and lowland spouses and of ethnically mixed children are disproportionately high at the peripheries. A historical factor accounts for much of this variation in the extent of intermarriage and racial mixing between river valleys. The direction of post-1880 Cuyonon pioneer settlement of mainland Palawan was from the north, from Roxas, and, later, from the south as the highway was extended from Puerto Princesa City, leaving the heartland Batak river valleys relatively unaffected until recently. Thus, while the Caramay area was settled by Cuyonon farmers as early as 1900, Langogan became an important settler destination only after 1960. Lowland settlement underlies one complicating factor in Batak demography after about 1940—the periodic fragmentation and relocation of entire local groups (see fig. 4). Such internal migration of local groups, coupled with a considerable amount of mobility by individuals and households *between* local groups, made study of the total Batak population (rather than some fraction of it) a practical necessity, even as its relatively small size made such study possible.

I eventually completed two thorough social anthropological censuses of the entire Batak population, the first in 1972 and the second in 1980. These censuses, particularly the second one, are the source of most of the demographic data discussed here. My methodological focus was on households and their memberships, with simple enumeration of each member's name, sex, age, previous place of residence, and kin relationships to other household members lying at the core of the census procedure.[1] In addition, I routinely obtained the marital and reproductive histories of all men and women who had ever been married. I interviewed samples of women about age at menarche, age at menopause, and duration of nursing. I made a careful record of all cases I encountered of disputed paternity and of adult men who had apparently never fathered a child. At Langogan, where I resided during 1980–81, I also monitored for a twelve-month period all visits by Batak from other local groups to Langogan, the visits Langogan Batak made to other areas, the periodic fission and fusion of households, and the periodic circulation of individuals among these households.

This turned out to be a more ambitious agenda for data collection than I had anticipated, and it led me to visit repeatedly every Batak local group and to meet virtually every living Batak adult in an effort to obtain demographic data I could use with reasonable confidence. In particular, I early recognized the difficulties of obtaining accurate dates and ages from a preliterate people, even as I was aware that much of the potential value of my later analysis would depend on the adequacy of such data. While formal techniques derived from stable population theory can be used to calculate the proper age distribution in a population of known fertility and mortality schedules, such techniques did not seem appropriate to the rapidly changing demographic circumstances of the Batak. Thus, I chose to make absolute age estimates myself.

In my estimation procedure I relied heavily, as have others (e.g., Van Arsdale 1978; Howell 1979), on the concept of relative age, culturally important among many peoples such as the Batak. Thus, observation and inquiry about kin terms of address enabled me to rank ages within and even between local groups. Then I estimated absolute ages based on appearance, birth order of siblings, comparison with known events (e.g., the Japanese occupation, postwar "liberation," and the 1969 PANAMIN project), and comparison with longtime lowland settlers of known age, some of whom were quite helpful in identifying their Batak "age mates." In the case of deceased children, I estimated ages at birth by reference to their placement relative to surviving siblings and by asking mothers to identify living members of the population born about the same time. Similarly, I estimated the age at death of deceased children by asking mothers about developmental stages the child had reached prior to death and about living children who were born about the same time as the death of the child in question (see Howell 1979:81–82).

Another area where accurate data were essential to my analysis but that had to be approached with considerable caution concerned female reproductive histories. Here I simply proceeded slowly and restricted my more detailed questioning to women I came to know reasonably well and whose reports I felt would be accurate. I was aided significantly by the fact that the Batak inhabit a part of the world where women are generally quite open in discussing matters pertaining to pregnancy and childbirth.

AGE-SEX STRUCTURE

Figure 6 illustrates the age-sex pyramid that results when the total population of 424 core Batak, part-Batak, and non-Batak spouses shown in table 10 is displayed according to age and sex. Several striking features provide our first indications of the nature of Batak demography. First, by lowland standards, there are relatively few old people—or rather, few Batak survive to "old age." By my estimates in 1980, the oldest living Batak was born in 1910, and a total of only six living Batak were born before 1920 and thus were 60 or older.

A second important feature, visible in the figure's central column, is the straight-sided nature of the population pyramid of core Batak. There are the same numbers of ethnic Batak in the younger cohorts as there are in the older cohorts. Given the high mortality of the Batak (below), there appears to be some cross-sectional evidence that the Batak are disappearing. Indeed, the relative absence of core Batak individuals in the younger age cohorts is such that age 30 separates the older 50 percent from the younger 50 percent in the core Batak population, rather than age 15 to 20 as in

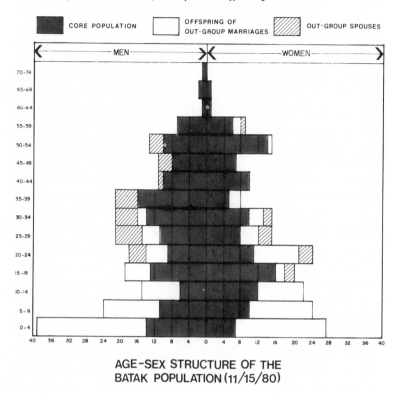

AGE-SEX STRUCTURE OF THE
BATAK POPULATION (11/15/80)

Figure 6

TABLE 11

COMPARISON OF THE BATAK POPULATION, 1972 AND 1980

	Batak	Part-Batak	Non-Batak spouses	Total
1972	275	68	31	374
1980	254	132	38	424

NOTE: Between 1972 and 1980 there were 61 births and 82 deaths in the core Batak population and 95 births and 31 deaths in the part-Batak population.

growing populations. (In the Philippines as a whole, for example, 55 percent of the population were under the age of 20 in 1975.)

But if we focus on ethnically mixed Batak, a different picture results. A third important feature of figure 6 is the predominance of mixed-parentage children at the lower reaches of the pyramid. In the age 0–4 and age 5–9 cohorts, such children outnumber core Batak children.[2] These children are numerous enough to suggest that the total study population, questions of ethnicity aside, might be constant or even growing.

COMPARISON WITH PREVIOUS POPULATION ESTIMATES

Is there any *longitudinal* evidence that can be brought to bear on the question of whether the Batak are increasing or decreasing in number? One possible benchmark for comparison is my 1972 census (table 11). At that time, the total population—core Batak, part-Batak, and non-Batak spouses—totaled 374 individuals. Hence, there was an increase in the total population, from 374 to 424, or about 13.4 percent, between 1972 and 1980. This increase consists entirely, however, of the growing numbers of ethnically mixed Batak (visible at the lower reaches of fig. 6), and there has in fact been a decrease in the numbers of core Batak, from 275 to 254. At least for recent years, the problem of whether the "Batak" are increasing or decreasing in number is therefore in part a classificatory one.

Several earlier population estimates also shed light on this problem. Miller (1905), who visited the Batak at the turn of the century, estimated that they numbered about 600 individuals. The 1911–12 Cummings expedition to the Philippines, led by Fay-Cooper Cole, estimated that there were 650 Batak (Field Museum 1983). Cole himself (1945:61) estimates the Batak population at 600 persons, but it is unclear if he is referring to data he obtained independently during one of his own visits or simply citing Miller's estimate. Several additional estimates are available for the period 1930–1940. Records of the Bureau of Non-Christian Tribes show that when the governor general of the Philippines proclaimed the establishment of the five Batak reservations in 1930, they were inhabited by a total of 160 "families" (presumably households). Whether some Batak may then have been living away from any reservation and thus escaped enumeration is unknown, but at contemporary household sizes, these 160 families included approximately 550 persons. A prewar census reported that the Batak numbered about 500 individuals (Commission of the Census 1939). I arrived at a similar estimate for the Batak population during the 1930s by asking longtime lowland Filipino settlers in different locales to report how many Batak households were present in their respective areas in the year they arrived (or in some other year for which the desired data could be easily recalled). Independent reports from different settlers in the same locale showed considerable internal agreement; apparently, village and other local officials had reasons to know these figures with some accuracy. This procedure yielded, for example, a total of 140 households, or (again at contemporary household sizes) about 480 persons, for the eve of World War II.

All of these earlier population estimates support the view that a significant decrease occurred in the Batak population—from about 600 persons to less than 400 persons—between 1900 and 1970.[3] We must now ask what the precise relationship is between the historical decline in the numbers of core Batak (who had dwindled to only 254 persons by 1980) and the historical increase in the numbers of ethnically mixed Batak (an increase that by 1980 had swelled the total study population back over the 400-person level). A key point here is that the Batak remained largely endogamous until well after World War II, in part because of simple lack of opportunity. The Tagbanua, the out-group with which Batak most commonly intermarry today, began to disperse from their central Palawan homeland for west coast and northern frontier areas early in the twentieth century (Fox 1982:26–33). But by the time of Warren's fieldwork among the Batak in 1950, they were still only recent arrivals at Babuyan, the southernmost Batak river valley (Warren 1964:27). Warren found no out-group marriages of any kind at either Babuyan or Sumurod (ibid.:73), observing that Batak in general had a "reluctance toward out-group marriage" and "seldom married Tagbanua" (ibid.:65). My own oldest informants corroborated such reports. At both Babuyan and Tanabag in 1940, for example, it was said that Tagbanua were already present but that no Batak marriages with them had yet occurred.

Batak today also marry lowland Filipinos, who intruded in Batak territory even before Tagbanua did. Unfortunately, turn-of-the-century reports on the Batak (see chap. 2) make little mention of the presence or absence of out-group marriage. Miller did observe that Batak "do not mingle or intermarry with the other native tribes" (1905:183). It certainly appears that Batak experienced little social intercourse with lowlanders until after World War II, and the cultural differences between them were far greater than between Batak and Tagbanua. The Batak themselves view out-group marriage as a recent phenomenon and claim that they were once far more numerous—and entirely endogamous.[4]

Table 12 musters some statistical evidence concerning the incidence of out-group marriage. It classifies all present and past marriages of living Batak (taking care to avoid double counting) by year of marriage and according to whether one spouse was an out-group member. This evidence confirms

TABLE 12
237 PAST AND PRESENT MARRIAGES OF LIVING BATAK, CLASSIFIED BY
DATE AND ETHNICITY OF SPOUSE

| Date of marriage | Batak | Ethnicity of spouse | Total |
		Tagbanua or Lowland Filipino	
Before 1950	43 (84%)	8 (16%)	51
1951–1960	48 (87%)	7 (13%)	55
1961–1970	44 (58%)	32 (42%)	76
1971–1980	28 (51%)	27 (49%)	55
Total marriages	163	64	237

that a high incidence of out-group marriage is a recent phenomenon, only becoming a significant factor after about 1960—well after the Batak had experienced considerable reduction (20–30%) in their numbers and extensive disruption in their socioterritorial organization (chap. 3), which made locating suitable Batak marriage partners progressively more difficult. Thus, more than the advent of a simple preference for out-group marriage explains the declining production of core Batak offspring: a genuine secular decline in the numbers of core Batak men and women forced many of those men and women to turn elsewhere to obtain mates. I will return to the notion of a threshold population size below which continued endogamy is not possible. First, however, let us examine more closely just what demographic processes were transpiring in the core Batak population which so reduced their physical numbers after about 1900.

Physical Extinction: Fertility and Mortality in the Core Batak Population

Small, preliterate populations such as the Batak pose special problems for demographic study which can only be partially compensated for by the relatively prolonged and intimate nature of anthropological fieldwork. Nevertheless, new explanatory interests in anthropology have generated considerable interest in the demography of such populations. Recent years have seen discussion of the theoretical and methodological problems involved (e.g., Howell 1973; Feeney 1975; Weiss 1976) as well as sophisticated demographic studies of anthropological populations (e.g., Neel and Weiss 1975; Howell 1979). In my analysis of Batak demography, I have eschewed application of the more complex methodologies of demographic analysis, such as stable population theory. This is, in part, because it seems to me that the Batak population has been so disrupted in recent decades as to violate the conditions under which such methodologies can profitably be used to model population dynamics and, in part, because of constraints posed by the data, in particular, small sample size and limited time depth. Instead, I have settled on an eclectic series of conceptually straightforward measures of fertility and mortality that, despite their simplicity, I believe to be adequate to the task at hand—trying to understand what was going on with births and deaths to cause such a reduction in the Batak population between 1900 and 1970. I begin with mortality, both because the relevant data are more readily ascertained and described and because the Batak experience with mortality— in contrast to Batak fertility—is comparatively unsurprising.

MORTALITY IN THE CORE POPULATION

One of the most straightforward and intuitively interesting measures of the mortality experience of a group of persons is their life expectancy at birth, which is also their average age at death (Howell 1973:256; Feeney 1975:34). Ideally, one would observe a large group of people throughout their lifetime, recording the ages at which each person died and when all had died, averaging the ages thus collected. Lacking such data for the Batak, it is possible to extract an estimate of life expectancy from observations of current

TABLE 13

Deaths by Age and Sex, for 83 People Who Died
between 1970 and 1980

Age group	Male	Female	Total
0–infant	10	16	26
1–4	4	5	9
5–9	2	1	3
10–14	1	1	2
Total, age 0–14	17 (41.5%)	23 (54.8%)	40 (48.2%)
15–19	1	1	2
20–24	0	3	3
25–29	2	2	4
30–34	3	1	4
35–39	4	1	5
40–44	2	1	3
Total, age 15–44	12 (29.3%)	9 (21.4%)	21 (25.3%)
45–49	2	6	8
50–54	4	2	6
55–59	5	0	5
60–64	1	2	3
65+	0	0	0
Total, age 45+	12 (29.3%)	10 (23.8%)	22 (26.5%)
TOTAL	41	42	83

Source: After Howell (1979:87).

mortality, that is, from the ages at which death occurs in a population during a given period. Table 13 classifies by age and sex the eighty-three deaths that occurred between 1970 and 1980 among the core Batak inhabitants of the Babuyan, Maoyon, Tanabag, Tarabanan, and Langogan River valleys (table 10), a group that numbered approximately 250 persons in 1970. (Although my first complete census of the Batak was not until 1972, I did some preliminary census work in the areas in question as early as 1966. Also, in the 1972 census, I systematically sought information on the whereabouts or date of death of close kin. Thus, I probably missed at most only a few deaths that occurred from 1970 to 1972.)

If we assume that the twenty-six persons shown in table

13 as having died before one year of age, died, on the average, at six months, then the average age at death for the entire group was 21.9 years. This figure, which can be taken to approximate Batak life expectancy at birth, is low but not surprisingly so. Comparable life expectancies have been reported for the Yanomama Indians (20 years; Neel and Weiss 1975:38) and for the Casiguran Agta (21.2 years; Headland 1986:365). Life expectancies of this order are at the low end of the normal range for human populations, which Howell (1973:261–262) estimates to be 18 to 20 years, "the highest level [of mortality] for which our limited human fertility can compensate." But while not extreme in the broadest sense, Batak life expectancy at birth is dramatically lower than that in many other populations, some of which are otherwise similar to the Batak. Howell (1979:114–116) calculates that !Kung life expectancy at birth was around 30 years when a relatively undisturbed hunting-gathering lifeway prevailed and has recently improved (depending on the data used) to 35 or 40 years. For the Semai, an aboriginal group of the Malay Peninsula whose natural environment and subsistence economy resembles that of the Batak, Fix (1982:179) also reports a life expectancy at birth of about 30 years.

Table 13 shows that one of the principal reasons for low Batak life expectancy is the high level of infant and child mortality; almost half the observed deaths occurred in the age 0–14 category. Infant deaths are particularly high. In another calculation, I tabulated all births that occurred to core Batak in the same area between 1960 and 1979. Of 130 children born, thirty-seven died before the age of one year, for an infant mortality rate (number of infant deaths per 1,000 live births) of 285. It is also shown that Batak life expectancy is limited by rapid attrition after about the age of 45. As figure 6 suggested, age 50 to 60 is already "old age" among the Batak. The !Kung again provide a revealing comparison: while virtually no Batak in the sample examined here survived beyond age 60, fully 35 percent of a similar sample of !Kung deaths occurred *after* age 59 (Howell 1979:87).

FERTILITY IN THE CORE POPULATION

From the standpoint of the direction of change in population size, particular levels of mortality must always be seen relative to particular levels of fertility. As Howell says, even at the levels of mortality experienced by the Batak (which are not that high, comparatively), fertility can and does compensate. Among the high-mortality Yanomama, for example, females of completed fertility average a high 8.2 live births each, and the Yanomama population is growing (Neel and Weiss 1975).

What about Batak fertility? We have already inferred that it in fact fails to compensate for Batak mortality, but it is necessary to be more precise. My best data come from the reproductive histories of seventy-one Batak women of completed fertility—women who had only been married to Batak men, who were over the age of 40 (see below) at the time I interviewed them, and whose birth histories could be ascertained with some confidence.[5] Such data must be approached with caution. A number of women will survive to reproductive age but die before completing their reproductive span, and the number of live births they experience will be less, on the average, than among the women whose birth histories are examined here. Further, analysis of birth histories provides more of a window to *past* fertility than to present fertility. Thus, particularly in situations of demographic change, one cannot uncritically assume that the levels of fertility observed still obtain in the present population. Nevertheless, the resulting statistic is interesting. It enables us to obtain, in effect, some measure of how many offspring (who will be subject to the mortality levels discussed above) each woman replaces herself with.

Table 14 shows that the seventy-one Batak women whose reproductive performance I studied averaged only 3.94 live births each. This is a low, even strikingly low, figure, yet I am confident that there was no significant underreporting of births. The figure may be immediately compared with an

TABLE 14

NUMBER OF LIVE BIRTHS TO 71 LIVING OR RECENTLY DECEASED
BATAK WOMEN OF COMPLETED FERTILITY

Total live births	No. of women	Total no. of children
0	7	0
1	10	10
2	12	24
3	5	15
4	14	56
5	6	30
6	2	12
7	3	21
8	5	40
9	2	18
10	3	30
11	1	11
12	0	0
13	1	13
Total	71	280

Mean number of children per mother = 3.94

average of 4.69 live births to a sample of !Kung women aged
45 and over (Howell 1979:123) and with averages of 4.03
and 4.08 live births to similar samples of other San women
(Harpending and Wandsnider 1982). While still low, these
figures are coupled with a mortality schedule less severe than
that confronting the Batak. Indeed, given the levels of mortality in table 13 and assuming equal sex ratios, Batak women
do *not* appear to be "replacing themselves," for the average
woman in our sample has but two daughters, only one
of whom, on the average, will survive to even *begin*
childbearing.

Why do Batak women average so few live births? A complete explanation of this phenomenon must account for the
considerable variation in female reproductive histories. As
table 14 shows, some women (about 10%) have no live
births, some women have two live births, and some women
have many live births. A complete explanation must also

address the characteristic scheduling of Batak births. Batak births are relatively few not because birth spacings are particularly long (as reported for the !Kung and other hunting-gathering peoples) but because women typically cease child-bearing altogether at an early age.

To pursue this last point, it is necessary to calculate age-specific fertility rates. Unfortunately, only for twenty-eight of the seventy-one cases in table 14 was I able to estimate the age of the mother as well as all of her offspring with the degree of confidence necessary for such calculations. This sample of twenty-eight mothers, while small, provides an invaluable window to an astonishing aspect of Batak fertility—a greatly foreshortened female reproductive span. Table 15 shows the number of these women in the age classes 5–19, 20–24, and so on, who gave birth to a child. The average number of live births for this sample of women is only 3.75, even smaller than that for the larger sample in table 14.[6] This figure, known as the total fertility rate, represents the total number of offspring that would be born, on the average, to a group of women, all of whom survive to the end of the childbearing period, who experienced these rates as they passed through the age groups (Howell 1979: 123).

A distinctive aspect of table 15 is the sudden decline in the age-specific fertility rate which begins with the age group 25–29 and leads to a complete cessation of childbearing before the age of 40. A useful comparison is again with the !Kung. Table 16 compares the age-specific fertility rates for sixty-two women aged 45 and over studied by Howell with the rates for the twenty-nine women considered here. Batak fertility rates are actually *higher* for the 15–19 and 20–24 age groups, but in later age groups they fall below !Kung rates and diminish even faster; !Kung women continue child-bearing for ten years longer than do Batak women. Low Batak fertility is even more surprising, given Howell's (1979: 124) opinion that !Kung fertility rates are somewhat lower for later age groups than would be expected based on the rates for earlier age groups.

TABLE 15
AGE-SPECIFIC FERTILITY RATES AND PARITY FOR 28 WOMEN AGE 40 AND OLDER

Age group	Parity											Total	At risk[a]	Age-specific fertility
	0	1	2	3	4	5	6	7	8	9	10			
15–19	0	2	7	2	2	1	0	2	3	0	4	23	140	0.164
20–24	0	2	5	4	8	5	0	8	4	0	5	41	140	0.293
25–29	0	0	0	0	5	3	0	5	4	0	6	23	140	0.164
30–34	0	0	0	0	1	0	0	5	3	0	4	13	140	0.093
35–39	0	0	0	0	0	1	0	1	2	0	1	5	140	0.036
40–45	0	0	0	0	0	0	0	0	0	0	0	0	140	—
No. of children:	0	4	12	6	16	10	0	21	16	0	20	105		0.750[b]
No. of mothers:	3	4	6	2	4	2	0	3	2	0	2	28		
Mean parity:														3.75[c]

Source: After Howell (1979:124).
[a] The number of person-years at risk of birth during each interval (29 women × 5 years).
[b] Computed by summing age-specific fertility rates for the 5-year intervals and multiplying by 5.
[c] 4.20 if four women at parity zero are excluded.

TABLE 16
COMPARISON OF !KUNG AND BATAK AGE-SPECIFIC FERTILITY RATES

Age group	Age-specific fertility rate	
	!Kung[a]	Batak
15–19	0.135	0.164
20–24	0.242	0.293
25–29	0.203	0.164
30–34	0.152	0.093
35–39	0.119	0.036
40–44	0.071	—
45–49	0.016	—
Total fertility rate	4.691	3.75

[a] From Howell (1979:124); n = 62 women at age 45 and older.

Batak women appear to utilize a very brief period of their potential reproductive period. Just how brief may be seen in table 17, which classifies the twenty-five women in table 15 who had at least one live birth according to their ages at first and final birth. Mean age at first birth is 18, about what one would expect for such a population and close to the !Kung mean of 18.79 (ibid.:128). (The clustering of Batak mothers with first birth at age 15 is suspicious and suggests that some of their ages may have been underestimated by a year or two.) Mean age at final birth, however, is only 26.3, far lower than the !Kung mean of 34.35 (ibid.:130). Thus, Batak women concentrate their childbearing within a mean reproductive span of about eight years, only a fraction of the thirty-four years (age 15 to age 49) theoretically available to them.

Any explanation of low Batak fertility, then, must center on the early age at which many women cease childbearing altogether rather than, say, age at menarche, age at marriage, age at first birth, or length of birth spacings. For the record, it can be said that the Batak are not particularly unusual in any of these latter respects. Age at menarche is somewhat high by lowland Philippine standards but is comparable to that in other anthropological populations. A small sample of nine

TABLE 17
AGE AT FIRST BIRTH AND AGE AT FINAL BIRTH FOR 25 BATAK
WOMEN OF COMPLETED FERTILITY AND AT LEAST ONE BIRTH

Age	Number of mothers with first birth at that age	Number of mothers with final birth at that age
15	6	
16	1	
17	3	1
18	6	2
19	3	1
20	2	2
21	2	2
22	1	2
23		
24	1	2
25		2
26		
27		
28		1
29		1
30		2
31		
32		
33		1
34		1
35		2
36		3
	Mean age at first birth = 18.0	Mean age at final birth = 26.3

teenage girls, whose birthdates I knew to the month and whose mothers were unusually cooperative in discussing the matter, averaged 15.1 years of age at menarche. Marriage (as in numerous other populations) and children (as we saw in table 17) soon follow. Birth spacings, finally, average about 28 months.

The obvious question at this point is whether Batak women, particularly older women, may *deliberately* restrict their fertility. The answer is inconclusive: some apparently do; most apparently do not. Both men and women spoke of indigenous contraceptive and abortifacient techniques. It is reported that some Batak women drink an herbal concoction, *tigaba'was*, to induce permanent sterility. The drug is said to be most efficacious when taken immediately following delivery of a new child, with the intention of preventing future pregnancies. In fact, it is said that the major incentive for use is experiencing a difficult childbirth and the ensuing fear, of the mother or her husband, that a future delivery might be unduly painful or even life-threatening. A number of older women with only one or two live births were cited as having taken tigaba'was; several confirmed that they had. I never sought the identity of the two species of vines said to be used to prepare the concoction, nor did I learn much about its possible mechanism. *Men* knowledgeable of medicinal plants traditionally prepare and administer the concoction. They claim it disrupts or even terminates menstruation. One insisted that the drug had to terminate menstruation to work as intended. Women were equally insistent, however, that tigaba'was worked even if it did not disrupt or terminate menstruation. In any event, while I am convinced that the drug exists and has prevented conception in certain women, by all accounts these women are a minority. Thus, of the seventy-one women shown in table 14, some of the thirty-four women with 1 to 2 live births can be presumed to have taken the drug. The principal explanation for low Batak fertility must therefore lie elsewhere.

Other customary practices and beliefs, for example, a prohibition on widow remarriage or seasonal or ceremonial sexual abstinence, while not perhaps regarded by the people themselves as reducing fertility, might nevertheless have this effect. No such factors seem important in the Batak case, however. Virtually all women marry early and stay married and sexually active throughout their reproductive lives. Although divorces occur regularly, most are preceded by an extramarital sexual affair that characteristically leads the woman to cohabit immediately with her new husband. (Lowlanders refer to Batak divorce practices as "wife stealing," calling attention to the fact that divorce among them rarely leads to simple separation. While Batak usually deny having any *kaupakat,* or "lover," relationships of their own, most will speak readily, if guardedly, of those of others.)

Most women, finally, seem to *want* to have children and, in fact, often express unhappiness that they do not have more. I did hear of one or two women who were suspected of inducing miscarriages or abortions in the interest of extramarital sexual freedom. Most of the married women rumored to be sexually active with other men, however, were presumed to be attempting to increase their chances of becoming pregnant. The Batak are pragmatists, and a charming custom governs fatherhood in those cases where such a woman does become pregnant: her lover may come forward and publicly claim a share of paternity. If this occurs, a meeting of elders is held, the appropriate ritual fine is paid, and the child, now known as a *lupaw,* will address both the mother's husband and lover as "father."

This brings us to those factors potentially explaining low fertility which are essentially biological and involuntary—a class of factors that I believe must principally afford the explanation for the early cessation of childbearing activity. The most dramatic, or at least the most immediate, is early menopause. Unfortunately, it is difficult for a male ethnographer to inquire about menopause, much less to attempt to date an event that is relatively unremarkable anyway. Certainly, one cannot *infer* that a woman has reached menopause simply because she ceases childbearing before age 50. As Howell (1979:129) says, such a woman may still be menstruating but not producing viable ova, or it could be that she is not having sexual relations or that she is sick or unlucky. But we have seen that lack of sexual activity does not appear to be a problem. Neither does sterility induced by venereal disease, to which Howell (ibid.:185−187) attributes a small portion of low !Kung fertility; to my knowledge, venereal disease has never been reported among the Batak or any other Philippine tribal population. Marriage to an infertile man is another possibility, made intriguing by the fact that about 20 percent of men age 40 and over have never fathered a child (although a number of these men claim a *share* in fatherhood). While a high incidence of apparent male infertility is inherently interesting, its impact on a woman's fertility is limited, as we have seen, because the parties to an infertile marriage characteristically seek sexual contact with others until pregnancy is achieved.

This brings us back to early menopause or some other early disruption in female reproductive function. I did interview six women, whose ages I knew with some certainty, on the subject. All were over 40 and reported that they were postmenopausal. In most cases, menstruation never returned following a final birth, which made dating problematic. Thus, the three women who gave birth at age 36 (table 17) reported that they never later resumed menstruation. The same was true of two women with a final birth at age 28. The sixth woman had a final birth at age 25; the child died at 2 weeks, and the woman's menstruation soon resumed, only to stop permanently the following year. Beyond these fragmentary quantitative data, there is a general impression among Batak women that they either enter menopause or become highly amenorrheic much earlier than their lowland counterparts. This issue cannot be addressed further without first examining Batak physiological well-being, the subject of chapter 5.

DEPOPULATION IN THE CORE GROUP AND THE
NOTION OF A THRESHOLD POPULATION SIZE

The diminishment in the core Batak population from approximately 600 persons in 1900 to approximately 400 persons in 1970 is particularly intriguing in view of the attention that has been given to 500 as a sort of magic number in hunter-gatherer demography (Birdsell 1968; Lee and DeVore 1968). While this figure was once regarded as a mean size about which many past and present hunter-gatherer populations were believed to cluster, recent demographic research suggests that the figure might more appropriately be regarded as a minimum, below which continued endogamy becomes increasingly difficult. Wobst (1975:80), for example, exploring the possible origin of the incest taboo, believes that ancestral human breeding populations might have had to reach a threshold size of approximately 500 persons before any cultural restrictions on mate selection (such as those posed by incest taboos) could have been instituted without working a demographic hardship. Adams and Kasakoff (1976:156–157), while recognizing the significance traditionally assigned the number 500, report that the majority of ethnographically known endogamous human breeding populations are larger than 500 and range from 850 to 55,000.

MacCluer and Dyke (1976) begin their exploration of the minimum size of endogamous populations by summarizing an earlier review of the relevant literature by Livi (1949), who

> concluded on the basis of observed population size that populations of fewer than 300 individuals are unlikely to survive; that populations of 300 to 500 individuals are in a state of *desequilibre*, on the borderline between survival and extinction; and that, in general, population sizes had to exceed 500 in order to insure survival. (P. 1)

The basic notion is the simple one that the number of potential marriage partners for each marriageable individual is inversely related to group size and as group size diminishes (at least in small groups), such individuals begin to experience increasing difficulty in *locating* marriage partners (McFarland 1970).

In practice, of course, all sorts of restrictions besides actual group size affect the availability of marriage partners. Much of the recent research on the subject concerns how these other restrictions—in particular, the incest taboo—would interact with absolute breeding numbers to produce thresholds of different sizes, depending on the number and severity of the restrictions in question, below which population survival would be threatened. Thus, for example, low-fertility, low-mortality populations can survive with fewer individuals than can high-fertility, high-mortality populations (MacCluer and Dyke 1976) and only the strongest marriage prohibitions (e.g., those extending to second cousins, as among the Batak) work a demographic hardship on populations in the low hundreds (Hammel et al. 1979). Some of this research concludes that under certain conditions, endogamous human populations can survive with as few as 200 persons (MacCluer and Dyke 1976:11; Hammel et al. 1979:977). But under the conditions the Batak faced at midcentury—low fertility, high mortality, disrupted settlement pattern, and a stringent incest taboo—it seems reasonable to conclude that a hypothetical population of even 500 persons (a threshold below which the Batak were then falling) would indeed be faced with extinction.

In any actual human population, individuals experiencing difficulty in locating customarily appropriate marriage partners would undoubtedly either explore alternative marriage possibilities within their own society or seek spouses in other populations (MacCluer and Dyke 1976:3). That is exactly what the Batak began to do at midcentury: they turned increasingly to cousins and outsiders for marriage partners. The increasing incidence of marriage between cousins, while statistically significant, was relatively unimportant demographically, and I defer discussion of it to another context (see chap. 7). Marriage to outsiders has become common (see table 12).

Out-group marriage underlies the recent stabilization in the total study population and thus represents the one sense in which the Batak appear to be adapting successfully to change. Of the thirty-seven Batak married to out-group members, twenty-eight were women married to Tagbanua or lowland Filipino men. As a group, these women are generally young and of uncompleted fertility. But mean household sizes are somewhat larger in those local groups where the most out-group marriage has occurred. Thus, in table 10, household sizes in local groups A1 and E average 4.8 and 4.1 individuals, respectively, whereas the corresponding figures for groups B1 and C are only 3.5 and 3.3. As households in all local groups consist predominantely of nuclear families, these observations suggest that out-married Batak women may indeed experience higher fertility than their in-married counterparts whose fertility was examined (see table 14). I have no comparable data indicating that mortality may be lower in the out-married population, nor do I have any evidence that out-marrying women marry non-Batak men because they perceive them to be better mates; the realities of demography and settlement pattern favor such marriages. But taken together, these data suggest that fertility in the intermarried population may now compensate for mortality and hence ensure, at least for the moment, the perpetuation of Batak genetic material. Out-group marriage, however, has had implications for cultural extinction as well as for physical extinction.

Cultural Extinction: Ethnicity in the Intermarried Batak Population

After about 1960, an increasing incidence of marriages between Batak and members of other ethnic groups began to change irreversibly the ethnic composition of the "Batak" population. Particularly striking was the decade 1970-1980, which saw out-group marriage on its way to becoming the most common form of marriage. Indeed, by the time I left the field in 1981, it appeared that few new marriages would ever be consummated between two core Batak. Figure 6 illustrated the consequences of this change in marriage patterns for the composition of the younger age cohorts in the population. Sometime during that decade, births of "mixed-marriage" children began to exceed births of core Batak children; the latter births apparently will soon cease altogether.

In a matter of decades, assuming that current trends continue—it is difficult to see how they could not—there will be few surviving individuals who can claim to have been born to two (pure) Batak. But there will be surviving individuals—descendants of members of the population studied here. Let us put aside the question of numerical change in this population and ask in what sense, if any, this ongoing change in the ethnic backgrounds of those who remain in fact also constitutes the *disappearance* of the Batak.

This question actually entails two related but distinct questions. On the one hand, there is the essentially etic question of how the social and cultural characteristics of the evolving population of mixed Batak compare with those characteristics of the dwindling population of core Batak. On the other hand, there is the essentially emic question of how the evolving population of mixed Batak is regarded—as "Batak" or as something else—by themselves and by others. The relationship between these two questions might be that members of the mixed population differ greatly from members of the core population in their values and behavior and yet continue to advance claims of Batak ethnic identity— claims that are accepted by others. In such a case, it would probably be more appropriate to conclude that the Batak are *changing* rather than disappearing, although many of their traditional values and institutions might, in fact, have become extinct. Conversely, members of the evolving mixed population might differ little from other Batak in their values and behavior and yet not advance claims of Batak identity, or they might find that their claims to such an identity are not accepted by others.

In practice, no such simple situation obtains. The mixed population, not surprisingly, resembles the core population in some respects, but not in others, and there are conflicting opinions—if not confusion—about what ethnic label to assign to individuals of mixed parentage. With respect to the objective characteristics displayed, and because outsiders (with a few exceptions) have "married in" rather than the

Batak having "married out," the mixed population lives together with the core population, that is, in Batak settlements and Batak houses. The Batak language, furthermore, continues to be the lingua franca in these settlements. Thus, what would appear to be two prerequisites for the maintenance of Batak ethnic identity, continued common residence and language use, seem to be met.

In practice, however, Batak language in the intermarried population survives only in simplified form. Out-group spouses are not usually fluent in Batak—nor, it is said, are their children. Communication in households formed as the result of out-group marriage often involves a mixture of Batak, Tagbanua, and Cuyonon. The offspring of out-group marriages also do not acquire many other, distinctively Batak cultural characteristics. Men do not dress in barkcloth, hunt pigs with bow and arrow, or climb trees to collect honey. Women do not dress in the traditional style or weave baskets with intricate designs. Neither do the offspring of out-group marriages learn to be shamanistic curers or follow traditional naming practices or play traditional musical instruments. Many of these same reductions in cultural inventory have taken place in the core population, particularly in those local groups where the most out-group marriage has occurred.

At the same time, neither do the offspring of out-group marriages, much less the core Batak themselves, acquire a full inventory of Tagbanua or lowland Filipino cultural institutions and practices. Such offspring, for example (with a few exceptions), do not attend lowland schools or religious services. But formal education, even if it only involves a few years of schooling, and identification with a world religion are important dimensions to the cultural inventory and ethnic identity of lowland Filipinos. Similarly, the offspring of mixed marriages, much less the core Batak, do not enjoy many of the political rights and economic goods and services that lowlanders enjoy. Again, with some exceptions, the Batak are nonliterate and therefore do not vote in government elections, they consume few of the foods and possess few of the furnishings and durables found in rural Filipino households, and so on. In short, and in comparison to the lives of their Filipino and Tagbanua neighbors, the cultural lives of both core and mixed Batak are relatively barren. I argue in chapter 7 that cultural impoverishment of this order in both the core and the intermarried population constitutes "deculturation" rather than merely "acculturation." I also examine the consequences of deculturation for Batak adaptive well-being. I defer until chapter 8 a discussion of the comparative question, Why do Batak-like peoples tend to suffer cultural impoverishment and marginalization instead of embarking on some more positive developmental trajectory vis-à-vis a wider, dominant society? For purposes of my argument here, it is sufficient to point out that considerable culture loss has in fact occurred among the Batak. Indeed, in those Batak groups where the most intermarriage has occurred, except for some persistent physical features and the use of Batak language, there appears to be little to distinguish the Batak, whether "core" or "mixed," from Tagbanua or from impoverished lowland Filipinos.

Does this mean that the Batak are *becoming* Tagbanua or lowland Filipino? The issue is not that simple. Indeed, the question of the perceived ethnic identity of the evolving population of intermarried Batak was the single most vexing problem I encountered in my fieldwork. It was a question about which Batak, Tagbanua, and lowland Filipinos were themselves genuinely perplexed and had little to offer. Several examples will illustrate this. First, in addition to the eight east coast river valleys currently inhabited by Batak (fig. 1), there is the west coast at Caruray, mentioned in turn-of-the-century reports as having a Batak population and generally acknowledged by present-day Batak as once having had a Batak population. Indeed, a number of contemporary Batak claim that some "Batak" still live there. None could be located, however. Those individuals actually identified by name as would-be Batak said they were "really" Tagbanua, a position also taken by other Batak. They said of these present-day Caruray dwellers, "People just think they're Batak, but they're not really" and "They used to be Batak but [because they lost their Batakness] now they're just like Tagbanua." Interestingly, these erstwhile Caruray Tagbanua— who, for that matter, display few traditional Tagbanua traits—are often referred to as *Caruraynen*, which means, in effect, "native of Caruray." Such a construction is a more specific version of the word *Tagbanua*, "from this place." It should be mentioned that the few Caruraynen I met were of quite dark complexion and had very curly hair. However, I could draw no genealogical connection between those Caruraynen I encountered and present-day east coast Batak, although it is generally acknowledged that the ancestors of Caruraynen somehow include both "Batak" and "Tagbanua."

Another of the perplexing consequences of intermarriage is seen in the situation at Buayan, the northernmost river valley still inhabited by Batak. As table 10 shows, there is extensive intermarriage at the Buayan settlement, and numerous Tagbanua and Visayans are present. The Batak at Buayan, who display few traditional Batak cultural markers, claim to be different from all other Batak and are in fact regarded by other Batak as distinctive "Buayan Batak" or "Buayanen"—natives of Buayan. In the earliest reports, Buayan Batak were said to be "more warlike" than other Batak, whatever that may have meant, but today their most visible difference is linguistic. Buayanen, as they call themselves, speak a dialect of the Batak language that is distinct from, although intelligible with, that spoken elsewhere. (In fact, less than ten Buayanen speakers still survive, and the last surviving speakers of a third Batak dialect, once said to have prevailed at Caramay, recently died.) Curiously, Buayanen (who claim to be related to the Caruraynen) say their version of the Batak language is the true and uncorrupted one, yet they *also* claim an affinity with Tagbanua that I never heard expressed in the more southerly Batak groups. "We're the ultimate in Tagbanua here in the north," said one. At the time, this statement struck me as mere ethnic chauvinism; since then, I have come to wonder if it might not be essentially correct.

A final example concerns the situation in the Caramay River valley, just south of Buayan, where extensive intermarriage has also occurred (table 10). In contrast to their counterparts still farther south, lowland residents at Caramay proper were often unable to specify whether certain of their upstream neighbors were in fact "Batak" or "Tagbanua." Comments such as "I don't know," "I think his father was really a Tagbanua," and "People say he's really a Tagbanua" were common. In river valleys farther south, where such ambiguities about ethnic identity are generally absent, lowlanders widely refer to the upstream regions inhabited by the Batak with the term *kabatakan*, "where the Batak live." At Caramay, in contrast, this term is not in use, and lowlanders instead refer to the area inhabited by the upstream population with phrases like *campo ng mga tribos*, "where the tribes camp," or *sa mga tribos*, "where the tribes live."

This reference to the evolving Batak population as "tribos" or "natives" is also common near Buayan, and it illustrates the future of those Batak who remain. That future is to be identified less as "Batak" and more as a kind of generic tribal population. As such, they will find themselves demarcated from others not by any distinctive, cultural markers (e.g., the use of the bow and arrow) but as presumed indigenes and by the same set of diagnostic social and economic factors—marginality, poverty, illiteracy, limited cultural inventory—that characterizes evolving Philippine tribal populations generally and for whom more vague ethnic designations are appropriate (e.g., Tagbanua). No lowlander would ever infer from another individual's marginal socioeconomic circumstances that that person was a Batak, but he might well infer that he was, somehow, an indigene and thus a kind of Tagbanua.

An evaluation of Batak adaptive well-being in terms of one central measure of adaptation, the ability to *persist* as a population, has shown that the Batak experienced a sustained decline in their numbers between about 1900 and 1970. I have argued that the magnitude and repercussions of this decline were such that they in fact constituted evidence that the Batak had entered a period of severe adaptive difficulty. On the question of whether the Batak are actually "disappearing," however, the data are ambiguous, for after about 1970, the population—increasingly intermarried with outsiders but still possessing considerable Batak genetic material—leveled off in number and now appears to be slowly growing. Thus, if the Batak do ultimately disappear, that disappearance will likely be cultural rather than physical. But our evaluation of Batak adaptive well-being is incomplete, for nothing has yet been said about the standards of living or quality of existence of those population members, regardless of numbers or ethnic identities, who *do* survive. This is the subject of chapter 5.

5

Physiological Evidence of Adaptive Difficulty

Here I continue the presentation of my evidence for the argument that the Batak are in serious adaptive difficulty but with the focus on the adaptive difficulties of individuals, in particular, the state of Batak physiological well-being. I begin by summarizing the results of anthropometric measurements and clinical observations made among two local groups of Batak during 1980–81. The anthropometric measurements show that by the standards of the West and even of the lowland Philippines, the Batak are not only short in stature but very lightweight for their height. Moreover, skin folds are quite thin, and both weight and skin folds show some seasonal variation. While my clinical observations of the Batak were untrained, experienced doctors and other medical personnel have visited the Batak. Their assessments of Batak health status have largely concerned the various diseases afflicting them; tuberculosis and other respiratory ailments, gastrointestinal illnesses, and malaria have been identified as the principal causes of sickness and death. It is the unanimous opinion of these medical specialists that the Batak are in poor health.

A case for individual physiological difficulties thus established, I turn to what I call the "proximate causes" of these difficulties. In particular, I discuss nutrition, emphasizing the well-known interactions of poor nutrition and lowered resistance to infection. The poor nutritional status of the Batak is a direct reflection of the contemporary diet: low in animal protein, low in vegetables and other greens, probably even low in calories. Despite the nutritional value and continued availability of many of the traditional subsistence foods cataloged in chapter 2, actual food consumption patterns are remarkably narrow and monotonous. Also examined here as a cause of poor health is the manner in which changes in living conditions, such as new house styles and preferences for Western clothing, have altered the transmission of disease.

My use of the word *proximate* to characterize the causes of physiological stress is deliberate; factors that are "causal" in one perspective are often, in a wider perspective, phenomena that must themselves be accounted for. In the case of the Batak, their current avoidance of some nutritious traditional foods has clearly helped to undermine their health status, but the attitudes and circumstances that lead the Batak to eschew such foods must be accounted for. Or, again, tuberculosis and other chronic ailments have clearly undermined Batak health, but why do the Batak fail to mobilize the kind of social support systems that help other people cope more effectively with these diseases than the Batak do? Questions such as these are pursued later, when I relate the causes of physiological stress discussed here to wider patterns of social stress and cultural disruption.

I close by suggesting that poor health may help to account for some of the characteristic features of Batak subsistence economy and Batak demography. Short workdays and a high incidence of rest days in the Batak subsistence round, I argue, likely reflect illness or lack of energy as much as any state of "primitive affluence." Similarly, the high infant mortality rate and the remarkably early age at menopause probably are consequences of Batak nutritional difficulties. Such consequences of physiological stress also provide powerful inferential evidence for the presence of physiological stress.

Indeed, high infant mortality is often treated as a virtual surrogate for poor health itself. But such phenomena are somewhat removed from poor health, and a relationship must be found by employing certain problematic assumptions, for example, assumptions about the relationships between weight and fertility.

An Assessment of Batak Health Status

To assess the status of Batak health, I rely on two major kinds of evidence about physiological well-being: anthropometric measurements and informal clinical assessment.

NUTRITIONAL ANTHROPOMETRY

My primary source of data on the health status of the Batak is their nutritional status and derives from my repeated measurements of the weights, heights, upper-arm circumferences, and skin fold thicknesses of men, women, and children over the course of a year. Given their relatively small numbers and dispersed settlement pattern, a major difficulty with obtaining such data among the Batak was simply locating adequate numbers of individuals to take measurements from. Children, in particular, were especially scarce, and instead of following any systematic sampling procedure, I simply tried to take measurements from as many individuals as possible. I limited my efforts to the two largest local groups: Langogan, where I resided during 1980–81, and Tanabag, where I had resided during 1972 and 1975 and which I continued to visit periodically during my stay at Langogan. But despite this concentration of my measurement efforts, there was still the problem that the Batak rarely come together as a group, and even at Langogan, I spent many hours carrying my anthropometric equipment along the trails to scattered field houses and forest camps, searching out the members of my "sample."

In these circumstances, it was essential that my equipment

be easily portable. For weighing, I employed a beam balance provided by the Nutrition Center of the Philippines. The balance was suspended from a tree limb or roof beam, and the individuals to be weighed sat in a sling suspended from the scale. The scale arm was calibrated up to 25 kilograms, but individuals of up to 75 kilograms could be weighed by hanging additional weights on the end of the beam. My other equipment consisted of an anthropometer and a pair of Harpenden skin fold calipers. When combined with a notebook and provisions, these items made for a somewhat ungainly pack. But it was essential to be mobile, and I was.

If locating adequate numbers of Batak was difficult, the Batak themselves proved highly cooperative. Adults and older children were weighed individually, without footwear and in minimal clothing. Infants were weighed with their mothers and their weights later determined by subtraction. I did not weigh at any particular time of the day, nor did I attempt to control for gut or bladder content. I did note what each individual was wearing at the time of weighing and eventually weighed samples of clothing and ornaments to determine average weights for each item—shirts, bark loincloths, skirts, brass ankle bracelets, and so on. I later deducted these weights, as appropriate, from my field measurements; thus, all weights discussed here are nude weights. I measured skin folds at two standard body sites: at midtriceps on the upper left arm and subscapular, on the left back. I took three readings at each site during each encounter and then averaged the three. At the same site where I measured the midtriceps skin fold, I also measured arm circumference using the tape measure. In the case of children, I also measured head circumference. After completing my measurements, I gave each adult a stick of tobacco and each child, some candy.

I eventually measured at least once 44 men, 40 women, and 24 children, a total of 108 individuals and more than 40 percent of the total population of "core" Batak shown in table 10. To explore the possibility that seasonal change in food availability might be sufficiently severe to be visible in

TABLE 18
BATAK HEIGHT, BY SEX AND AGE

Age	Height (cm)	
	Men (n = 44)	Women (n = 40)
15–24	152.2	144.4
25–34	155.9	143.9
35–44	152.7	141.6
45–54	153.8	144.5
55–64	151.2	137.6
65–	149.7	138.4
All	153.1	143.2

seasonal variation in weight and fat accumulation, I repeated my measurements three times over the course of the year. I took my first set of measurements on January 31 in Tanabag and between February 20 and March 29 in Langogan, a dry-season period of average food abundance. I took my second set of measurements on August 1 in Tanabag and July 16–23 in Langogan, at the height of the preharvest "famine season." I took my third set of measurements on October 18 in Tanabag and November 11–14 in Langogan, during a period of postharvest leisure and rice abundance. Weighed at least twice were 35 men, 28 women, and 16 children. The 44 adult men measured once or more averaged 153.1 centimeters in height and 46.5 kilograms in weight; the 40 adult women measured once or more averaged 143.2 centimeters in height and 40.5 kilograms in weight. Tables 18, 19, and 20 classify height, weight, and midtriceps skin fold thickness, respectively, as a function of sex and age.[1]

With what should we compare these data to determine what they tell us of Batak nutritional status? One possible comparison is with comparable data for other equatorial hunter-gatherer groups. Table 21 presents such data for the Agta and the !Kung Bushmen. This comparison is intriguing because of the considerable similarity in body measurements among these three groups, but it does not resolve the question because there is no consensus about whether these other

TABLE 19
BATAK WEIGHT, BY SEX AND AGE

| Age | Weight (kg) | |
	Men (n = 44)	Women (n = 40)
15–24	47.3	42.8
25–34	50.0	41.5
35–44	46.2	38.0
45–54	46.1	41.0
55–64	43.2	33.8
65–	41.0	29.6
All	46.5	40.5

TABLE 20
BATAK MIDTRICEPS SKIN FOLD THICKNESS, BY SEX AND AGE
MIDTRICEPS SKIN FOLD THICKNESS (mm)

Age	Men (n = 44)	Women (n = 40)
15–24	5.9	10.3
25–34	4.7	8.4
35–44	4.6	7.4
45–54	4.9	10.5
55–64	5.4	6.9
65–	6.3	4.6
All	5.0	9.0

TABLE 21
HUNTER-GATHERER ANTHROPOMETRIC MEASUREMENTS

	Batak	Agta[a]	Bushmen[b]
Height (cm): male	153.1	153	160
female	143.2	144	150
Weight (kg): male	46.5	45	49
female	40.5	38	41

[a] From Headland (1986:544); n = 115 Casiguran Agta.
[b] From Lee (1979:285); n = 573 Dobe San.

groups suffer from nutritional stress. In the Bushman case, for example, there is disagreement about whether their small stature and their physique are evidence of chronic or seasonal undernutrition (Truswell and Hansen 1968, 1976) or of efficient adaptation to a particular climatic and subsistence regime (Tobias 1964: 76; Lee 1979: 289–292). Interpreting his Agta data, Headland (1986: 394–396) takes the former position. After his own careful evaluation of Agta health status, he concludes that their extreme thinness is not the result of physiological or genetic adaptation but of nutritional deficiencies. Griffin (1984: 22–23), describing the deteriorating health of women in another group of Agta, does not report anthropometric data but similarly concludes that they suffer from "malnutrition." The ultimate problem, however, is that no one knows exactly what the weight of a well-nourished desert or tropical forest forager should be.

In the absence of such knowledge, Tables of Standards derived from measurements of other populations provide another basis for comparison of anthropometric data. Such tables allow one to calculate the proportions of a population sample that stand in particular relationships to the standard value, which is taken to be the most desirable value. The most widely used such standards are the Harvard Standards, which appear in Jelliffe (1966); selected for comparative purposes here are the weight-for-height standards. This widely used evaluation of body proportions is presumed to reflect current nutritional status and to be relatively independent (in comparison to weight or height for age) of genetic influence (Waterlow et al. 1977). Table 22 displays the comparison between these standards and the weight and height data in tables 18 and 19. Table 23 makes a similar comparison using the midtriceps skin fold data in table 20. Table 22 shows that the median weight for height for both sexes is only about 85 percent of standard, with about half of the adult men falling below 80 percent of standard.[2]

Lee (1979: 289) makes the same comparison using his data and with the same result: the average !Kung male and female

TABLE 22
WEIGHTS FOR HEIGHTS OF ADULT BATAK MEN AND WOMEN,
CLASSIFIED AS PERCENT OF STANDARD

% of standard	Number of adult men[a]	Number of adult women[b]	Total
105–109	0	3	3
100–104	1	0	1
95–99	1	5	6
90–94	5	6	11
85–89	11	4	15
80–84	4	5	9
75–79	12	4	16
70–74	5	3	8
65–69	3	0	3
Total	42	30	72

Source: Jelliffe (1966).
[a] From tables 18 and 19, less two men shorter than the minimum height (145 cm) shown in Jelliffe (1966).
[b] From tables 18 and 19, less ten women shorter than the minimum height (140 cm) shown in Jelliffe (1966).

each weigh only 83 percent of the standard weights for their heights. Again, however, Lee questions the validity and applicability of the standards more than he does the nutritional well-being of the !Kung. My feeling is that Lee, anxious to defend the hunting-gathering way of life, is too ready to dismiss such comparisons. However, after exhaustively pursuing the possibility that any seasonal food shortages might be visible in marked seasonal weight fluctuations, Lee found almost insignificant weight losses and gains over the course of a year—on the order of only 1.0 to 1.5 percent of adult body weight.[3] Seasonal weight fluctuation of only about 1.0 percent has also been reported for the Efe Pygmy, who resemble the Batak and !Kung in body proportions and who depend on agricultural food for a large part of their subsistence (Bailey and Peacock n.d.).

The Batak present a sharp contrast. Although I only weighed nineteen adult men and nineteen adult women three times, I found considerable seasonal weight fluctuation

TABLE 23
TRICEPS SKIN FOLDS OF ADULT BATAK MEN AND WOMEN,
CLASSIFIED AS PERCENT OF STANDARD

% of standard	Number of adult men	Number of adult women	Total
100	0	0	0
90	0	1	1
80	0	5	5
70	0	2	2
60	4	7	11
Below 60	40	25	65
Total	44	40	84

Source: Jelliffe (1966).

among them (see table 24). (As we saw in chap. 3, the Batak do suffer a famine season, albeit an agricultural one.) Adults lost 3.2 to 4.2 percent of their body weight between February and July and gained back 2.6 to 3.1 percent between July and October. Skin folds fluctuated considerably—on the order of 15 to 20 percent. These data suggest that the Batak, while otherwise anthropometrically similar to peoples like the !Kung, may indeed be in greater nutritional difficulty.

Turning to the twenty-four children, a local basis for comparison is provided by the weight-for-age standards employed by the Philippine government in its "Operation Timbang" program to assess the extent of rural malnutrition. While these standards are clearly closer to home, they are meant to apply to the lowland Filipino population, not to Negritos. The validity of the comparison is again problematic as these two populations do differ genetically. If the comparison is valid, however, the Batak children I measured were in a poor state. Table 25 shows that half weighed less than 75 percent of the standard weight for their age, and a few weighed less than 60 percent of standard. All of the school-age children in the sample would be considered underweight, three severely so. My arm circumference measurements suggest a similar conclusion. Arm circumference

TABLE 24

SEASONAL VARIATION IN THE MEAN WEIGHTS AND SKIN FOLDS OF THE 19 ADULT BATAK MEN
AND 19 ADULT BATAK WOMEN WEIGHED THREE TIMES

Measurement	February average	July average	% change Feb.–Jul.	Oct./Nov. average	% change Jul.–Oct.
A. Men					
Weight	47.5	45.5	−4.2	46.9	+3.1
Triceps skin fold	5.3	4.1	−22.6	4.7	+14.6
Subscapular skin fold	8.3	7.1	−14.5	6.9	+2.8
B. Women					
Weight	39.3	38.0	−3.3	39.0	+2.6
Triceps skin fold	8.9	7.3	−18.0	8.5	+16.4
Subscapular skin fold	8.6	6.9	−19.8	7.9	+19.7

Forest clearance by lowland settlers near the mouth of the Langogan River. The Batak reside twelve kilometers upstream.

Batak on the move between their settlement and a forest camp.

The Batak are agile tree climbers. Here a man collects wild honey, a favorite food.

Wild pigs are hunted at night, from blinds in trees.

A typical leaf shelter at a forest camp.

A woman processes
wild yams.

Dry season forest camps may be out in the open. The woman is weaving a mat for drying rice after the harvest.

A girl pounds a poisonous tree bark used for stunning fish.

Batak children: two sets of siblings related as first cousins.

A Batak man.

A rice field house.

An upland rice field.

Batak men hired by a lowland settler to help clear his homestead.

A man guards his rice field against the intrusions of wild pigs and monkeys.

A woman harvests
upland rice.

A girl helps her family
move its possessions from
one forest camp to another.

TABLE 25

WEIGHTS FOR AGES OF 23 BATAK CHILDREN,
CLASSIFIED AS PERCENT OF STANDARD

% of	Number of children with age														
standard	0	1	2	3	4	5	6	7	8	9	10	11	12	13	Total
91–100	3														3
76–90			1		1	2	2	1							7
61–75	1	1			1	1	1	1	3				1		10
51–60		1										1		1	3
															23

NOTE: The 24 children weighed one or more times, less one premenarchal 15-year-old girl (standard tables include ages 1–14). Philippine standards (Operation Timbang); separate standards apply to boys and girls.

is considered a good index of muscle wasting and hence of protein-calorie malnutrition in children (Berlin and Markel 1977:75). Of the nineteen children whose arm circumferences I measured one or more times, only six exceeded 85 percent of the reference value (classified by age and sex) shown in Jelliffe (1966). Of the remainder, eight children fell between 75 and 85 percent of the reference value and six fell between 65 and 75 percent.

INCIDENCE AND SEVERITY OF INFECTIOUS AND COMMUNICABLE DISEASES

Even if the Batak are somehow "too thin," what difference does it make? With this question in mind, it is appropriate to turn now to my other major kind of evidence of Batak health status—the diagnoses that physicians and other medical personnel have made of the conditions they have observed among the Batak. Given the influence exerted by nutritional status on resistance to and recovery from infection (Scrimshaw et al. 1968), the conclusive proof of whether Batak thinness should be judged dysfunctional may in part be sought in the incidence and severity of infectious and communicable diseases. If, on the one hand, the Batak go through their lives relatively free of serious illness and survive in large numbers to old age, perhaps one may justifiably dismiss as irrelevant comparisons of Batak anthropometric measurements with Western-derived standards. But if, on the other hand, the Batak do not enjoy such lives, we may indeed want to regard their nutritional status as marginal.

In addition to making (admittedly untrained) clinical observations of Batak health problems, I often inquired about causes of death of deceased individuals in the course of obtaining my census data. Of course, in the absence of a physician's diagnosis, it is often difficult to determine precisely kinds of illnesses and causes of disability and death, particularly among people like the Batak who do not subscribe to the germ theory of disease and who do not normally classify their health problems in the fashion of Western medicine. The Batak were of some help in this enterprise, however; in cases of death due to illness, for example, they readily described the part of the body most affected and the most visible symptoms prior to death. Some illnesses (e.g., tuberculosis) could be deduced with relative confidence from such descriptions, although others could not (thus, the Batak usually describe any illness accompanied by severe fever as malaria, and they probably attribute more deaths to malaria than it actually accounts for in practice). Fortunately, doctors have visited the Batak from time to time, and I am able to draw on some of their appraisals as well as my own.

Epidemic disease, the great depopulator of tribal societies, has played its role in the demographic history of the Batak. They have apparently been spared the devastating epidemics that reduced some tribal groups to small fractions of their aboriginal numbers (Dobyns 1966; Driver 1969). Rather, the Batak have been swept repeatedly by smaller, more localized epidemics—measles, cholera, and influenza have all taken their toll. A case in point is a measles epidemic that occurred in Langogan in December 1980. Of the fifty Batak present at the start of the epidemic, twenty contracted measles during December. Among these twenty were virtually all of the small children, most of the teenagers, and four adults who had previously escaped the disease. Four children, ages one to three, died; two adults almost died and were said to have survived only because of intervention by City Health Department personnel. In addition, two children of Tagbanua families living among the Batak also died. The impact of this same epidemic on the lowland Langogan population was strikingly different. Approximately three times as many lowland adults and children contracted measles during December, but all survived (without medical assistance).

The Batak were particularly vulnerable to contagious disease in December; as we saw (chap. 3), in November and December the Batak are concentrated in their settlements, often with two or three families sharing a single dwelling. But despite a more dispersed settlement pattern, many lowlanders contracted measles as well. It is unknown whether their higher survival rate reflected genetic or immunological factors or better nourishment or care.

Over the longer term, however, chronic, rather than epidemic, infectious and communicable diseases have likely been the single greatest cause of Batak mortality. Those diseases that most seriously plague the Batak are malaria, tuberculosis and other respiratory infections, and gastrointestinal infections. Palawan, in general, has a serious problem with malaria; both vivax and falciparum are endemic. The latter, now chloroquine resistant, is probably the biggest single cause of hospital admissions on the island. All Batak adults claim to have had recurrent bouts with malaria, and on many occasions, I saw individuals apparently suffering from malarial fever. In 1980, a team of health workers examining spleens and blood smears estimated that 70 percent of the Langogan Batak harbored malarial parasites. Only occasionally do Batak obtain and use antimalarial drugs. Rai (1982:134) believes that malaria only became a significant health problem for the Agta after lowland Filipinos entered their environment and established agricultural fields. I cannot assess whether this interesting contention applies to the Batak as well, but there is some evidence that malaria is more prevalent among indigenous peoples living at the fringes of an altered forest than among more nomadic peoples living within an intact forest (Wirsing 1985:314). In any case, while malaria itself may account for relatively few deaths, the disease is debilitating and likely decreases Batak resistance to other, more life-threatening infections.

Among these other infections is tuberculosis. Unfortunately, no tine tuberculin tests have ever been administered among the Batak; they frequently attribute deaths to a set of symptoms—chronic coughing, coughing up blood, prolonged weight loss—indicative of tuberculosis. Indeed, "the chest" is probably the most commonly cited locus of terminal illness, although chest ailments are not limited to tuberculosis but probably also include bronchitis and pneumonia. An instructive comparison may again be drawn with the Casiguran Agta, who closely resemble the Batak in general health status as well as in anthropometric measurements. Headland (1986:394) reports that respiratory diseases are the most common causes of death, with tuberculosis being the single biggest killer among adults and pneumonia being the biggest killer in the population as a whole. Recently introduced tuberculosis is a serious threat to many tribal peoples, and there are places where mortality from this disease has for many years exceeded the birth rate (Wirsing 1985:307).

Another locus of terminal illness often cited is "the stomach," with "disenteria" or "loose bowels," sometimes said to contain blood, as the most visible symptom. Again, it is likely that these terms gloss a variety of medical conditions—from amoebic dysentery to severe infestations of intestinal parasites. No stool samples have ever been examined among the Batak, but they would undoubtedly show a variety of helminths (see Dunn 1972). Two unverified accounts of deaths involving high fever mentioned worms leaving the ears and nose of the dying individual.

Such difficulties with epidemic and chronic infections—
and the levels of infant and child mortality discussed in
chapter 4—strengthen my earlier conclusion that Batak nutritional status is indeed marginal. In the developing world
generally, for example, mortality due to measles is said to be
a result largely of poor nutritional status (Scrimshaw et al.
1968 : 15—16). Along the same lines, Buchbinder (1977) has
demonstrated that local Maring populations in New Guinea
which suffered the greatest mortality from introduced infectious diseases also suffered the greatest degree of chronic
malnutrition.

The Batak have apparently been spared the ravages of
venereal disease. I saw little evidence of degenerative disease. Teeth and eyes do often fail in older individuals, and I
observed several adults with cataracts or opaque lenses.
There are no living blind Batak. One adult is blind in one eye,
and there is one living deaf-mute, age 42. I saw only a few
individuals who appeared to suffer from rheumatoid arthritis.
Leprosy and rabies, occasional health problems on Palawan,
are known and feared by the Batak, but I learned only of one
death attributed to rabies.

Less serious, but highly visible, are a variety of skin lesions
and diseases, notably, tropical ulcers, scabies, and ringworm.
They are a source of much discomfort and embarrassment to
the Batak. I have known entire families to be infected with
scabies; they would lie awake all night, scratching themselves
in agony. And for the fastidious lowlander, the stereotypical
Batak is covered with ringworm (or "doubleskin," as it is
known locally) over 70 to 80 percent of his body. Many
Batak escape such diseases, but many do not: I estimate that
scabies or ringworm, or both, is a chronic problem for almost
half the Batak at Langogan. Lowlanders blame poor hygiene
for these conditions, but individual Batak appear to differ not
only in their hygienic practices but also in their predisposition to skin diseases. The living conditions and cultural
practices that affect the transmission of these and other diseases are discussed below.

There are, to be sure, other causes of disability and death among the Batak besides disease. Most distinctive for outsiders are the various occupational hazards associated with the hunting-gathering life (Howell 1979:54–59). Snakebites, falling from trees, being gored by wild pigs, accidents with weapons—these are the things that might appear to make Batak life dangerous. In fact, however, although the Batak do often talk about and even fear such hazards, actual incidents involving them are uncommon. My data on this subject are not systematic; they concern the number of cases of various kinds of accidental deaths that several adults, questioned together, could recall as having occurred since they were young among the Langogan and Tagnipa Batak, today totaling 23 households but once totaling many more.

The only fatal snakebite recalled in these two districts occurred during World War II. (In late 1981, a Babuyan Batak died of snakebite; it was likely the only such death in the entire population for at least ten years.) Only two Langogan Batak have ever been bitten by venomous snakes, probably by the common Philippine cobra. The only Langogan Batak recalled as having been attacked by a wild pig survived it. No individuals could be recalled who died because they were accidentally shot by another or because they fell out of a tree while collecting honey, although two men who limped slightly were pointed out as having experienced precisely these kinds of accidents. Similarly, no deaths were reported in these districts as the result of weapons malfunctions, although in 1977, a Tanabag Batak did die after a homemade "pigbomb" he was carrying exploded prematurely.

Somewhat more important may be accidents not related to hunting and gathering per se but to forest life in general. For example, a man was said to have died at Langogan several years before my arrival as the result of a severe infection from a foot wound he sustained while walking in the forest. Similarly, my informants recalled one small child who accidentally fell into a river and drowned and two infants who apparently smothered in their blankets. Childbirth, of course, can also be hazardous; a number of women were said to have died during or after childbirth. Such deaths are not common, however. In addition to the likelihood of rigorous selection against any genetic predisposition for difficult childbirth (Howell 1979:58), women who experience a difficult childbirth and survive may take an herbal preparation to prevent future pregnancies (see chap. 4). (Headland [1986:538], however, estimates that about 14 percent of adult Agta women die as a result of the complications of childbirth.) In summary, even allowing for some undercounting, the risks and accidents associated with the Batak way of life are not a major cause of death. Rai (1982:133), reviewing the causes of Agta mortality, similarly concludes that occupational hazards are infrequent causes of injury or death.

Finally, there are the injuries and deaths that can occur as a result of interpersonal violence, but such incidents among Batak are truly exceptional. From Howell's (1979:59–62) account of interpersonal violence and homicide among the !Kung and her estimate that such violence accounts for 5 to 10 percent of all deaths known, it appears that the !Kung are not the "harmless people" Thomas (1965) thought them to be. But such a characterization could be applied with some accuracy to the Batak. Landor (1904:145) reported them to be a "most peaceful people, shy and retiring," who never fought among themselves or with others. (Similar peoples inhabiting the Malay Peninsula have been described as remarkably nonviolent; see Howell 1984:34–38.)

After years of inquiry, I failed to turn up one case, present or past, in which one Batak had killed or intentionally injured another Batak. Such behavior is quite simply unthinkable. Furthermore, despite the variety of frictions and intimidations associated with contact with lowland Filipinos (see chap. 6), only on two occasions within the memory of living Batak has a lowlander actually killed a Batak. In 1968, a lowlander shot a Batak in Tanabag while both were drinking. This incident was widely discussed among the Batak as the first of its kind. A second murder in 1975 at Tagnipa was more threatening. A Batak involved in a land dispute with an influential lowlander was found hanging from a tree, an apparent suicide. No one familiar with the case believed it to be a suicide, but no arrests were made. Only on one occasion, apparently, has a Batak killed an outsider: in 1971, incensed at having been cheated in an economic transaction, a Caramay Batak shot a widely disliked lowlander with a bow and arrow. He was not apprehended until some years later when, during a drinking spree, he bragged publicly about the murder. He remains in detention today.

The Batak may have suffered more violence at the hands of outsiders prior to 1900. As we saw in chapter 2, the sultanates of Sulu and Brunei long raided Palawan for slaves, and every adult Batak can recount how the feared "Moros" surprised and carried off one of his or her kin as a young child. But it is impossible to assess the quantitative impact that such raiding had when it was practiced.

Infectious and communicable diseases, in synergistic interaction with poor nutrition, are by far the most significant cause of disability and death, if only because other causes of disability and death are absent or unimportant. I now turn to the causes of poor nutrition and the factors governing the transmission of disease.

Poor Health: Proximate Causes

The discussion has largely concerned the physiological conditions I observed among the Batak. Causally related to these conditions—but not to be confused with the conditions themselves—are a variety of activities and circumstances. Foremost among these activities is food intake. While food intake, an activity, is closely related to nutritional status, a physiological condition, the two *are* different, and the relationship is incompletely understood. But a strong prima facie case can be made that the contemporary Batak diet contains less variety and fewer nutrients than in the past and does in fact underlie the Batak's marginal nutritional status. A similar case can be made that changes in living conditions accompanying partial sedentarization have—in the absence of compensatory cultural changes—likely increased Batak susceptibility to infectious and communicable diseases.

BATAK DIET TODAY

My data on dietary patterns are limited and consist of qualitative observations of the kinds and relative amounts of foods consumed by particular households during periods of several days, in different locations, and at various times during the year. With the exception of a trial effort in 1975, I never attempted to weigh the portions of food consumed. Given the nature of Batak food preparation and consumption habits and the priorities I placed on the use of my time, quantitative monitoring of food intake on a large scale would have been too difficult and time-consuming. Because such monitoring on a small scale would have had an uncertain research payoff, I chose not to do it at all. As much as possible, however, I did make note of what people were eating as I went about my other business. To supplement these notes, I turned at times to recall interviews to round out my dietary records for sample days and weeks.

My most systematic set of such data consists of the foods consumed by one five-member household during four sample weeks over the course of a year—in February, April, July, and September. During the four weeks, the household was residing in the settlement. Thus, my observations may not be taken as typical of the Batak diet in general, but they are typical, I believe, of their diet when living in their settlements. I was particularly interested in the settlement diet, because settlement living is a relatively recent, but increasingly important, part of Batak adaptation.

During the four weeks, or 28 days, I collected data, my sample family did not consistently eat a meal on rising in the morning. On ten mornings, they ate cold rice or plantains. On most of the others, they had coffee and sugar, but occasionally, they had nothing at all. The family consumed a noon meal and an evening meal on each of the 28 days, however, for a total of fifty-six meals. All of these meals centered on rice; a few included other starches, such as cassava or plantains. Of the fifty-six meals, fourteen (25%) were accompanied by no sidedishes at all (except salt). As this family never consumed sidedishes in the morning, on 25 percent of the days observed, only starches were consumed. Thirteen of these meals were accompanied by a vegetable sidedish—unripe jackfruit, palm or rattan pith, mushrooms— or some kind of animal protein, in some cases cooked with greens. The kinds of animal protein consumed during the sample days were mollusks (7 times); fresh, dried, or canned fish (14 times); wild pig (2 times); eel (2 times); chicken (1 time); and jungle fowl (1 time).

Two observations are in order. First, while some animal protein did accompany approximately half the meals, the amounts were often exceedingly small. The only occasion when "chicken" was consumed by the members of this household, for example, was during a noon meal prepared by a lowland employer as partial payment for a day's agricultural labor. Only one chicken was killed and cooked with jackfruit and coconut milk, but more than twenty people shared the meal. Again, on three of the occasions when "canned fish" was consumed, a single small can, cooked with green papaya, served the same number of people. Even when this family was eating in its own home (which was most of the time), it never enjoyed a surfeit of animal protein. On the two occasions when "pig meat" was consumed, it was a gift from another Batak. On one occasion, the meat was spoiled, and on the other, the "meat" consisted only of a small piece of fat. Only rarely in this household did each person's portion of edible animal protein amount to more than about 50 grams.[4] Second, while the Batak only consume small quantities of wild greens, at least some of these greens are quite rich in nutrients. Table 26 presents the nutritional compo-

TABLE 26
Nutritional Compositions of Selected Wild Greens and Cultivated Vegetables

Composition, 100 grams, raw edible portion

	Cal.	Gm. protein	Gm. fat	Gm. CHO	Gm. fiber	Gm. ash	Mg. CA	Mg. P	Mg. FE	Mg. Na	Mg. K	I.U. Vit. A	Mg. Thia.	Mg. Ribo.	Mg. Niac.	Mg. Vit. C
Wild greens																
Gnetum gnemon L.	104	7.4	2.0	19.4	11.5	0.6	44	15	0.1	?	?	1680	0.10	?	1.2	121
Escape taro	69	4.4	1.8	12.2	3.4	2.0	268	78	4.3	11	1237	20385	0.10	0.33	2.0	142
Fern fronds	37	3.8	2.1	2.9	1.3	1.3	23	67	4.4	15	554	3775	0	0.09	1.7	9
Escape pepper	50	6.3	1.2	6.9	0.9	2.2	264	56	1.2	41	671	11505	0.52	0.34	1.9	77
Cultivated vegetables																
Okra	34	1.8	0.1	8.2	0.7	0.8	120	49	0.8	4	246	270	0.08	0.09	0.8	17
Yardlong bean	38	2.8	0.2	8.2	1.5	0.7	42	46	0.9	5	230	570	0.12	0.13	1.2	22
Eggplant	24	1.0	0.2	5.7	0.8	0.6	30	27	0.6	4	223	130	0.10	0.10	0.6	5

Source: FNRC (1974).

sition, per 100 grams of edible portion, of some of the principal traditional plant resources discussed in chapter 2. Similar data for several locally important cultivated vegetables are included for comparison.

Other households, as I have said, followed a similar dietary pattern while residing in the settlement—a pattern of two meals a day, with small quantities of animal protein consumed at about half of them. It was my distinct, albeit subjective, impression that the sidedishes consumed were inadequate in variety and quantity to consistently provide necessary amounts of protein, vitamins, and minerals. It was also my distinct, and again subjective, impression that the Batak were scarcely getting enough *caloric* nourishment. Members of the household discussed here, and other Batak whom I know, complained periodically (even regularly) of hunger during the periods I lived among them, and I take their complaints to be genuine. Doctors who have seen the Batak and also lowlanders who know them describe the Batak diet—again, as seen in the settlements—in precisely these terms. Their observations and mine suggest that failure to get enough to eat is probably the biggest single shortcoming of the evolving Batak adaptation.

On the one occasion, in July 1975, when I did attempt to monitor the *quantity* of food consumed by a settlement family, I obtained data that support a general picture of caloric undernourishment, although not of protein or vitamin malnutrition. For eight days, I weighed all of the food consumed by a four-person household. I did not weigh separate portions. Average total daily caloric intake during this period was only 78 percent of the Food and Nutrition Research Institute's (FNRI) per-day recommendation for a Filipino household of this age and sex composition (FNRI 1981).[5] These data are only fragmentary. Moreover, they were obtained during the preharvest famine season, probably the most nutritionally stressful time of the year. But, at least for this time of the year, I believe this finding accurately reflects the dietary circumstances of most Batak households.

We have already seen in chapter 3 a number of the circumstances that account for the nature of food intake patterns among settlement-dwelling Batak. Local resource depletion, for example, makes the provision of varied subsistence more difficult, and the sometimes frenetic pace of settlement life gives some credence to the Batak claim that they often have "no time to look for food." Batak food consumption practices, however, also reflect motivational patterns that must be understood in the context of the wider patterns of social and cultural change discussed in chapters 6 and 7.

These observations suggest that the Batak do not eat very well, at least during those periods when they are residing in their settlements. Whether their diet was better in the past is a matter we can only speculate about. However, the Batak *say* they did. They explicitly identify the past as a time of dietary plenty, of "fat Batak," and compare it invidiously with the privation and hunger they claim to experience today. Certainly, the dietary record presented here contrasts markedly with the range of traditional food sources discussed in chapter 2.

Further, the Batak today appear to eat better when living in forest camps and even, perhaps, when in their swidden fields than they do when residing in settlements. I have already expressed my reservations about drawing inferences about the aboriginal foraging economy from observations of contemporary foraging camps and activities (see chap. 2). Nevertheless, it seems reasonable to assume that food intake patterns at such camps today more closely resemble those of aboriginal times than do the dietary patterns of settlement households.

In any event, at the series of forest camps I visited during 1980–81, food was visibly and consistently more varied and more abundant than at the settlement. The same general pattern of a noon meal and an evening meal was followed, but eating at other times of the day, particularly if honey was available, was common as well. Indeed, at any given moment, it often seemed that *someone* in the camp was eating *something.* The main meals usually centered on honey or wild yams obtained nearby, although rice was sometimes brought to camp from the settlement. At least in the camps I visited, virtually all meals were accompanied by animal and vegetable foods, often of several kinds. Because of the communal manner in which food was shared and consumed in Batak camps, I did not attempt to monitor a specific household's individual meals, as I did at the settlement. I did, however, routinely monitor and sometimes weigh all the foods that were brought into a camp and consumed during my visit.

The record of the foods consumed in one camp that I visited in April 1981 stands in marked contrast to the dietary regime of settlement households. This camp, larger than most, included 14 adults and some children. The principal foraging activities at this camp were honey collection and fish stunning. During the four days I remained at the camp, 7 beehives were obtained, providing all the honey needed during this interval. In addition, the members of the camp obtained and consumed one large wild pig (sufficient for two days), 4.15 kilograms of fish, 4 eels (totaling 1.65 kg), 4 turtles (2.3 kg), 3 Palawan peacocks (1.5 kg), one wild chicken (0.5 kg), one flying squirrel (0.5 kg), one crayfish (100 g), and a variety of greens (all weights shown here are live weights). At another camp that I observed for 72 hours in May, which consisted only of a married couple without children, some rice had been brought from the settlement. Locally procured foods included one wild piglet (4.4 kg), 2 flying squirrels (1.0 kg), 2 eels (1.7 kg), mollusks (2.0 kg), fish (950 g), honey (3 hives), and some land crabs, rattan pith, and greens. It is fair to say that the Batak rarely, if ever, eat this well in their settlements, yet the cases I have cited seem reasonably typical of the way they eat in the forest.

The third type of evidence indicating that Batak diet has deteriorated is the large and compelling comparative literature on the negative impact of economic development and change on indigenous diets in general. Australian aborigines and Kalahari hunter-gatherers who have become sedentary, for example, have suffered declines in their nutritional well-being (Taylor 1977; Hitchcock 1982:254–255). More broadly, the available data suggest that the nutritional status of indigenous peoples of all kinds is endangered when subsistence production and food self-sufficiency give way to commercial production and purchase of food (Fleuret and Fleuret 1980). These general trends have been shown to be particularly acute among poor and marginal people like the Batak.

LIVING CONDITIONS TODAY

Dietary change is only one element in a skein of changes in the Batak lifeway; others also may have had detrimental health consequences. Such effects have resulted not so much from the advent of new activities as from the new consequences of old activities as the Batak have become more sedentary. Traditionally casual Batak attitudes and practices concerning sanitation and hygiene, while appropriate to nomadic, forest-dwelling conditions, provide, under more settled conditions, greatly enhanced opportunities for the transmission of disease and parasites. A greater disease and parasite load, in other words, appears to be part of the price the Batak have paid for "settling down" (Wirsing 1985:306, 311).

Most Batak get their drinking water, for example, from streams or rivers. But particularly near settlements, watercourses are also regularly used for washing, bathing, and defecating. Thus, contaminated drinking water is one likely cause of gastrointestinal disease. Another is unhygienic methods of garbage disposal. Waste is typically discarded in the bushes at the edges of house yards, which are also another popular place for defecating. Flies abound in such areas and likely contaminate unguarded food. Pots and cooking utensils are typically not cleaned until just before they are needed for the next meal. Then they are washed in the river, without soap. Nor do the Batak regularly employ soap to wash themselves, their blankets, or their clothes. Such practices no doubt contribute to Batak difficulties with scabies and ringworm. Gomes (1982:37–38) and Turnbull (1983:148–149) similarly conclude that unhygienic water procurement and sanitation practices likely promote the spread of infectious disease among recently settled Semang and Mbuti Pygmy.

More speculatively, the Batak practice of using cooking fires inside or immediately under their houses for warmth may exacerbate their difficulties with respiratory disease. The Batak have long used fires to provide warmth, but under forest living conditions, lack of adequate ventilation is not as great a problem as it seems to be in their lowland-style settlement houses. While ignorance does play a part in these various practices, poverty is by far the most important factor. Even such a simple item as soap, while scarcely beyond the means of the Batak as an occasional purchase, would be expensive (and difficult) for them to procure on a regular basis.

The kinds of health problems discussed here probably help to account for some of the characteristic aspects of Batak subsistence economy and demography discussed earlier (chaps. 3 and 4). For example, poor nutrition or a high disease load can erode work capacity and motivation (Spurr 1983). It seems reasonable to suspect that such problems underlie the Batak penchant for short workdays and for alternating workdays with rest days as much as does any cultural preference for leisure. Similarly, the high levels of infant, child, and adult mortality reflect, as we have seen, the synergistic interactions of poor nutrition and infectious disease. More interesting is the possibility that Batak fertility has been influenced by poor nutrition or infectious disease. Malaria, for example, can increase the incidence of miscarriages, premature births, and stillbirths, and it has been cited as a cause of population decline in previously uninfected populations (Bayliss-Smith 1975:437–438). Other endemic tropical diseases have also been implicated as causes of subfertility in both men and women (McFalls and McFalls 1984).

There is also the attractive "Frisch hypothesis," which relates malnutrition to depletion of fat storage below a certain "critical minimum," thence to reduced reproductive performance by some combination of delayed menarche, earlier age at menopause, and increases in the incidence of anovulatory cycles, the risk of spontaneous abortion, and the duration of lactational amenorrhea (Frisch and McArthur 1974; Frisch 1978). Frisch's work has been widely cited by anthropologists, and nutritional regulation of population has become a popular form of explanation in both archaeology and demography (Huss-Ashmore 1980:61; see, e.g., Binford and Chasko 1976; Howell 1979). Certainly, it is tempting to assert a causal connection between nutrition, fatness, and fertility in the Batak case, which appears to involve both deteriorating nutritional status and population decline due (in part) to reduced fertility.

Unfortunately, the status of the proposed relationship between nutrition and fertility remains uncertain. The Frisch hypothesis has been extensively criticized on both statistical and physiological grounds (e.g., Trusell 1978; Huffman et al. 1978). Some current reviewers of the evidence (e.g., Bongaarts 1980; Menkin et al. 1981) conclude that moderate, chronic malnutrition has only minor influences on fecundity and fertility. However, research on anorexia nervosa does show that malnutrition in women can indeed be associated with irregularity and anovulation in menstrual cycles (e.g., Wentz 1977; Gold et al. 1986). Furthermore, recent research suggests that fecundity in women is directly responsive to energy expenditure, independent of any changes in body composition, with suppression of reproductive hormone levels occurring even at moderate levels of exercise (Shangold 1984; Loucks and Horvath 1985). The question remains open, although my opinion is that the strikingly short mean total reproductive span of Batak women has *something* to do with poor nutrition.

6

Increased Stress Levels as the Cause of Adaptive Difficulty

This chapter and the next place the group- and individual-level adaptive difficulties documented previously in the context of wider patterns of social stress and cultural disruption. Limitations imposed by my data make this enterprise somewhat speculative. But I am motivated by a firm belief that just as physiological stress (e.g., epidemic disease) can overwhelm a tribal people, so too can social stress and in ways that have in fact been important among the Batak. Here I examine the ways in which economic, political, and ideological pressures from the outside world have created an array of stressful situations that are affecting individual Batak as members of domestic families, local groups, and Batak society as a whole. Before proceeding, however, I want to discuss briefly the theoretical and empirical justification for my use of the concept of social stress.

Social Stress

Anecdotal reports of illnesses that seemed to occur during periods of major change in people's lives have long intrigued physicians, social scientists, and lay people alike. That the recently widowed or divorced, for example, are subject to higher mortality rates in comparison to otherwise similar persons has helped to stimulate a considerable body of research exploring the possible relationships between the "stresses of life" and human health and illness (Bieliauskas 1982:6). Many definitions of stress and many models of how it works have been proposed (McGrath 1970; Scott and Howard 1970), but three principal conceptual domains are involved: origins, mediators, and manifestations (Pearlin 1983:4).

The basic idea underlying stress research is that certain "stressors," or stressful situations in the social environment, cause, in turn, certain "disorders" because of a failure in "coping" ability (see, e.g., Levine and Scotch 1970). In much of the literature, "stressful life events"—marriage, birth of a child, and the like—are still the stressors of interest (e.g., Holmes and Rahe 1967; Dohrenwend and Dohrenwend 1974). Similarly, the resulting disorders, or "harmful consequences" of stress, are usually conceived as the physiological or psychological difficulties of individuals. Thus, Levine and Scotch (1970:2) identify "physiological dysfunction, disease, mental disorder, and socially pathological behavior" as the possible outcomes of social stress. Much of the research on coping ability, finally, concerns the availability of "social support" and other kinds of response-mediating resources to the individual exposed to the stressful stimuli (see, e.g., Lumsden 1975:213–214).

The scientific literature on social stress is vast, and it is not my purpose to review it here. Nor is it my purpose to treat stress as a rigorous scientific model, from which testable hypotheses might be deduced. Rather, I find the concept heuristically valuable for connecting seemingly diverse aspects of Batak existence in a way that helps to illuminate some crucial causal relationships relevant to the detribalization process (see McGrath 1970:11). While the concept of stress has not been extensively utilized in anthropology, it has proven similarly valuable in at least one other, related endeavor: the study of the human consequences of forced resettlement (e.g., Lumsden 1975; Coelho and Ahmed 1980; Hansen and Oliver-Smith 1982).

I agree with Lumsden (1975:210) that much of social change arises through adaptation to stress and that the concept of stress must therefore be an integral part of any meaningful theory of change. But for many anthropological purposes, a significant limitation of many existing models of stress is in fact their preoccupation with life events and other sorts of extreme or traumatic circumstances as the precursors of stress (Scott and Howard 1970:266; Farrington 1982:2–3; Pearlin 1983:4). According to Scott and Howard:

> This association has had the effect of diverting attention away from the stimuli that are wearing to the organism, and that have important physiological and psychological consequences for it, but which are neither dramatic or especially unusual. The relevance of such stimuli for the study of stress is suggested by the findings of an investigation by Scott of patterns of illness in a group of female employees in a large commercial enterprise.... The study revealed that traumatic events such as the sudden death of a family member or friend, a recent divorce, or similar personal crises often produced acute illnesses. It was also clear, however, that such events were comparatively rare, and therefore of little value in helping to explain the very large amount of illness that routinely occurred on a day-to-day basis. An analysis of the data revealed that the life style of the individual, and especially the quality of her social role relationships with others, was much more determinative of the amount and severity of illness she suffered than the occasional traumatic situations that arose. (1970:266–267)

Some studies have found that life events appear to explain as little as 9 percent of the variation in health outcomes (Kessler et al. 1985:534). As Scott and Howard (1970) suggest, the search for the causes of stress should thus be broadened to include its "more structured and durable social and economic antecedents" (Pearlin 1983:4). Pearlin, for example, explores the notion of "role strain" as a potential source of personal stress; such phenomena as role captivity and role restructuring, he argues, can create stress by altering or intensifying important aspects of key social roles. In short, there are many different kinds of potentially stressful situations in the human social environment.

Efforts to take a broader view of the social origins of stress are particularly appropriate to the study of tribal peoples in situations of extensive social change. Like all "situation-based" approaches to stress, however, such efforts share a significant weakness—the problem of delimiting just what kinds of social situations, and which of their properties, in fact make for stress (McGrath 1970:13). As Levine and Scotch (1970:5) say, "only a lack of imagination limits the extent to which social conditions found to be associated with a disorder can be interpreted as being stressful." Furthermore, the study of chronic stress poses methodological difficulties. It is easier to determine, for example, whether a particular life event, such as the death of a spouse, has occurred than to objectively measure the level of stress entailed by a chronically stressful marriage (Kessler et al. 1985:538–539), much less the overall stress level in an entire society (Savishinsky 1974:217). These comments recall my earlier criticisms of assumptions that all tribal social change is stressful and of approaches to the concept of adaptation which provide few guidelines about what is being adapted to, other than all of life itself.

These are serious difficulties, but they should not impede efforts to develop a more eclectic view of the origins of stress. If life potentially poses many different kinds of stressful situations, one can at least attempt to monitor change in the nature, amount, or perception of those situations. Meanwhile, methodological advances (e.g., chronic strain inventories; Stone and Neale 1982) and new research on stress-related illnesses promise to clarify the ways in which the social environment affects human health and well-being.

Another significant limitation of many approaches is that

the *manifestations* of stress have traditionally been conceived only at the level of individual actors and their experiences. In fact, however, stress-related disorders may occur at many levels of human existence and affect social groups as well as individuals. According to Scott and Howard (1970:265), "studies of stress have shown it to be a phenomenon that largely transcends the arbitrary levels of analysis designated by the terms biochemical, physiological, psychological, and sociocultural. Stress manifests itself in all of the environmental fields to which the organism simultaneously adapts."

Again, of course, there are difficulties with an expansionist view. But according to Farrington, who has also advocated such a multilevel conceptualization of stress,

> the "parallelism" between individuals and social systems implied here with regard to the experiencing of stress is not meant to suggest that stress manifests itself identically at the various levels of human activity, nor should it be taken to imply that I advocate "psychologizing" the study of social reality. As Lazarus (1966:401–407) has clearly demonstrated, the confusing or blurring of stress at these different levels of human activity can result in serious conceptual difficulties. However, it is meant to suggest that, just as an individual actor can be said to be under or to be experiencing "stress," so too can a unit of social reality, such as a social group, social system, or social organization. (1982:4)

Linsky and Straus (1982) provide some empirical support for this view. They found a relationship between socially patterned stress and patterns of pathologies within social systems which was not predictable solely from a knowledge of the individual members. For example, a given rate of unemployment affects not only those persons who are actually out of work "but also their families and local businesses, and may have a socially and economically depressing effect on communities throughout a state" (ibid.:7). More generally, the emergent qualities of social stress are such that a new level of causation occurs at the group level which cannot be accounted for merely by grouping stress-related effects at the individual level (ibid.:6–7). A poignant illustration of the emergent qualities of social stress is found in Shkilnyk's (1985) account of the relocation and subsequent disintegration of an Ojibwa community in Ontario. The more visible costs of relocation—alarming increases in the incidence of homicide, suicide, alcoholism, and child abuse—were borne by individuals. But it was the collective trauma precipitated by relocation—the unraveling of the community's social fabric, the deterioration of community morale—which was ultimately to blame.

Finally, a broader view of stress mediating and stress coping is necessary. In much of the literature, social support and other resources affecting vulnerability to stress are characteristically examined in terms of the response capabilities of individual actors. But it seems to me that one of the most important contributions that anthropology, with its unique emphasis on the concept of culture, can make to a greater understanding of stress is to demonstrate and explain the variations in ability to respond to stress which occur not only between individuals but between different kinds of social groups—including entire social systems. In the Batak case, the relationships between cultural disintegration and the diminished stress-coping abilities of individuals and social groups is such a critical issue that it merits extended discussion in a separate chapter (chap. 7).

Stress in the Batak Environment Today

The kinds of systemic, everyday social stresses that affect the Batak as they go about their lives are all ultimately experienced by individuals, but the primary social contexts of these stresses vary widely. Batak experience role strain, one significant source of stress, primarily as members of domestic families, but they experience threats to their ethnic identity as members of a much larger social group. I will focus, in turn, on the kinds of stresses that I believe are best conceptualized as experienced within Batak society as a whole, within particular local groups of Batak, and within particular domestic families. This is not meant to be a tight classificatory scheme but a convenient means for bringing some order to a large and chaotic portion of Batak social reality.

SOCIAL STRESS AND THE BATAK AS A WHOLE: RELATIONSHIPS WITH OUTSIDERS

Despite one hundred years of sustained contact with lowland Filipinos, the Batak continue to find relationships with them stressful. The more immediate *economic* stresses entailed by contact have already been discussed in some detail (chap. 3) because they so directly affect contemporary Batak economic behavior. I argued that such factors as continued land tenure insecurity and debilitating relationships of trade and dependency account for the Batak's desultory economic life.

A second set of stresses affecting Batak society as a whole is *political* in nature and concerns the relative impotency of the Batak in the face of a variety of demands and intrusions by outside individuals and agencies. Government officials, forest guards, missionaries, anthropologists, college students on field trips, and tourists on holiday all find reasons to visit the Batak and interfere in their lives. The attitudes of such individuals are often paternalistic or authoritarian, and many, if they do not simply cheat the Batak outright, fail to reciprocate for Batak time and hospitality. Worse, most such visitors make no genuine effort to ascertain that their presence or assistance (if such is alleged) is in fact desired by the Batak, mistaking acquiescence for approval. In fact, the Batak find it difficult to say no, not so much because of some cultural premium on hospitality or cooperation as because of a lack of institutionalized means for resisting outside interference and a fear of the consequences should such resistance be attempted. Thus, the Batak frequently find that they are objects of curiosity, study, or assistance, without having first been consulted in any meaningful way. Summoned here and there to meet this visiting dignitary or to participate in that government program, the Batak are continually reminded of their inability to control their own lives.

A local group is visited by a team of foresters from a government research institute in Puerto Princesa City. They summon all the adult men from their rice fields to the settlement for a series of 15-minute interviews about forest resource use. No payment for the resulting half-day's loss of labor is made because, it is said, the Batak "don't have anything to do anyway," and in any case, the results of the research project will ultimately redound to the Batak's own benefit. A school is opened for the first time in another Batak local group. The teacher assigned there "buys" some of his food supply from the Batak but regularly fails to pay for it as agreed. The teacher reasons that the Batak owe him their gratitude for accepting a hardship assignment. Batak adults bearing fresh food avoid the teacher but otherwise feel helpless to deal with his behavior. Elsewhere, no schools are available exclusively for Batak, but the school district periodically encourages them to enroll their school-age children in the nearest lowland school. Infected with the spirit of the latest such program, a lowland community leader issues a proclamation that all parents whose school-age children are not attending school will be jailed. The Batak are duly impressed and excitedly round up and bring to the lowland community a small group of would-be students. After several days, the threat of imprisonment appears to wane, and the Batak children drift back to their settlement.

Individuals and agencies convinced that they are somehow helping the Batak often do the most damage. In my opinion, the single most stressful event affecting the Batak since World War II occurred in 1969, when virtually the entire population was forcibly resettled by PANAMIN, an agency of the government expected to look after the welfare of the nation's "cultural minorities." While the PANAMIN resettlement was only a single and ultimately unsuccessful effort, the stresses associated with the forced resettlement of indigenous peoples are everywhere serious and lasting. According to Scudder and Colson (1982:269–271), who have undertaken extensive research in compulsory relocation in Africa, three sorts of stresses characteristically attend such relocations: physiological stress, seen in increased morbidity and mortality rates following removal; psychological stress, visible in such phenomena as guilt, depression, anxiety, and a "grieving for a lost home" syndrome; and sociocultural stress, which concerns the economic, political, and other cultural effects of relocation. In the Batak case, the attempted PANAMIN resettlement was so economically, socially, and psychologically destructive that the Batak today remain deeply suspicious of any government efforts to "help" them.

This resettlement, like PANAMIN itself, was conceived by Manuel Elizalde, an egotistical and politically ambitious scion of a wealthy industrialist family. Once a media darling, Elizalde has since fallen from public and official favor. PANAMIN itself was discredited by persistent reports that the agency was a vehicle for Elizalde's personal ends and the government's political ends, the latter often at variance with the welfare of the tribal populations PANAMIN was supposed to serve (Rocamora 1979). In 1981, PANAMIN was disbanded, and the welfare of all Philippine tribal populations was made the concern of a new office, Muslim Affairs and Cultural Communities.

But in 1968, the heyday of PANAMIN, and after years of inaction by the moribund Commission on National Integration, it was felt that action was finally going to be taken to improve the lot of tribal Filipinos. What was to be done for the Batak was explained to them, with much fanfare, at a meeting of the entire group held on the Babuyan River. The meeting was called by Elizalde himself. The Batak were to be resettled on an isolated tract of land on the west coast of Palawan near Ulugan Bay, where PANAMIN would pay them to construct their houses and provide their subsistence needs during a transition period while they were taught the practice of wet rice agriculture. Gathering the Batak together at one site would protect them from the depredations of lowland Filipinos, guarantee some land for them (although PANAMIN, not the Batak, would own the land), and make possible the provision of educational and health services. Including the time necessary to travel to and from the meeting site, this preparatory meeting lasted several weeks, during which Batak rice fields lay unburned or unplanted. The Batak remember 1968, the first of the PANAMIN years, as a year of hardship.

The next year, the Batak were again taken from their settlements. This time they were carted off in military vehicles—like cattle, some said—to the new PANAMIN project. Only the Langogan group escaped resettlement; they tricked their escorts and fled to the forest far upriver from their settlement, which lay completely abandoned from 1970 to 1972. Those Batak who did go to "PANAMIN" later complained bitterly of the unfamiliar locale, the privations and difficulties of making a living, the social tensions and conflicts, and the unrealistic expectations, cavalier behavior, and outright corruption of the PANAMIN officials. Poorly planned, mismanaged, and underfunded, the project was a disaster. Batak started leaving immediately, and they continued to leave over the weeks and months that followed. One woman was said to have died as the result of injuries sustained during a fall while "escaping" PANAMIN; many were said to have fallen ill. As the result of the attempted resettlement, few Batak were able to make upland rice fields in 1969, the second of the PANAMIN-caused hardship years. By mid-1970, only about ten households remained at PANAMIN, and the project was virtually defunct.

In 1975, PANAMIN attempted a second, "voluntary" resettlement scheme. A site on the Babuyan River where the last participants in the first project had moved in 1972 was designated as "PANAMIN II," and some services were provided. Here, too, the local school district has provided the only school that directly serves the Batak. Batak have come and gone from this project site, and a small number remain. Together with a larger number of Tagbanua and lowlanders who also live here, these Batak comprise local group A1 in chapter 4. The land this group occupies, however, is apparently no more secure than that of other local groups.

In addition to the obvious stress imposed by this loss of political autonomy, some further aspects of the Batak case merit special attention. First, lack of political control is often economically costly; all of the incidents described wasted Batak time or resources. Second, the political stresses brought to bear on Batak society as a whole tend to precipitate negative feelings and conflicts among the Batak themselves. PANAMIN was probably the worst offender in this regard, not because of any explicit "divide-and-conquer" strategy but because of the repercussions of its heavy-handed and culturally insensitive approach to helping the Batak. During my stay at Langogan, for example, a PANAMIN agent appeared one day and informed the Batak that they were soon to be visited by a Manila-based evaluation team of PANAMIN executives as part of preparations to establish a pan-Batak service center at another Batak settlement. The Batak were warned to hide any radios and lanterns, lest they be deemed insufficiently needy. Against the possibility that the visit would be made by helicopter, they were also to construct a helipad within fifteen days. A work schedule was devised, and the Batak were divided into "voluntary" labor groups. Many of the adult men eventually worked on the helipad (little more than a large clearing in the middle of the settlement), but others did not. In any case, the evaluation team never arrived, the helipad was never finished, and the service center was never constructed. The only significant outcomes for the Batak were some wasted labor days and a good deal of bickering between those who worked and those who did not.

On another occasion during my stay, a PANAMIN official

in Puerto Princesa City decided that the Batak should be better organized. Each local group was to elect two "councillors," with the overall "kapitan" being a PANAMIN designee. When a PANAMIN agent visited the Langogan group, an election was held and the two Langogan councillors were duly elected. After the PANAMIN agent departed the next day, however, the Batak held a second election and selected two different councillors, one of them a Tagbanua married to a local Batak. The latter went to Puerto Princesa to inform the PANAMIN office of the results of the new election. PANAMIN officials were dismayed and later spoke darkly to me about the interference of the Tagbanua in Batak affairs. Meanwhile, back in Langogan (where neither election had been a model of the democratic process), Batak argued for days about who their real councillors in fact were. But all of this mattered little, as no further action involving the new pan-Batak organization was ever taken.

Tourism has also created interpersonal conflicts among the Batak. In 1980, an interesting incident occurred involving the Tanabag Batak, whose permanent settlement was then a major destination for tourists wanting to combine a trek in the jungle with a chance to see some "primitives." Batak there had already tired of the invasion of privacy and demands on time entailed by regular tourist visits and had acquired a reputation for hiding from arriving tourists and their Filipino guides, much to the dismay of the local luxury hotel sponsoring the tours. The Puerto Princesa City government was alerted to a threat to Palawan's nascent tourist industry, and representatives of the mayor's office exhorted the Tanabag Batak to be more hospitable to their tourist visitors. This pressure came at a difficult time for the Batak, for it was the start of a new swidden season. As we saw, Batak usually vacate their settlements at this time for a period of langsan camp residence and field clearance. But a solution, which seemed quite ingenious at the time, was devised by the Batak: they divided themselves into groups that would rotate residence in the settlement, such that some households would always be present to entertain any tourist arrivals, while others could work in their rice fields upriver. Unfortunately for those who elected to remain in the settlement first, those who went upriver never returned on the timetable agreed upon, instead continuing to live in their langsan camps. Ill-feeling resulted, and the entire scheme immediately disintegrated.

Tourism has also provoked conflict among the Batak over money. The Batak have scarcely grown rich from tourism, and there is a widespread feeling that they have not been adequately compensated for the interference of tourists in their lives. Thus, virtually all Batak bows and arrows have been sold to tourists, and few Batak have been motivated to make and sell new ones. Similarly, although groups of Batak have been paid in money and alcohol to stage "curing ceremonies" for tourist groups, they seem to find such stagings more trouble than they are worth. The feelings of indifference and even disgust toward tourists visible in the 1980 Tanabag incident are widespread. Tourists, for their part, seem to feel that having already paid the hotel and tipped the guide, any compensation for the Batak is unnecessary, or at least not their concern. Tourists, furthermore, may have unrealistic notions about Batak life. Some spoke earnestly to me about their desire to help the Batak but confided that they did not want to give them any money for fear of further "corrupting" them (manufactured clothing and other purchased goods being evidence that such corruption had already begun). On numerous occasions, however, Batak *have* been given money by tourists, and acrimonious discussion has followed between those who were given money and those who were not about whether and how widely the money was to be shared. (Greater bitterness is reserved for the tour guides, who the Batak correctly suspect have often received from tourists, but failed to pass on, sums of money intended for the Batak.)

One further example, again of an incident that occurred during my stay at Langogan, nicely illustrates how the various kinds of stresses associated with the Batak inability to control their own lives are intertwined. A city government medical team was to visit Langogan to examine the Batak and to treat any illnesses. As the team only had one day to devote to this effort, it was impractical for them to visit the Batak at their settlement. Rather, the Batak would be brought to the lowland community at Langogan and examined there. A Filipino settler who had commercial dealings with the Batak and who enjoyed a quasi-official status as a local PANAMIN representative was asked to inform the Batak of the planned visit. He himself only learned of the visit the day before it was to occur, but early the next morning he hiked upriver and "rounded up," as he put it, as many Batak as he could. In fact, with some cajoling, he was able to assemble most of the adults and older children, with only a few ill individuals (being unable to travel) remaining behind, together with two households at a distant forest camp.

The medical team arrived as promised, and all the Batak who appeared were examined at a makeshift clinic set up in the yard of the village captain's house, across from the school. Numerous lowland adults and children watched the proceedings, for many rarely see the Batak and find them objects of considerable interest. There was some demeaning talk, audible to the Batak, about Batak physical and cultural characteristics. The doctor treated some conditions, mostly skin diseases, and a technician took blood smears from everybody. (Antimalarial drugs would be given later, it was said, for those persons who tested positive for malaria, but although I later learned that most of the smears were positive, no drugs were forthcoming during the balance of my stay.) All Batak, finally, were given one or more bottles of vitamins, cough syrup, or sulfur ointment. There was little communication during the examinations, and Batak questioned later had only the vaguest understanding of the purpose of the drugs they received. Some, for example, received bottles of vitamin B6; others received bottles of tablets to take "if they became ill." (Local governments in the Philippines often receive substantial quantities of "surplus" drugs from the World Health Organization and other international agencies. Labeling can be sketchy and the names of the drugs unfamiliar to local settlers who might otherwise be able to assist the Batak with their use.)[1]

By the time the health team departed and the Batak left for their settlement, it was late afternoon. The settler who had assembled the Batak earlier in the day asked them to stop at his own house for a while to help process some coffee beans. This project took several hours, until after nightfall, but the Batak were not compensated for their labor, other than with some bottles of gin while they pounded the berries. The settler reasoned that *he* had not been paid by the medical team for his efforts, and since the Batak were the beneficiaries of their visit, it was only fair that they should somehow compensate him. Since a number of the group had outstanding debts to this settler, they could scarcely refuse. The Batak finally arrived home at about 10:00 P.M., tired, hungry, and argumentative about the day's work lost and the free labor extracted, and some blamed others for having been talked into going to the lowlands.

Still other sources of stress on Batak society as a whole can be identified by examining the economic and political subordination of the Batak to wider Philippine society. First, this subordination leaves little or no room for the Batak to pursue any sort of entrepreneurial involvement, whether economic or political, with lowland Philippine society (see, e.g., Gould et al. 1972:278–279). The Batak lack the necessary skills, and lowland Filipinos already occupy the relevant niches. The capitalist milieu of wider Philippine society, to which the Batak are expected to adjust, places considerable emphasis on individual initiative. But the emerging political economic pattern is everywhere one of Batak clientage and dependency.

Second, there is a subjective dimension to the economic and political subordination of the Batak which helps to provide lowlanders with a rationalization for that subordination even as it makes the overall Batak-lowlander relationship more stressful for the Batak than it might be otherwise. Similarly, Rai (1982:199–201) speaks of the "sociosymbolic subordination" of the Agta to their non-Agta neighbors. In the Cagayan Valley, he says, there is a caste-line, hierarchical ranking of ethnic groups, with the long-Christianized Ilokano at the top and the Agta at the bottom. More generally, common throughout the Philippines is the notion that Negritos (like tribal peoples generally) are a people inferior in mind and culture.

The Batak are aware of their subjective position in wider Philippine society—indeed, through word and deed of lowlanders, they are constantly reminded of it. They know, for example, that they are variously regarded as unclean, lazy, ignorant, superstitious, or easily fooled or intimidated. The Batak resent and speak bitterly of these attitudes. "Why must we be treated like this?" I was once asked. "Even if we haven't been to school, we're people, too." Daily reminders that most outsiders regard the Batak as an inferior people contribute to undermining such important stress-coping resources as self-esteem. I will return again to the notion of sociosymbolic subordination in chapter 7.

SOCIAL STRESS AND BATAK LOCAL GROUPS:
RELATIONS BETWEEN NEIGHBORS

Many of the social stresses that the Batak experience arise not from their gross economic and political subordination, as an entire ethnic group, to the "outside world" but in the more mundane context of everyday life in particular local groups. Each local group of Batak—in particular, each of the permanent settlements associated with these local groups— experiences a unique set of stresses of its own which adds to the total amount of stress that each individual Batak must cope with.

We saw (in chap. 3) that maintenance of, and periodic residence in, a permanent settlement today reflects both the emerging rhythm of Batak economic life and formal and informal pressures from government officials and lowland neighbors to the effect that that is the way the Batak *ought* to live. In their settlements the Batak are expected to live in lowland-style houses rather than the leaf shelters characteristic of forest life. In practice, however, their settlement houses are often unconstructed, uncompleted, or in various states of disrepair. In these circumstances, several families often reside together in one desultory house. The settlements themselves are often overrun with regrowth and may look as if they had been abandoned altogether some months previously. Nowhere do the Batak look more impoverished either to themselves or to outsiders than when they are living in their settlements. Here, too, they appear to have the greatest difficulty getting along with one another. Indeed, it seemed that for many Batak, their settlement was more a place to avoid than to live.

One reason is that settlement living brings together at a single residential location more individuals, and more unrelated individuals, than Batak ever customarily shared food with, resulting in ambiguities and negative feelings about such sharings. More generally, sedentary living magnifies a number of everyday difficulties and conflicts long associated with Batak life but which under more traditional residential conditions would be less noteworthy. The stresses created by the Batak's famine season nicely illustrate this point. That the Batak today must endure a famine season itself reflects the Batak's increasing involvement with a wider agricultural economy. Under the preagricultural regime, it is said, Batak may have gone hungry from time to time but never for more than a day or two. Now, however, the belt-tightening that culminates in July may begin in May or April.

First, and foremost, of course, this famine season is physiologically stressful, a point discussed previously. But the circumstances and aspirations of settlement life, even when those settlements are not continuously occupied, make the hungry season psychologically stressful as well. Rice is the desired staple throughout the year, but efforts to obtain it during July not only may be time-consuming but frustrating as well. These frustrations can lead to outbursts of anger or even accusations of laziness or dishonesty against neighbors or family members who, at the moment, seem somehow responsible for economic difficulty. Such seeming nonessentials as coffee and sugar become essential, and neighbors who once casually shared such commodities become irritable and calculating as they become scarce. This situation seems to be exacerbated by a preharvest settlement pattern in which men take to the trails in search of food while women, having finished in May and June the baskets and mats for the harvest, remain relatively mobile and unemployed, in swidden clusters or in settlements, waiting for the grain to ripen. More generally, and throughout the year, the Batak seem to experience greater difficulty "doing without" when living in their settlements or swidden houses than when living in the forest. Sedentary living, in short, has created new ways of feeling and being poor.

Other kinds of interpersonal conflicts in Batak settlements arise from the competitive consumption or display of consumer goods obtained in the lowlands—conflicts that arise, in effect, from the Batak's own efforts to emulate the modern consumer society. Kerosene pressure lanterns and battery-operated phonographs were the most sought-after items during my stay at Langogan. Those who had these items reminded those less fortunate of this fact in ways that even the Batak themselves described as childish. Like gossip, another of those human foibles that seems magnified by sedentary living, petty jealousies about the display, the borrowing, or the failure to loan or return consumer durables were decried by all even as they involved all.

Sedentary lowland Filipinos, of course, also engage in competitive consumption of consumer durables, and many must also endure a famine season. But it appears that settlement-living Batak have more difficulty coping with such stresses; they have not yet satisfactorily "adapted" to the exigencies of sedentary living. While stress coping is more properly the subject of chapter 7, I do want to emphasize here that other observers of hunting-gathering peoples who have recently turned to part-time or full-time settlement living have similarly emphasized the heightened patterns of tension and conflict that such living seems to create (e.g., Lee 1972; Headland 1981; Rai 1982:65).

Writing of the Hare Indians of Canada who, like the Batak, now alternate residence between permanent settlements and the "bush," Savishinsky (1974:132) observes that the less acculturated Hare in particular find the drinking, tension, and lack of privacy of the "more concentrated village situation" hard to take. Excessive drinking, it should be said, is not yet a major social problem among the Batak, although settlements (and stores in lowland villages) are the usual sites of those episodes of drinking that do occur. Even were they so inclined, however, the exigencies of poverty and geographic distance are such that the Batak would find it difficult to regularly obtain alcoholic beverages in any quantity. Other aspects of Savishinsky's analysis, however, apply as well to the Batak.

White (1977) provides an additional and provocative perspective on the question of why recently settled hunting-gathering peoples seem to find their own settlements such inhospitable places. She studied the effects of sedentary living on a group of Australian Aborigines at Yalata, in South Australia. She explains why Aborigines, particularly women, find living privately in permanent houses a source of boredom by appealing to a distinction between "firsthand living" and "secondhand living" (ibid.:103). In traditional Aboriginal society, most living was firsthand and centered on the variations in activities, experiences, and social relations generated by periodically moving camps and rearranging living shelters. In industrial societies, in contrast, much living is of the more vicarious, secondhand sort entailed by such activities as reading newspapers, watching television, and attending schools and movies. But settled Aborigines lack the skills and wherewithal necessary for much secondhand living: they may be unable to understand written or spoken English or to afford a television set. Ennui and social disorder arise in settled Aboriginal communities, White reasons, because the opportunities for firsthand living have been drastically curtailed without any compensating increase in secondhand living (ibid.: 103–105). Life in Batak settlements, I believe, suffers from a similar qualitative shortcoming.

One further stressful aspect of Batak settlement life merits special attention here: the conflicts caused, in some settlements, by Tagbanua who have chosen to live, work, or marry among the Batak. Batak feel a much greater affinity for and get along better with Tagbanua, as members of another tribal population, than they do with such lowland peoples as Cuyonon and Visayans. Although Tagbanua have probably only entered traditional Batak territory in the past one hundred years, many Batak claim to be a "kind of Tagbanua." While sentiments of affinity are partially reciprocated by the Tagbanua, they too tend to look down on and ridicule the Batak. Nevertheless, themselves the objects of discrimination in the lowlands, some Tagbanua have visited or joined Batak settlements. Here they escape much of the economic, political, and symbolic subordination that lowland-living Tagbanua must endure, but, in turn, they tend to push the Batak around.

Such behavior is visible in the groups of Tagbanua youths who periodically visit Batak settlements in search of good times, temporary sexual liaisons, or marriage partners. Such visits may last for days or weeks and are not, in principle, resented by the Batak. Indeed, they seem to welcome such visits for the excitement and news of Batak in other settlements they may bring. But such visitors would be more welcome if they were more respectful and made some contribution toward their subsistence during their stay. Moreover, some of these Tagbanua youths are a little dishonest in the way they pursue their romantic interests or, at the very least, are less readily influenced by Batak elders in these matters than the latter would like.

An incident involving a Tagbanua that occurred at Langogan during my stay is worth recounting in detail, for it illustrates the ultimate helplessness of the Batak in the face of those who would make trouble for them, even single individuals with no other resources with which to intimidate the Batak except their own presence. A lowland-raised Tagbanua youth of about twenty, the half-brother of a Langogan Tagbanua married to a Batak at the Mangaping settlement, had stayed at Mangaping for more than a month. Intelligent, physically strong, and aggressive, he was not on particularly good terms with his half-brother and drifted from household to household. He drank a lot during his stay, flirted with some women, and became involved in a series of minor arguments with some of the men. He was, in short, a troublemaker with few friends and no apparent reason for wanting to stay at Mangaping (although some suspected he was hiding from trouble he had caused in the lowlands).

The Batak had no effective means of making this Tagbanua leave. Then one argument escalated to the point that the youth, who was quite drunk, fired his gun in the air and threatened to strike a bystander with his bolo. All Batak present immediately fled the scene, as they had on previous occasions when he became menacing. This time, however, the Batak agreed that a community meeting would be held the following morning to investigate the incident and, more generally, the Tagbanua himself. This meeting was less an investigation than a sort of latter-day "meeting of the elders." One Batak, relatively articulate and experienced in traditional modes of dispute resolution, publicly gave voice to many of the sentiments that residents were feeling privately. "Are you visiting here or living here?" was one widespread sentiment thus expressed. Others offered, "There have always been problems here since you arrived" and "What kind of drinking are you doing, anyway—drinking to drink or drinking to make trouble?" The youth denied hurting anybody but otherwise said little during the proceedings. In demeanor, he was alternately contrite, smug, and resentful.

There was some remarkably frank talk during the discussion about limiting or prohibiting his drinking at Mangaping or even throwing him out altogether if he failed to reform. But in the end, he was simply enjoined to drink peacefully and to sleep afterward, rather than seek trouble.

In the days that followed, the Tagbanua did appear somewhat chastened by the episode, but he eventually returned to his former behavior. About a month later, he finally drifted back to the lowlands. As one sympathetic lowlander put it, it was a shame that the Batak had retreated as far into the mountains as they had to escape the freeloading and troublemaking of outsiders only to find that there were those outsiders who would bring these things to them.

SOCIAL STRESS AND BATAK HOUSEHOLDS: RELATIONSHIPS WITHIN FAMILIES

The Batak experience a final set of stresses in their roles as parents and adolescents or husbands and wives within particular domestic families. These stresses, too, appear to have increased with the changes that have overtaken the Batak. Pearlin's (1983) notion of "role strain" as a potential source of stress is helpful here. According to him, "it is around daily and enduring roles such as breadwinning and work or marriage and parenthood that much of our lives are structured through time" (ibid.:5). Roles, furthermore, are particularly potent sources of stress because people usually attach considerable importance to role activities even as a variety of social forces converge on these roles (ibid.).

Differential participation in lowland Filipino society may have increased role strain among the Batak in several ways. More than older people, for example, adolescents and young adults have found affective satisfactions by joining or emulating the leisure-time activities of lowlanders. The same popular songs, Western dancing, and domino games that interest youths in rural Philippine villages now attract Batak youths as well. Older Batak do not generally disapprove of these activities, but they appear to be related to a general loss of interest among the young in learning the traditions from their elders. The importance of the role of parent has diminished rapidly. Older people, in general, seem to find the significance of their positions in society to be less than they were in the past, in part because opportunities to earn money in the lowlands allow youths to become *independent* of their elders in ways without precedent in traditional society.

Other observers of tribal societies undergoing traumatic social change have reported similar stresses and strains in the relationships between parent and child and between young and old. Van Arsdale (1981) reports that a majority of elderly Asmat in New Guinea now live in a "ritual void," social and cultural change having carried away much of what once lent structure and significance to their lives. In the relocated Ojibwa community discussed earlier, family life has deteriorated as parents and grandparents appear unable to provide for or to guide their offspring (Shkilnyk 1985:34–49, 80–85). In Yanomamo villages exposed to contact with Brazilian society, Saffirio and Hames (1983) were struck by the degree to which the young had gained status and authority at the expense of the old, particularly in villages located on highways. The young owed their enhanced positions and increased independence to their greater abilities to conform to Brazilian expectations, acquire Brazilian goods, and speak Portuguese (ibid.: 26).

> The introduction of Western goods and the practice of wage labor is altering the very basis of Yanomamo social organization. Age, sex, and individual achievement in traditional skills no longer dominate the integration of Yanomamo society, especially in highway villages. Traditional skills are devalued because they fail to facilitate interactions with Brazilians. The young view the traditional knowledge and values held by elders as impediments to successful relations with Brazilians. Thus, as the Yanomamo become more dependent on Brazilians for economic resources, the bonds of kinship and marriage among them deteriorate. Modern

medicine has eroded the position of the shaman. Finally, many of the younger Yanomamo from the highway villages no longer wish to be considered Yanomamo. (Ibid.: 27)

Differential involvement in external socioeconomic systems has also visibly eroded the status of Batak women. More than their wives, Batak husbands have visited and even worked in the lowlands, learned lowland languages, and found opportunities to participate in the market economy. Most Batak men, for example, are reasonably fluent in Cuyonon, and a good number can get by in Tagalog. Batak women, in contrast, speak almost no Tagalog and while many understand Cuyonon, relatively few are comfortable communicating in it. Again, such significant income-earning activities as copal, honey, and rattan collecting are male activities. Men, in general, are far more skilled than women in handling market sales and purchases.

The changing economy has also rearranged traditional Batak husband-wife roles as they pertain to child care. Under forest camp conditions today (the closest Batak still come to their pre-1880 foraging lifeway), the burdens of child care appear to be shared fairly equally between the sexes. At settlements or swidden field houses, however, men may go off to work for a day or more at a time, leaving their wives behind to care for the smaller children.

Outside market involvement does not *necessarily* depress the relative status of women or strain husband-wife roles. In a study of development and sex roles among the Batek, Karen Endicott (1979) reports that women as well as men may work for Malays as agricultural laborers, collect and trade forest products, or trade and buy goods in Malay towns. Agta women, again unlike their Batak counterparts, also trade meat, fish, and other subsistence goods directly with lowland traders (Griffin 1984). Hence, local economic opportunities and cultural patterns are always important. Even among the Batak there is significant local variation. At Langogan and Caramay, for example, coffee berry picking is an important cash income source, and both men and women pick berries.

But, in general, studies of other foraging peoples suggest that sedentarism and its attendant social and economic changes usually undermine the relative sexual equality characteristic of such people (Leacock 1978; Dahlberg 1981). Nomadic !Kung women, for example, enjoy greater status, authority, and decision-making influence than do their settled counterparts (Draper 1975). Among the Chewong, a hunting-gathering people of the Malay Peninsula, men rather than women took advantage of the opportunity to collect and sell rattan. Subsequent male purchases of consumer goods became a preoccupying focus of public attention and social discourse and, for the first time, colored the sexual division of labor in a way that made the male domain seem more important (Howell 1983). Such changes are not limited to foraging peoples; market involvement has brought growing sexual inequality and dependency among indigenous peoples everywhere. Thus, in Mesoamerica, Indian women traditionally enjoyed higher relative status than Ladino women because they were economically complementary to men, while Ladinos were not. But as Indian men have entered the capitalist wage sector, Indian women have been left behind to pursue subsistence and domestic activities or, at most, informal self-employment, and their status and power has quickly declined (Bossen 1983:40–47). Based on a comparative study of South American Indians, Johnson and Johnson (1975) similarly conclude that economic complementarity helps women maintain an independent economic posture, while individualization of their labor makes women more isolated and vulnerable.

The actual amount of new stress introduced by such changes, whether it is experienced as role strain or in some other form, is of course a matter of speculation. But among the Batak, where male and female roles were traditionally complementary and men and women were relative equals in social skills, mobility, earning power, and child care responsibility, emerging inequalities in these roles may indeed have taken their toll. Thus, visits to the lowlands by groups of men may later precipitate domestic discord as wives complain of their husbands' alleged adultery or reckless spending on alcoholic beverages.

Finally, as we saw in chapter 4, it has become more difficult for individual Batak even to *find* husbands and wives. Batak often range far afield in search of spouses, and even then they may marry cousins (traditionally proscribed for marriage) or non-Batak. Steve Pruett, a missionary living with the Tanabag Batak, reports how in 1981 two young Batak women there were ready to marry and were under some social pressure to do so. But only one Batak male at Tanabag was of the appropriate age, still single, and of sufficient distance genealogically. Neither woman, apparently, found this particular Batak attractive (his body was extensively covered with ringworm). One woman precipitously married a Tagbanua she knew only casually; the second was left to marry the Batak man. This case is extreme, but nowhere do Batak men and women today have as much choice in selecting marriage partners as they did in the past.

In the face of these observations, it would be convenient to report that frequency of divorce has been increasing in recent decades. This does not appear to be the case, however. While many adults have been divorced at least once, Batak have always divorced and remarried with relative ease. But under the old foraging regime, with its lack of fixed agricultural assets, divorce had fewer economic repercussions than it does today. Thus, divorces, when they do occur, may entail more stress than they did in the past.

In summary, Batak do not enjoy the carefree lives that many lowlanders believe them to lead. Families, local groups, and the population as a whole are caught up in a world of pressures, tensions, and conflicts that result in a stress load on the Batak which can only be described as daunting. It is a basic premise of my analysis that when the level of social stress on a people exceeds their individual and collective stress-coping abilities, that stress will exact its costs. It may be objected that many of the stresses experienced by the Batak are, after all, only (if painfully) contemporary. But members of contemporary industrial societies have had many generations to develop and adopt more effective individual and collective means for dealing with the tensions and conflicts arising from the patterns of economic exploitation, political subordination, sexual inequality, and rapid culture change that affect *them*. The Batak have not, and they have suffered accordingly. The following chapter concerns the reasons Batak are unable to cope adequately with stress and how, precisely, uncontrolled stress exacts the costs that it does.

7

Decreased Stress-Coping Ability as the Cause of Adaptive Difficulty

Were Batak culture to persist in a more viable form than it actually does, the Batak might have routinely accommodated themselves to increasing stress levels. But the same changes that have augmented stress levels in the Batak environment have also undermined Batak ability to *cope* with stress. This decrease in "stress-coping capacity" may be traced directly to *deculturation*—the loss, without replacement by functional equivalents, of many traditional cultural beliefs, practices, and institutions (Isaac 1977:139). These beliefs, practices, and institutions once traditionally equipped the Batak, individually and collectively, with the resources necessary to cope with the exigencies of everyday life. Today, however, Batak resources—and I speak now of both the "core" and the "mixed" Batak—are no longer adequate for this purpose.

I will distinguish here between social network resources and ego resources that functioned in this fashion. While this distinction is analytically useful, many beliefs and practices function in a variety of ways to cope with stress and therefore resist classification under any one heading. But my aim here is not to classify cultural beliefs and practices but to examine, as comprehensively as possible, the costs to individual Batak of the reduction in cultural inventory that has accompanied incorporation into lowland Philippine society.

Culture loss, as opposed to simple culture change, is not a common theme in anthropological literature. The notion that cultural inventories can somehow be richer¹and poorer appears to run against the discipline's characteristic stance of cultural relativism. Further, there is the presumption, certainly appropriate in many cases, that wherever marriage or other significant social interaction occurs between members of the society in question and members of outside groups, any resulting losses in the traditional cultural inventories of the former will be offset by new acquisitions, as it were, from the inventories of the latter. Anthropology's long-standing notion of "acculturation" rests on precisely this reasoning, but, as I showed in chapter 4, it does not apply very well to the Batak.

Attempting to refine the notion of acculturation to come to terms with differences in "acculturative outcomes," Berry (1980) divides it into several varieties of adaptation, one of which is deculturation. According to Berry, deculturation occurs in situations of high "acculturative stress" and entails loss of cultural identity and (unlike, say, "assimilation," another variety of acculturation) a "negative relation" to a wider, dominant society (ibid.: 13–17). The notion that some tribal populations have in fact been deculturated by contact with outside social systems has been noted from time to time, particularly in the literature on South American Indians and most explicitly in the work of Isaac (1977) and Stearman (1984) on the Siriono. An analogous notion is the debilitating (but probably more temporary) "erosion of cultural inventory" observed to accompany forced resettlement, because at least part of the relocatees' traditional cultural inventory is not relevant to the new setting (see, e.g., Trimble 1980; Scudder and Colson 1982:271).

My particular interest is with the role of culture in constituting or mobilizing the social and psychological stress-coping resources that figure in adaptation and thus with the consequences of deculturation for the efficacy of those resources. For each type of resource, I begin by continuing a discussion initiated in chapter 6 about the general nature of social stress, now focusing on the roles of such phenomena as social support and self-esteem in facilitating stress coping. Then I detail the circumstances that have eroded such stress-coping resources among the Batak. Most important, I want to relate, through the medium of individual behavior, the kinds of stresses discussed in chapter 6 with the adaptive difficulties or "costs of stress" discussed in chapters 4 and 5. I want to explain, in effect, how stress hurts.

The relationships in question are multiplex, for a particular stress may exact a variety of costs, and a particular cost may reflect a range of stresses. Nevertheless, it is possible to identify more specifically some particular relationships between stress and its apparent costs. Some such relationships, I argue, arise because while the Batak do continue to cope with some of life's stresses, their coping efforts often create still other or adaptive difficulties. And some stress simply is not being coped with at all; this circumstance also has costs that I will examine.

Some readers may be uncomfortable with the functionalist, even speculative, nature of my analysis. Therefore, I close this chapter by presenting a detailed case study of the demise, during the 1950s, of one particular Batak cultural institution, the *umbay* ceremony. Here I will eschew further functionalist assertions and simply invite the reader to judge whether the disappearance of this unique institution in fact represents a loss to the Batak themselves.

Deculturation and Traditional Stress-Coping Resources

SOCIAL RESOURCES

The idea that social bonds and supportive interactions with other people are important to a person's health and well-being is widely shared, both in the industrial West and in numerous other cultures. While the notion long remained within the realm of folk wisdom, a considerable body of hard evidence now attests that "social support," as such bonds and interactions are commonly called, is indeed a major variable "buffering" or "mediating" how an individual is affected by or copes with the stress of life (Turner 1983:108). The emphasis on bonds and interactions is a vital part of the concept, for more than the mere presence of other individuals is involved. According to Johnson and Sarason (1979:155), "in the most general sense social support refers to the degree to which individuals have access to social resources in the form of relationships, on which they can rely, especially in time of need, but at other times as well. These resources might include spouse, family, friends, neighbors, community groups, and social institutions."

"Reliance" on the support of others can of course take many forms, but there is considerable agreement that the quality of an individual's social resources is paramount and that it is the *perception* of being supported that is the central issue. Thus, in an influential definition, Cobb (1976:300) conceived social support to be "information leading the individual to believe that he is cared for and loved, is esteemed and valued, and belongs to a network of communication and mutual obligation."

While some researchers (e.g., Turner 1983) follow Cobb and limit the concept of social support to the provision of emotional support, others (e.g., Caplan 1974) would include the provision of material assistance as well. But however broadly or narrowly the concept is defined, a compelling body of literature demonstrates that social support assists the individual in coping with or adapting to all sorts of stressful physical and psychological events, including pregnancy and childbirth, hospitalization, and illnesses as diverse as arthritis, tuberculosis, and alcoholism (see, e.g., the reviews in Cobb 1976; Kaplan et al. 1977; Berkman 1981). Social support is thus fundamentally protective of the individual, and far from fostering dependency, it fosters independent behavior and mastery of the environment (Caplan 1974:7; Cobb 1976:301; Johnson and Sarason 1979:156).[1]

How does social support "happen"? While some, to draw a contrast with more organized or institutionalized support systems (e.g., Caplan 1974), speak of spontaneous or natural support systems, it is important to recognize that such support is never automatic. Particularly outside the domain of the nuclear family (probably the most important support system in most societies), support is *mobilized*, in culturally constituted ways. It seems to me that if effective communication of those sentiments said to underlie social support is to take place, at least in the case of a dispersed, preliterate, and low-technology society like the Batak, some sort of regular and organized face-to-face contact between support givers and support seekers must occur. This would require, in turn, some physical movement by at least some of those involved. If so, there would appear to be two logical possibilities: the person in need of support can seek out would-be supporters, or those supporters can be brought to the person in need. This distinction, while simplistic, provides a useful way of calling attention to the disruptions that have occurred in two major Batak support systems: a system of intergroup mobility, in which persons in need of support seek out friends and kin in other local groups, and a system of shamanistic curing, in which the friends and kin of an ill individual are mobilized and brought together by a curer in an appeal for supernatural assistance in effecting a cure.

DISRUPTION OF TRADITIONAL MOBILITY PATTERNS

At least beyond the level of the nuclear family, unrestricted individual and household mobility was a central element in a Batak's ability to mobilize social support from friends and kin. That mobility among foraging peoples has important social as well as economic functions is well known; the most obvious and most widely reported such function is to *escape* the interpersonal tensions and conflicts that characterize everyday life in small bands. For example, in his study of stress and mobility among the Hare Indians, Savishinsky states that

> the pronounced physical mobility of the people during the course of every year, which is primarily a response to their traditional survival requirements, has also been developed by band members as a way of coping with ... other sources of stress and anxiety. That is, socially, psychologically, and ecologically provocative situations are dealt with, in part, by leaving undesirable environments and shifting to more manageable or familiar ones. The people, in trying to manipulate and control the context of their lives, consequently resort to travel and residence changes as primary coping strategies. (1974:xv)

It should be emphasized, however, that in those societies where mobility is a characteristic means of escaping stress, the individuals and households that are leaving stressful situations are usually seeking out and joining socially supportive kinsmen. Among the Batak, some such support seeking occurs within forest camps and settlements and is visible in the ubiquitous visiting between households, the constantly shifting composition of task groups, and the periodic realignments in household membership.

Other support seeking occurs between local groups. Marriage patterns ensure that all Batak have kinfolk dispersed in several local groups, and men and women traditionally traveled long distances to visit such kin for days, weeks, or even months at a time. Being a source of variety in life, such visits were pleasurable in their own right. But they also helped to reinforce a system of material obligation and exchange, to guarantee that an individual would have a place to turn in the event of distress, and to remind an individual that he was esteemed, valued, and loved—that is, that he was socially supported (e.g., Appell 1982:41–42).

Many observers of band-level societies have been struck by the intensity of their members' cultural and emotional commitment to unrestricted mobility. Based on his observations of Hare mobility patterns, Savishinsky concluded that

> the social and psychological value of movement seemed to
> be as significant for them as was its ecological utility. Their
> great emphasis upon freedom and self-sufficiency placed par-
> ticular stress upon mobility as a means to the independence
> which they so highly prized. Travel, then, became something
> of an end in itself, taking on the dimensions of an expressive
> activity, besides being an instrumental aspect of survival and
> subsistence. The flexibility of the people's relationship to
> their social and physical reality thus drew much of its
> strength from the fluidity which mobility allowed.
> (1974:118)

An emphasis on travel as an end in itself has also been attributed to Philippine Negritos. Garvan (1955:788), for example, spoke of their love of "liberty" and "forest freedom," which he apparently attributed to some sort of inherent Negrito wanderlust. Equally striking, however, is what Garvan describes as the Negrito's love of "home and forest homeland." According to Rice and Tima (1973:15), for example, Zambales Negritos who were forced to leave their own territories for other areas reported that they became ill and were unable to work. The resolution of this apparent paradox—that such peripatetic travelers are also relative homebodies—lies in part in the connection between traveling and support seeking: mobility within one's own territory has vital economic and social functions; outside, it is irrelevant or worse.

Batak mobility patterns, however, have changed dramatically. Incorporation into lowland society has constrained traditional patterns of movement, and the Batak, increasingly tied to their swidden fields, their copal lots, and their local creditors, are settling down. True, the Batak scarcely reside full-time in their settlements, and it was a major point of my analysis in chapter 3 that the Batak have in fact become almost hypermobile. At least some of this continuing mobility is concerned with support seeking. But social support today may be sought or obtained at considerable economic cost.

For example, most of the cases of "farming failure" described in chapter 3 involved the breakup of a household due to the departure of a key member to seek support in another locale. Such was the case of Wawa, the old man who prevailed on his nephews to make a rice field for him which he was ultimately unable to care for. Another case involved marital discord. Husbands and wives who quarrel seriously, for whatever reason, traditionally coped with the stress of their disagreement by separating, temporarily or permanently, each to seek the support of relatives—wherever they might be. While such behavior is common enough in kinship-based societies, among the Batak it seems to result, under the new economic regime, in unusually severe economic dislocations. On several occasions during my stay with the Batak, marital differences resulted in the temporary or permanent abandonment of agricultural fields prior to harvest, with the resulting loss of months of labor invested. Lowland husbands and wives quarrel as well, but such quarrels rarely lead to field abandonment.

Other cases of field abandonment occurred during my stay because illness or some other crisis prompted an entire household to temporarily move to another local group. During one harvest time, a woman at Babuyan was reported to be seriously ill. Two households at Tanabag, two days' walk away, decided to visit her and help her with her harvest. They intended, it was said, to return to Tanabag in time to harvest their own fields, but they stayed away longer than planned. By the time they did return, their own fields had been extensively damaged by wild pigs and inclement weather, and little standing rice remained to harvest. Again, under the old subsistence regime, such support-giving or support-seeking strategies were less costly, because a household's "economic operations" could more readily be transferred to a new location. The Batak themselves, of course, recognize the economic costs of intergroup mobility.

Today, intergroup visiting by entire households is generally restricted to the postharvest months. Travel at this time entails fewer immediate economic dislocations, but it still has significant opportunity costs.[2]

DEMISE OF CURING CEREMONIES AND OTHER ELEMENTS OF THE TRADITIONAL BELIEF SYSTEM

Like members of other human societies, the Batak traditionally not only sought the support of friends and kin but of spirit beings or deities as well. An emphasis on the presumed functional benefits of religious beliefs and practices has a long and distinguished tradition in anthropology. Recently, Appell (1982:47) has sought to develop an explicit link between indigenous belief systems and adaptive well-being, arguing that it is "through belief and meaning that the cognitive models are built that enable people to organize their lives and their coping capacities."

The adaptive significance of religious belief systems stems in large part, I believe, from the fact that while such beliefs ostensibly function (by definition) to mobilize supernatural support, they typically mobilize considerable social support as well. Caplan (1974), examining the kinds of support systems that contribute to community mental health, was struck by the importance of religious denominations:

> Setting aside the primary theological aspects of religions for the purpose of this discussion, what impresses me most about them are the following support system characteristics: Most denominations are organized in congregations of neighbors. They hold regular meetings and provide a range of opportunities for their members to become friends and to identify with each other. This process is fostered by their joint allegiance to a shared theology and to a common value system and body of traditions. Members are usually enjoined to help each other, especially in times of acute need; religious ceremonials as well as service programs are provided to accomplish this, especially at predictable crisis times such as birth, marriage, illness, and death. These organized social

supports are significantly buttressed by the internal supports
of a meaningful value system and set of guidelines for living,
so that the religious person does not feel that he is dependent only on his individual wisdom in grappling with life's
problems. He can rely on the wisdom of the ages enshrined
in his religion. He can also rely on the positive and negative
sanctions of a present and cohesive reference group to help
him control and direct his impulses and chart the course of
his life. (P. 25)

To be sure, Caplan is writing about organized religions in
a complex industrial society. But his appraisal of their importance has a definite Durkheimian ring to it, and anthropologists who have studied religions in tribal societies have
commented in similar fashion on their supportive functions.
According to Endicott (1979*b*: vii), the ultimate source of the
"remarkable vitality and optimism" of the Batak can be found
in a set of religious beliefs that give meaning and value to
their lives and reassure them that the way they live is right
for them and in harmony with the forces of nature. (Endicott
also observes that Batek religious beliefs reinforce their characteristic "Negrito" emphasis on freedom of movement.) In
the same vein, Rice and Tima (1973:60), preparing a development plan for a Negrito reservation in Luzon, Philippines,
warn against the possible deleterious social consequences
of cosmological breakdown: "it is their present cosmology
which provides the necessary integration of the various customs and social institutions into a reasonable framework for
their entire life style."

Little remains, however, of what was once Batak religion.
It has fallen victim to forces of change already discussed.
Indeed, attempting to reconstruct what Batak religion once
was is a difficult and speculative enterprise. Little was recorded on the subject until Warren's fieldwork in 1950–51,
and the resulting account (Warren 1964:98–112) is of a
system of beliefs and practices that we must assume was
already extensively disrupted. Certainly, by the time I
studied the Batak, only the oldest men and women could

give a coherent account of Batak cosmology. Even then it seemed to have nothing of the elegance that Fox (1982) attributes to the religion of the Tagbanua, the Batak's horticultural neighbors to the south. Fox maintains that Tagbanua religion centers on a "cult of the dead" that mirrors the social order of Tagbanua society and reflects their world view. Thus, among Tagbanua, "one social and moral order encompasses the living, the dead, the deities, and the total environment" (ibid.:252). Any such centeredness or cosmological integrity in Batak religion had apparently disappeared by midcentury—in part, ironically, because of borrowings from the Tagbanua, who have much influenced the Batak in ritual and jural realms (Warren 1964:107).

What can be said is that the central elements of Batak religion apparently resembled those of other Southeast Asian tribal societies. The Batak traditionally lived in a world inhabited by a variety of nature spirits and supernatural beings, and they relied on mediums or shamans to mediate their relationships with these spirits and beings (ibid.:98). Most Batak can still identify by name a considerable number of such supernaturals. Most nature spirits fall into two broad classes: malevolent *panya'en* or capricious, but benevolently inclined, *diwata*. Visible only to shamans, panya'en and diwata inhabit specific trees, bamboo thickets, rocks, caves, streams, and other places in the natural environment. Such spirits are very humanlike in their lives, actions, and desires. They are said to affect Batak welfare in a variety of ways, most notably, with respect to illness (below), for humans may provoke them by unwittingly violating their territory, destroying their dwellings, or injuring their families (Shimizu 1983:134).

Other supernaturals fall into neither category but are unique and rather fearsome individuals. One is like a large goat in appearance and voice, eats, wild pigs, and chases unwary hunters. Another is humanlike and no bigger than a small boy, but it is extremely aggressive and given to shouting and throwing rocks if disturbed. Finally, there is a group of powerful supernaturals who are the "leaders" of wild pigs and bees, capable of summoning them or sending them away and thus exerting a powerful influence on the outcome of hunting activities.

Mediating Batak relationships with a world of such supernaturals are the *babalians*, mediums capable of interceding with spirit beings on behalf of some human enterprise or misfortune. The opening of a new swidden field, a consanguineal marriage, or a local epidemic of illness are all occasions when spirits either are angry or may become angry and thus for which a babalian must organize the appropriate ritual action. Batak rituals are brief and involve little paraphernalia, but glossolalialike chants are performed and all local group members participate. Babalians also pass on the traditional knowledge about the supernatural that all must know, for example, that the human soul leaves the body during sleep and is vulnerable to capture by a panya'en and that violent thunderstorms arise because somewhere a Batak has laughed at an animal or failed to visit a relative.

It is admittedly difficult to draw any specific connections between such beliefs and practices and the kinds of supportive functions that Endicott (1979b) and Rice and Tima (1973) allege characterize Negrito religions. In consequence, it is speculative to attribute any of the Batak's current adaptive difficulties to the general demise of those beliefs and practices. With respect to *beliefs*, furthermore, we have the additional uncertainty of not being able to know conclusively just what people "believe" and thus whether their beliefs are in fact even changing. With respect to *practices*, which can be directly observed, we are on firmer ground.

Thus Scudder (1975:468), viewing the human consequences of compulsory resettlement—a process not unlike rapid culture change—argues that the truncation or cessation of traditional rituals that often follows relocation decreases people's ability to cope with the stresses of uncertainty, misfortune, ill health, and death. While such attributions may still seem speculative, Scudder does muster evidence that the relocatees he studied in fact suffered increased ill health and death. Many possible causes are still involved, but ritual disruption is indeed a likely one. At least some traditional rituals involved curing, and curing rituals, in whatever society they are held, typically mobilize highly visible social support for ill individuals (Wood 1979:300). Considerable comparative evidence suggests that the indigenous institutions that mobilize social support do make a genuine contribution toward preventing disease and speeding recovery from illness (e.g., Dressler 1982). Thus, we are on firmer ground in asserting that the observable demise of traditional Batak curing ceremonies—one element of their traditional religion—may indeed have undermined Batak adaptive well-being.

The babalian (always a male among the Batak) is the central figure in the curing ceremony. Only he, through song or dance, can enter a trance. Hence, only he can communicate directly with the diwatas, familiar to him from previous trance states, who may be able to intercede on behalf of an ill individual. The nature of the intercession sought depends on the babalian's diagnosis of the illness. Some illnesses arise because an individual accidentally stumbled on and damaged the house of a panya'en or unthinkingly misspoke or misbehaved in a fashion offensive to a panya'en—perhaps by carrying a sack of rice around at midday or by jesting about the guardian spirit of the bees. In such cases, the angered panya'en may throw some object at the person which lodges in his body and causes the illness. To effect a cure, the babalian appeals to his diwata familiars for assistance in drawing out the offending object.

Other illnesses arise because a panya'en has captured the soul of the ill individual, which had wandered during a dream. To effect a cure in this circumstance, the babalian must ask a diwata familiar to attempt to determine what the panya'en's conditions are for the return of the soul. Depending on the symptoms, a babalian may also administer some herbal medicines, which may be the only treatment proffered in those illnesses with relatively straightforward symptoms (e.g., diarrhea or cough). While only a few Batak ever specialized in curing, many of the adults in each local group would attend and participate in curing ceremonies, thus demonstrating considerable social support for the ill individual and the babalian's efforts to restore his or her health. (A detailed account of a Pinatubo Negrito curing "seance," similar in many respects to a Batak curing ceremony, is found in Shimizu [1983].)

Today, the traditional Batak curing system is virtually moribund. What is most striking is that the occupation of babalian is disappearing with the current senior generation. Three of the eight Batak local groups have no surviving babalians at all. Furthermore, of the other five groups, only at Tanabag and Maoyon are babalians still actively practicing their trade, and even then their performances are often for tourists. In none of the groups, finally, are any Batak youths preparing to *become* babalians. While change in cultural values has been important, particularly among the young, simple depopulation has also taken its toll on the status of babalian and the institution of curing. Among the Amahuaca of eastern Peru (Dole 1961) and the Mundurucu of Brazil (Murphy 1958, 1960), depopulation so reduced both the number of suitable individuals available to fill shamanistic roles and the number of individuals available to attend shamanistic ceremonies that these ceremonies simply could not be held (see also Isaac 1977:146–147).

The situation with respect to curing ceremonies at Langogan is typical of that prevailing in other Batak local groups. One babalian still lives at Langogan; two others died recently, in 1971 and 1979. No youths have apprenticed themselves to the present babalian, who last performed a curing ceremony in 1979. No such ceremonies were performed at all during 1980–81, while I lived at Langogan; the babalian lacked motivation, it was said, and the rest of the people lacked interest. This situation was not expected to change. Even Tanabag and Maoyon, the present strongholds of Batak culture, will eventually go the way of Langogan, and it seems likely that Batak curing ceremonies—at least those aimed at curing and not at tourists—will disappear entirely by the end of the century.

In these circumstances, what kinds of care *do* the Batak provide for ill individuals? There is still periodic use of herbal medicines. Knowledge of plants with medicinal properties is not limited to babalians, and at times of illness or injury, many adults are capable of suggesting or preparing an appropriate root or leaf concoction. Batak knowledge and use of herbal medicines seems surprisingly scanty, however, for a foraging people who otherwise still preserve a remarkable inventory of knowledge about their forest environment.

The demise of curing ceremonies notwithstanding, Batak do continue to provide care and emotional support to the ill. They are visited frequently by others, and there is always someone, usually a close family member, to provide food, water, and company. In many cases, however, it seemed that little more was provided. During my stay at Langogan, a number of cases of serious illness involved infants or small children. One child had a fever and a bad bronchial condition, another had a fever and suffered from vomiting and convulsions, and so on. In each case, the mother attended to the child constantly, but neither she nor those around her seemed to know what else to do. No herbal medicines were sought or offered, no curing ceremonies were held, little interest was expressed in my own supply of medicines, and not even the most basic precautions were taken to avoid further deterioration in the child's condition. Those adults present to "see the child through" simply seemed to be waiting to see if it would survive or not. In short, and speaking only of the cases of illness that I knew of personally, people were obviously *concerned* for the ill person's welfare but they did not seem highly *motivated* to do much about it. Such fatalism reflects, in part, Batak beliefs about causation in illness. Also, in the case of ill children, a mother's own nutritional and disease status may affect the quality of her mothering.

One particular health problem, tuberculosis, deserves special mention. It is suspected to be a major cause of death among the Batak. Many lay people probably believe that tuberculosis is a straightforward infectious disease, with the appropriate medicine and professional supervision being the keys to cure. But both contraction of and recovery from the disease are known to be powerfully influenced by factors in one's social environment. Jackson (1954), for example, showed that alcoholics who tried to stop drinking on their own were many times more likely to develop tuberculosis symptoms than those alcoholics who attempted to stop drinking with the support of an organized program, such as Alcoholics Anonymous. Holmes (1956) showed that the incidence of tuberculosis in Seattle was highest among people who were "socially marginal": those living alone in one room; those single or divorced; those of minority status in their neighborhoods; and those who experienced the death of a parent, or divorce of their parents, before age 18. Reviewing a variety of such studies, Chen and Cobb (1960) conclude that tuberculosis is a disease of social isolation, that is, a disease of the failure of social support systems. This circumstance helps to explain, for example, why Bantu working in South African cities suffer one of the highest tuberculosis rates in the world, while Bantu who remain behind in their native villages are largely resistant to infection, despite exposure to their severely ill, city-working kin, many of whom return to their native kraals to die (Dubos and Dubos 1952:194). Thus, more than changes in diet, working conditions, or exposure to the bacilli explain outbreaks of tuberculosis in a society, for such outbreaks reflect as well "the complex of disturbances brought about in the community as a whole by most forms of social upheavals, be they abrupt changes in ancestral habits, rapid industrialization, or wars" (ibid.:195–196).

It must be added that besides disrupting traditional social support systems, incorporation into lowland Philippine society has made available to the Batak some *new* support systems. I argue in chapter 6 that some interventions by outside individuals and agencies aimed at assisting the Batak in fact made life more stressful for them. But, paradoxically, potential sources of stress in life may also be potential resources for coping with stress. Over the years, for example, some lowland farmers have been genuinely supportive of individual Batak. Patron-client relationships aside, such farmers have provided everything from friendship to material aid to political backing or legal assistance. The same is true of those missionaries, Summer Institute of Linguistics workers, and World Vision project personnel who have worked with Batak in various local groups. Finally, new cosmologies (e.g., Catholicism) and new health maintenance systems (e.g., occasional visits by rural health personnel) that also help cope with the physiological and psychological stresses of life have begun to penetrate Batak society. But in my opinion, these things have not offset the reductions in stress-coping capacity that have resulted from the loss of the traditional social support-providing institutions discussed here.

Ego Resources

Besides seeking social support in the face of stress, people can fall back on their own individual psychological resources. Considerable evidence suggests that a strong sense of self is a vital aspect of one's ability to successfully cope with stress (Appell 1982:33–37; Pearlin 1983:26–28). But among the Batak, such important aspects of the self as mastery and self-esteem have been badly undermined by contact with lowland Philippine society. Mastery, or the belief that one can manage or control the events or forces that importantly affect one's life (Pearlin 1983:27), has been eroded by repeated demonstrations of Batak's patent *inability* to control such forces. Self-esteem has been eroded by daily reminders of the achievement gap between the Batak's present level of living and the lowland level of living to which they have come to aspire. Yet efforts to close this gap, and restore self-esteem, have proven costly and ultimately unsuccessful.

POLITICAL IMPOTENCY AND THE EROSION OF MASTERY

Feelings of self-efficacy—that one is, in effect, the master of one's own fate—are among the most important stress-coping resources possessed by the person (Kaplan 1983:226). But a notable attribute of the demands and intrusions of outside individuals and agencies on the Batak is their *unpredictable* and *uncontrollable* nature. The PANAMIN resettlement project was extreme, but as the other examples of political impotency also illustrate, the Batak never know when the representative of this or that agency will suddenly appear and expect them to drop what they are doing for some length of time.

Psychologists who have studied stress have found that the less control a person judges himself or herself to have in an unpleasant or threatening situation, the more stressful it will be (Houston 1972; Johnson and Sarason 1979:158–159). In contrast, when individuals can exercise some control over the timing of unpleasant events, they are able to plan their lives around these events, and the events themselves are then less stress provoking (Glass and Singer 1972:87). At the extreme, loss of control over one's life is a serious business. Seligman (1975) argues that people learn to be "helpless" on continued exposure to uncontrollable, aversive stimuli; over time, they become progressively less motivated to devise strategies to *escape* from these stimuli. Deci, who believes that people have a "generalized need" to be "self-determining," says that "when people are denied the opportunity to be self-determining they lose motivation, their performance and learning become impaired, they may become ill, and in some cases they may die" (1980:45, 208). Turning again to the literature on forced resettlement, Trimble (1980) follows this line of reasoning to emphasize that one important reason that relocatees characteristically have trouble adjusting to their new circumstances is their lack of decision-making power.

EMULATION OF LOWLAND FILIPINO CONSUMPTION PATTERNS AND EROSION OF SELF-ESTEEM

Simply "feeling good about oneself" is also a central element in one's ability to manage stress. But Batak self-esteem has been eroded by sustained contact with lowlanders who, despite their negative actions and attitudes, have nevertheless become vital "important others" to the Batak. Not surprisingly, perhaps, the lowlander the Batak sees almost daily is as important an influence on his feelings and behavior as a kinsman in another settlement whom he may see only several times a year. But contact with lowlanders has devalued the traditional Batak system of prestige allocation while confronting them with an alternative system, based on capitalist consumption patterns, that the Batak lack the wherewithal to successfully compete in. But they are expected to compete in it, and they do try to do so. As a result, new kinds of stresses are created, such as the interpersonal conflicts arising from the consumer goods competition (see chap. 6), even as self-esteem is diminished by ultimate failure.

Batak efforts to emulate lowland dietary patterns, particularly with respect to such basic lowland foods as coffee, sugar, and polished rice, illustrate these difficulties. Running out of coffee and sugar in a forest camp today is certain to precipitate a morning of complaints about the hardships of Batak existence, just as an evening meal of wild yams will occasion much comment about how much better rice tastes. Batak desires to obtain and consume such foods stems from their powerful, "double reinforcement effect" (Erasmus 1977:107). The foods are simultaneously utilitarian (they taste good) and a source of prestige and personal good feelings. These good feelings arise because consumption of foods such as coffee and rice enable the Batak to demonstrate, to themselves and to outsiders, a modicum of participation in the life-style of lowland Filipinos—a life-style the Batak want desperately to achieve. Clothing similarly has more than utilitarian appeal. Writing of the importance of Filipino-style clothing to the Tagbanua, Warner (1979: 166) speaks of its "camouflage effect": wearing it makes Tagbanua feel more comfortable in a social world composed increasingly of lowlanders. Batak sentiments are much the same.

Batak desires to obtain lowland consumer goods run deeper, however, than a mere need for "camouflage"; they are tied up with an individual's own sense of identity and self-worth. Reporting an incident reminiscent of Batak behavior, Savishinsky (1974) describes how Hare Indians, dispersed in wintertime fur-trapping camps, vary in the number of trips they make back to their main settlement in the course of the winter according to how "acculturated" they are. Men from acculturated households make the most trips—but out of psychological, not ecological, necessity. One such individual's journeys were particularly frequent; "his family's shortage of even minor supplies was a sufficient excuse for most of these trips, and between the 'shopping' and the drinking he did at the village, he was away from his traplines for about a third of the time" (ibid.: 100–102). While only an anecdote, the case illustrates that an individual's efforts to obtain life's new necessities, however understandable in social-psychological terms, may undermine his longer-term welfare.

To help satisfy their newfound lowland food wants, the Batak divert some high-quality traditional foods (wild pig, wild honey) to the external market. As I showed in chapter 5, outside foods obtained in this fashion tend to be of lower nutritional quality than the indigenous foods they replace. Lacking longitudinal production data, it is impossible to determine whether the Batak today obtain wild pig and honey in greater quantities than in the past or whether they have simply cut back on home consumption. However, circumstantial evidence—sedentarism's depressing effect on foraging yields in general, the competing demands on Batak time—make the first possibility unlikely.

Further, Batak have simply reduced or eliminated entirely consumption of a wide variety of traditional but less desired foods, such as fungi, insects, wild bananas, and certain species of roots, greens, fruits, and animals. This change is a result, in part, of the availability of alternative lowland foods. Mostly, however, it reflects Batak response to the disdain that lowlanders express for many traditional Batak foods. The outcome has been a dramatic decline in diet diversity over the past one hundred years.

To be sure, the Batak do find ways to husband their self-esteem and to otherwise feel good about themselves. Settlement living, for example, was said to breed social tensions, and I suggested that at least some Batak seemed to treat their settlements as places to avoid as much as places to live. But settlement life does have its pleasures, as the following cases illustrate. Like poor and socially marginal people everywhere, however, the Batak are often led to seek pleasure—to feel good about themselves—in ways costly to individual and family welfare.

In May, a settlement-dwelling Batak went to Langogan to borrow 20 kilograms of unhusked rice, ostensibly to feed his family during the weeks ahead. Half would later be paid for with a delivery of roofing material, and half by weeding the lender's rice field. By the afternoon, several neighbors appeared and helped pound about 8 kilograms of the newly arrived rice, inviting themselves, in effect, to dinner. By nightfall, more rice was pounded, for still others arrived and were expected to eat. Meanwhile, someone had produced a battery-operated phonograph, and some Batak began dancing. A kerosene pressure lantern also appeared, and a domino game ensued. Some women brought their mat-weaving materials. Still more rice was pounded, cooked, and consumed; sixteen adults ultimately ate dinner at this man's house. Despite the absence of meat or fish, many spoke of what a fine evening it was, "even if there was nothing else" (but the rice itself) to celebrate. The host did not seem particularly upset by the outcome of his rice-borrowing efforts. Indeed, he expressed not merely fatalism but considerable satisfaction with himself for having fed and otherwise entertained neighbors and kin whose needs, as he put it, were so great. It is fair to say, though, that this was not his intention at the beginning of the day.

One morning in February, two Batak were preparing to set out from the settlement to work, the one for some overdue weeding in his rice field, the other for a day of labor owed a settler. Just as they were leaving their house, a neighbor came by on his way to the lowlands and jokingly asked if it was time for a drink. A bottle of gin appeared from the house, and each took a drink; at this point, everyone apparently still intended to proceed with their plans for the day. But before the bottle could be put away, still others arrived, and the drinking continued for several hours. Soon it was apparent that no work would be done that morning. A long-simmering dispute over a borrowed homemade gun came to a head during the drinking, and some men spent the afternoon discussing it. The first two Batak did engage in some minor subsistence pursuits in the late afternoon, but neither reached his intended destination for the day.

Both these cases are extreme, but they illustrate how readily time and resources can be shared or squandered in the pursuit of happiness in the crucible of settlement living. Such living is desultory on a day-to-day basis, but it is punctuated by debilitating and dependency-breeding episodes of "high living" that bring the Batak a modicum of satisfaction with life even as they help maintain economic and social marginality.

There are other possible connections between disruption of an individual's psychological stress-coping resources and the kinds of demographic and physiological impairments in Batak adaptive well-being discussed in chapters 4 and 5. Some evidence, for example, connects high levels of stress and anxiety with low fertility. An early version of this argument in anthropology was Rivers's (1922) claim that such psychological factors as "lack of interest in life" explained declining birth rates in Melanesia and thus helped to account for the widespread depopulation in the region following European colonization. Later generations of anthropologists were critical of such arguments (e.g., Pentony 1953), with the prevailing tendency to explain depopulation attending colonial contact largely or exclusively in terms of the impact of introduced diseases in mortality (e.g., MacArthur 1968). Recent evidence, however, suggests that humans may indeed react to stress with reduced fertility (Harrell 1981:804), and seasonal variation in anxiety levels have recently been used to explain birth seasonality (Malina and Himes 1977). But the evidence for such connections is not yet conclusive (Mosher 1979:173).

More compelling is a body of evidence relating such psychological factors as reduced self-esteem with heightened levels of illness and mortality. Turning again to an early analysis of depopulation in the Pacific, Hogbin (1930) attributed population decline on Ontong Java, a Polynesian atoll, to the interactions of cultural decay, psychosomatic malaise, and disease-related mortality. While disease was the primary variable, the other factors contributed, Hogbin believed, to a fatally passive state of mind that "acquiesces in extinction" (ibid.:65). Bayliss-Smith (1975) has recently reviewed the evidence and arguments concerning Ontong Javanese depopulation and repopulation and views Hogbin's argument favorably. As for the actual mechanisms involved, the prevailing view seems to be that psychosocial malaise somehow results in compromised resistance to disease in general (Berkman 1981:63; Turner 1983:106), a theme I return to.

Deculturation: A Case Study

I will now examine, in some detail, the circumstances surrounding the decline and disappearance during the 1950s of one particular cultural institution, the umbay ceremony. A kind of puberty ceremony or rite of passage, it initiated adolescents into a status whose associated behavioral expectations, it is said, helped to prepare them for adulthood and marriage. The umbay ceremony apparently combined elements of the traditional belief system with mobilization of neighbors and kin and reaffirmation of Batak ethnic identity. But because I never observed Batak society with the umbay ceremony and related practices still present, I have no direct evidence to offer that the disappearance of this particular institution in fact significantly altered Batak ability to cope with stress or significantly undermined Batak adaptation in some other way. Thus, the account that follows consists of a straightforward documentation of how and why the decline and disappearance in question occurred, with the assumption that much Batak deculturation occurred in analogous fashion.

The umbay ceremony marked the transition, at about the age of fourteen, from the childhood statuses of *sumandak* (male) and *pamuklan* (female) to the adolescent status of umbay, a status occupied until marriage. The ceremony consisted of a mock sexual intercourse scene between the initiate and an opposite-sex partner, the latter already an umbay. Plans were made without the knowledge of the umbay-to-be. Apparently because of the behavioral expectations involved (below), adolescents did not want to become umbays and could be expected to hide or resist. The following description concerns a male initiate, but the practices applied to both sexes equally.

When an adolescent male was to be made an umbay, a female opposite was chosen and a time and place agreed upon. When the Batak gathered for the ceremony, some went to take the umbay-to-be by surprise and drag him bodily into the dwelling where the ceremony would occur. Here he was forced to lie down in the center of the floor and was held in place until he abandoned attempts to escape. His partner was then brought in and made to lie next to him, and the pair were covered with a blanket. In this fashion, they were expected to lie quietly for as much as an hour. During this interval there was singing and story telling—and, it is said, a good deal of laughter about the discomfort of the pair on the floor. Removal of the blanket terminated the ceremony. The following day, the partner visited the initiate to present him with the *todol*, or body ornaments, that he was now entitled to wear. There was no expectation that umbay partners would later marry each other, although they could do so if they wished.[3]

Umbays were expected to do all the work activities peculiar to their sex without adult assistance or supervision. Young males, for example, who once searched for wild honey in the company of their fathers or other older relatives, were now expected to go into the forest alone or with their age-mates. At the same time, umbays were also expected to refrain from the play activities that previously occupied much of their time. A new umbay who continued to play at the river with friends would soon hear someone shout, "Aren't you ashamed! You're already an umbay, but you keep on playing! All the other umbays are working!" To be so reprimanded would make one *uyangyangen*, a state of embarrassment peculiar to umbayhood.

The most distinctive feature of umbay status was lexical substitution. When umbays spoke, either to each other or to other Batak, they employed a vocabulary uniquely their own. Certain objects and actions were, for umbays, *lagah*: they could not be spoken of using their normal Batak term. Prohibited words include many major features of the Batak natural and cultural environments, particularly useful plants and animals. For each prohibited word there was a *pandiin*, or substitute word, that umbays were expected to learn and use. It was believed that umbays who failed to use pandiins as required risked breaking out in boils. (The personal names of certain affinal kin likewise require use of a pandiin; see Eder 1975.)

When did this institution disappear? Classifying a sample of 65 Batak of all ages according to birthdate and cross-classifying them according to whether they became umbays, we find that of 22 Batak born during 1930 or before, all but 2 became umbays. Of 15 Batak born between 1931 and 1940, 5 became umbays and 10 did not. Of 28 Batak born after 1940, only 3 became umbays. If we assume a lag period of about fifteen years between birthdate and initiation, then clearly the major period of stress on this institution began about 1945 (when the children born between 1931 and 1940 began to come of age) and ended by about 1960 (since only a few of the children born between 1941 and 1950 actually went on to become umbays). The last three umbay ceremonies involving Batak in this sample (which I believe to adequately represent the entire Batak population) were in fact dated to 1956, 1958, and 1959. After 1959, no further Batak were made umbays, for, as I was told, *da' na paumbayen*, there was no one left to be made an umbay with.

The nature of the pairings made during the umbay ceremony thus provides the key to understanding why the institution disappeared. For an acceptable partner was not only himself or herself already an umbay but was also, in the ideal view, an appropriate marriage partner. The Batak say that known consanguineal kin should not marry, and umbay pairings reflected this belief. (Batak genealogical reckoning extends to third cousins.) In practice, as we shall shortly see, known consanguines do in fact now marry, but no umbay initiate was ever paired with a consanguineal kinsman. Less explicit, but also strongly felt, is the belief that marriage should be locally endogamous, that is, within the same local group. A common cause of argument between husband and wife is the question of postmarital residence, and inability to resolve this question is a common cause of divorce. (The Batak are nominally uxorilocal, but residence choice is strongly influenced by personal preference and the developmental cycle of the family.) In any case, local endogamy clearly obviates much of this problem. Again, many marriages are, in practice, locally exogamous, but the Batak say that umbay partners, like ideal marriage partners, were always drawn from the same local group. Finally, there was the implicit understanding that Batak only married other

Batak, and while there has always been some outgroup marriage, no Batak was ever paired with a non-Batak in an umbay ceremony.

What kinds of changes were occurring in Batak society between 1945 and 1960 which would account for growing difficulty in finding umbay partners? These were the same years that saw the five coastal reservations disband and the Batak retreat to the interior. Depleted in number, they were fragmented into smaller and remoter groups. With changing economic activities, intergroup and interpersonal contact not only declined in frequency but changed in nature, in ways we have examined. Such contact today consists largely of brief and purposive individual visiting, rather than periodic coalescence and dispersion of families or entire local groups. Most significantly, local groups themselves drifted toward growing interrelatedness, and individual Batak found themselves surrounded by a dense network of consanguineal kin.

In these circumstances, many would-be initiates found that the only umbays present in their own local groups were cousins, with whom they could not be paired. True, there were potential umbay partners in other local groups. But intergroup pairings would not only have violated cultural ideals about marriage. Lacking the milieu of the reservation as a centralized meeting place, any intergroup pairings would have required advance planning and would thus have robbed the umbay ceremony of much of its spontaneity. While Batak acknowledge that going farther afield to obtain umbay partners was a logical possibility, their failure to exploit it is perhaps not surprising.

The case of Salimbag is typical of the situation that confronted growing numbers of Batak after 1945. Salimbag is the youngest of three brothers. The eldest two became umbays; Salimbag did not. His brothers had in fact been paired (in different ceremonies) with the same female umbay, but by the time Salimbag came of age, this particular female was already married. The only female umbays then present were his consanguineal kin, and Salimbag married without ever becoming an umbay. As time went on, other Batak likewise failed to become umbays—and thus removed themselves from the diminishing pool of potential umbay partners for those who would follow.

There were, no doubt, always occasional Batak who failed, for whatever reasons, to become umbays. The institution must certainly have been flexible enough to tolerate such failures. But it is also easy to see that once large numbers of Batak began to "miss their turn," the institution would necessarily disappear quite rapidly. That is precisely what happened during the decade 1950–1960.

If the umbay ceremony fell into disuse because the Batak literally ran out of culturally acceptable umbay partners, then recent years should presumably have seen a substantial increase in the frequency of marriages between those very classes of individuals which could not be paired as umbays. The pairing of umbays is primarily a ceremonial statement of how things ought to be in a Batak society; the pairing of marriage partners is primarily a practical statement of how things actually are. Retrospectively, pairings, such as those between cousins, that could not be tolerated under the first institution, at the level of ideals, had to be tolerated under the second institution, at the level of practice—at least if Batak society was to preserve any reproductive viability at all.

We already saw, in chapter 4, that the incidence of marriage between Batak and members of other ethnic groups increased dramatically after about 1960. The rest of the proposition, that there has also been an increasing incidence of marriages between consanguineal kin and between members of different local groups and outgroup members, can also be tested against my census data, for I routinely obtained information on the past and present marriages of all individuals who had ever been married. But while these marriages vary widely in date, most were consummated after 1945. Thus, taken together, they do not provide adequate time depth for purposes here. One group of twenty-seven households re-

TABLE 27

109 BATAK MARRIAGES: CONSANGUINEAL RELATIONSHIPS

| Year of marriage | Consanguineal relationship between spouses | | Chi-square | Significance |
	Absent	Present		
1945 and before	46	3	6.07	0.02
After 1945	46	14		
	92	17		
Total		109		

ceived more intensive study, however. Here I obtained complete marriage data not only for all living individuals present but also for their parents (regardless of their status or whereabouts at the time of the census). Taking care to avoid double counting, data on 109 such marriages were obtained in this fashion. These 109 marriages were consummated between 1910 and 1974, and they provide the sample for analysis here.

Table 27 shows that there has been a marked increase in the incidence of marriage between consanguineal kin in marriages consummated after 1945 when compared to those consummated before. A chi-square test shows this association to be significant at the p = 0.02 level. In a longer time perspective, this increase may have still greater significance. According to the Batak, the earliest consanguineal marriage in the sample, which occurred in 1939 and involved second cousins, was in fact the first such marriage to have occurred in anyone's memory. This is certainly not literally true, for no doubt there were always Batak who married consanguineal kin. But recent decades appear to have seen a genuine qualitative change. It is significant that the Batak still talk about the 1939 marriage. They recall the furor it created at the time—it was strongly condemned and the focus of much ritual activity—and claim that it was this particular marriage that precipitated the growing numbers of marriages between consanguineal kin that were to follow.[4]

TABLE 28

109 BATAK MARRIAGES: LOCAL GROUP ORIGINS OF SPOUSES

Year of Marriage	Origin of spouse		Chi-square	Significance
	Same group	Different groups		
1945 and before	34	15	2.91	0.10
After 1945	32	28		
	66	43		
Total		109		

The evidence for a possible increase in local exogamy is more ambiguous.[5] Table 28 reclassifies the 109 sample marriages according to whether they were endogamous or exogamous, again before and after 1945. While the trend seems to be in the expected direction, the association ($p = 0.10$) is not significant. There are other reasons, however, to believe that locally exogamous marriage is indeed becoming more frequent. If we look, for example, only of the twenty-three marriages in our sample of those consummated after 1965, we find that ten were endogamous and thirteen were exogamous. Thus, the trend indicated by the post-1945 marriages, with the majority of marriages now locally exogamous. Better dating for the earlier marriages and a more sophisticated statistical procedure might show that this trend is in fact statistically meaningful. Furthermore, we have failed to take account here of those exogamous marriages consummated by living Batak who left the census area as single persons before the time of the census to marry elsewhere. The impact of this omission is proportionately greater on the post-1945 marriage sample. Most marriages in the pre-1945 sample involved persons in ascending generations, now deceased, for whom data were obtained from offspring and thus were not contingent on whether they themselves resided as married individuals within the census area. Inclusion of this aforementioned class of exogamous marriages would strengthen the association in question. In any case, the

Batak themselves say that "marriage between persons of different local groups," at least as they understand this notion, is on the increase. Certainly by the 1980s, men and women were having to go farther and farther afield to find a spouse.

It has become a truism that incorporation into wider social systems can literally overwhelm tribal societies. The overwhelming nature of such incorporation derives, in part, from its capacity to destroy indigenous cultural traditions in so many different ways. Some traditional institutions in changing tribal societies are lost directly—because they are perceived as useless, or replaced by substitutes believed to be more desirable, or abandoned in the face of explicit or implicit pressures from more powerful and sophisticated people.

Some cultural practices disappear, however, not because they are replaced by substitutes or otherwise deliberately abandoned but because these practices simply become untenable in the evolving social order. The umbay ceremony depended on a socioterritorial organization that assured adequate recruitment of opposite-sex partners, themselves already umbays and not consanguineally related to the would-be initiate. The demographic changes that resulted from incorporation into lowland Philippine society—sedentarization, local group fragmentation, and population decline—rendered such recruitment difficult and, eventually, impossible. When that happened, a part of Batak culture died too, not because of a frontal attack on the cultural tradition itself but because demographic change destroyed the ecological and social organizational foundations on which the tradition rested.

The Batak are caught between increase and diversification in the total amount of stress on their social environment and reduction in the efficiency of their traditional ways of coping with stress. (Savishinsky [1974:219] arrives at a similar conclusion for the Hare.) Both social resources and ego resources for coping with the exigencies of life have been disrupted by the deculturation attending incorporation of Batak society into lowland Philippine society. Excessive stress, as it is said, hurts, and we have also seen here how stress may be related to some of the demographic and physiological adaptive difficulties discussed in chapters 4 and 5. On the one hand, some Batak efforts to cope with stress have been dysfunctional with respect to their longer-term adaptive interests; on the other hand, some stress is simply not being coped with at all. In the next chapter, I place these concerns with social stress and adaptive well-being on a broader stage.

8

Ethnic Identity, Human Motivation, and Tribal Survival

In my conclusion, I return to the observation I made at the outset: it seems that the Batak could somehow "do better" in the circumstances that confront them; despite the presence of genuine adversity, they could perhaps survive and even prosper. In particular (limiting my consideration only to those tribal peoples who, like the Batak, still have access to some land and to reasonable economic opportunities), I explore the role that a strong sense of ethnic identity—and the associated, culturally constituted patterns of motivation that such identity helps to foster—may play in helping such peoples resist marginalization to wider social systems. I return, in other words, to an issue raised previously, that is, the importance of group memberships or *social identities* to facilitating a people's coping responses to environmental demands—responses that help them, in effect, to stay individually and collectively *healthy*.

This is necessarily a speculative enterprise, and it may be that my conclusions go beyond what my data nominally permit. Whether any group of people could actually do better in a given set of circumstances is difficult, perhaps even impossible, to document. I speak, therefore, to a lingering impression—rather than an empirical finding—formed from living among the Batak, from the data discussed in this volume, and from a reading of the comparative literature. It is not my intention to diminish the ecological and economic disruptions that have overtaken the Batak; these topics have been discussed extensively. I recognize that some readers—the same readers, perhaps, who are uncomfortable with the functionalist, even speculative, nature of chapters 6 and 7—may believe that these disruptions are alone sufficient to explain the adaptive difficulties documented.

In such a view, to dwell further on such relatively elusive notions as ethnic identity and human motivation unduly complicates efforts to explain, in more general terms, the detribalization process. Worse, it could be maintained, they divert attention from the economic issues (e.g., control of ancestral lands) that are already known to be of vital importance to tribal survival. Thus, in the Batak case, it could be maintained that the data concerning economic dislocations (chap. 3) are necessary and sufficient to account for the data on adaptive difficulty (chaps. 4 and 5). Such a position would certainly fit with the strong materialist emphasis in current anthropological explanations of change in the tribal world. Further, it has the advantage of simplicity: as the world system expands, tribal peoples in its path become its victims, overtaken and eventually destroyed by circumstances they cannot control.

But, as I argued in chapter 1, such a view of detribalization is deficient. It is superficial, and it is an overgeneralization. The superficiality of the victims-of-progress explanation can be demonstrated most effectively by reference to another "hypothesis" about detribalization—the view held, in the Batak case, by many lowlanders. Lowlanders ascribe Batak adaptive difficulties to such personal shortcomings as laziness and lack of foresight. While there is some basis for this explanation, it fails to look beyond the Batak themselves to account for their economic performance (and alleged personal shortcomings). The victims-of-world-system-expansion explanation, again excluding cases of outright land alienation, habitat despoliation, or epidemic disease, is similarly superficial. While the locus of blame is moved from the individual to the wider social system, the relationship between the two is still not satisfactorily developed: local history is omitted, the precise sequence of economic, social, and cultural changes leading to tribal ruin is not detailed, the responses of the people themselves are not identified, and so on.

A second deficiency arises from overgeneralization. Some tribal peoples have in fact survived and seemingly prospered following their incorporation into wider social systems; they have maintained their numbers, their physical well-being, and their cultural integrity. There is probably no one necessary and sufficient condition that accounts for such survival. Instead, there are a series of necessary conditions that are not yet completely known. I will, therefore, have little further to say here about the importance of ancestral lands, precisely because it is already well known that such lands are necessary to tribal survival. Rather, I want to pursue other necessary conditions whose importance is not as well understood. Some may still see a retreat from anthropology's characteristic stance of cultural relativism, or even political danger, in this enterprise. Thus, I explicitly disavow any Social Darwinistic leanings: I do not regard those tribal peoples who *have* survived as somehow more virtuous, or more deserving of survival, than those who have not. They were simply and ultimately luckier, in ways I explore below.

Detribalization as Marginalization

One of the most important social scientific understandings of the last thirty years is the recognition that development has a dialectical relationship with underdevelopment, such that the increase in living standards enjoyed by the major industrial powers has occurred, in part, at the expense of the rest of the world. Despite the explanatory limitations of a global economic approach for understanding the nature and causes of change among peoples like the Batak, the dialectical relationship of development and underdevelopment provides the overall context within which detribalization must be understood.

Swift (1978), surveying the current status of tribal societies in Asia and Africa, has usefully placed this change in the context of class formation:

> The process by which isolated small-scale societies are incorporated as marginal components of a larger universe is usually also the process by which class formation is started. The commercialization of previously subsistence economies leads to the emergence of new and more permanent economic and social inequalities; the new institutions and roles that are created to mediate between the small society and the larger often become the institutions of a new class system. As a result, the problem of a marginal society begins to become a problem of class as much as ethnic or cultural identity, although it may continue to be perceived and formulated solely as the latter. (Pp. 13–14)

Of course, this is only one of several ways of envisioning detribalization. But I find Swift's concern with the notion of marginality useful for focusing attention on the evolutionary trajectories characteristically traveled by tribal societies as they are incorporated into larger societies. In fact, along such trajectories, it becomes less and less appropriate to speak of two distinct societies, as if each, despite growing economic interdependence, remained somehow distinct in language, culture, or social boundaries. What is more relevant is that a single, wider society has grown more complex and more specialized internally.

It is from this perspective that Fox (1969:141) provocatively reevaluates the status of South Asian hunter-gatherers, emphasizing that they are not so much "independent, primitive fossils" as they are occupationally specialized productive units whose economic regimens are geared to trade and exchange with the more complex agricultural and caste communities within whose orbits these peoples live. In consequence, according to Fox, Indian hunting-gathering groups are best seen as "marginal economic specialists for traditional Indian civilization." Their economic incorporation into the wider society, furthermore, mandates that their traditional social organizations be "transformed to meet the expectation of collection and exchange with the outside world" (ibid.: 143).

The point here, however, is not simply that tribal peoples tend to get incorporated into wider social systems but that the incorporation is on disadvantageous—that is, marginal—terms. Thus, my own image of the future of the Batak, discussed briefly at the close of chapter 4, is that they will come to be identified less as "Batak" and more as a sort of generic tribal population within wider Philippine society. They will be demarcated less by any distinctive cultural markers (e.g., use of the bow and arrow) than by the same set of diagnostic social and economic traits—poverty, illiteracy, political impotency—that characterizes evolving Philippine tribal populations generally. In the same vein, Friedlander (1975) observes that to be an "Indian" in Mesoamerica today means little more than to be poor, uneducated, and lacking in land and political power.

Marginalization, in short, is *destructive*, a point recently explored by Adams (1974) in some detail. The central element of the marginalization process, Adams says, is that the controls some peoples traditionally exercised over their local societies (and their own lives) are taken from them, such that their remaining autonomy of action does not conflict with the wider system (ibid.: 49). He notes that just as expanding industrial societies make waste out of portions of their habitat, they also "make waste out of portions of the populations and cultures of the participating societies" (ibid.: 39). Adams's use of this notion is not entirely metaphorical; in fact, massive deculturation often accompanies the development process, particularly among marginal peoples (ibid.:57). To be sure, deculturation occurs in industrial, or "primary," areas as well.

> There is a crucial difference, however. Culture change in primary areas usually occurs with replacement by new elements, new forms, new sets of meanings and often new social relations. When it occurs in secondary areas, as often as not it is simply deculturation, a restriction of social relations; and where replacements occur, they may be leftovers from the primary areas. New cultural forms in secondary areas have greater problems of acceptance, and when one turns to marginal populations, it is sheer deculturation, with little or no cultural replacement and few new cultural forms developing from local sources of technological and economic growth. Obviously, since these populations do not have access to the productive resources of the primary areas, their cultural regrowth has to depend upon residues of their earlier culture and the limited possibilities that a damaged environment permits. (Ibid.)

Anyone who subscribes to the view that culture is somehow "adaptive" must agree with Adams that the deculturation accompanying marginalization "calls for considerably more than sentimentality" (ibid.). A people's culture is tied up with everything from the way they make their living to what they live *for*. Marginalization, in short, destroys not only culture but *motivation* as well. A common observation of distressed tribal peoples is that they suffer from ennui, lethargy, or "lack of interest in life" (e.g., Brain 1972:11). A particularly poignant statement of this condition is found in von Fürer-Haimendorf's (1982) contrast of the atmosphere prevailing in two types of Konda Reddi villages in India, those relatively isolated in the hills and those along rivers in more populated areas:

> In Gogulapudi, where the Reddis live much in the same style as their parents lived forty years ago, I found the same cheerfulness and relaxed mood which I observed in 1941. In Koida, on the other hand, where the Reddis now dwell side

by side with cast Hindu immigrants from the coastal districts, all joie de vivre seems to have evaporated, and Reddis and Koyas have turned into sullen and dispirited drudges, resentful of the tyranny of merchants and moneylenders but incapable of any concerted action which might lessen their dependence on these newcomers. (P. 151)

Development and Tribal Societies: Are There Any "Successes"?

Are all tribal peoples destined to become "sullen and dispirited drudges," economically and politically exploited by outsiders? Or can marginalization—at least in its severer forms—be resisted? As the case of the Gogulapudi Reddis demonstrates, simple geographic isolation may confer a modicum of protection against detribalization. Obviously, if this were the only relevant factor, the prognosis for the world's remaining tribal societies would be even more discouraging than it is. But other factors are also involved, as an examination of several tribal societies said to be "successfully adapting" to change illustrates.

It is difficult, certainly, to locate unambiguous examples of successful tribal adaptation to a developing world. And with respect to assessing the impact of social and cultural change on human beings, anthropologists are notorious equivocators. Moreover, anthropologists are characteristically suspicious of any claims by others of tribal adaptive success. It is tempting to argue that any apparent successes are only temporary, pending further (and ultimately deleterious) historical developments, or that any allegations of such successes are based on inadequate data. A major problem arises from the variety of kinds of data (and kinds of theoretical perspectives) on which an allegation of successful adaptation might rest (see chap. 1).

Such difficulties notwithstanding, anthropologists have occasionally singled out—correctly, in my opinion—certain tribal peoples as evidencing *relative* success in coming to terms with incorporation into wider social systems. These cases are worth examining briefly for the light they shed on the causes of the more numerous cases of relative and outright adaptive failure. The first concerns a group of Australian aborigines, known as the "Jigalong Mob," described by Tonkinson (1974). Today, the Jigalong aborigines inhabit a mission station in western Australia. Like other aborigines, they traditionally exploited a desert environment by means of a seminomadic hunting and gathering lifeway. But in contrast to most aborigines, despite a common experience of sedentarization and economic change, members of the Jigalong Mob have preserved many of their core cultural values and retained much of their traditional kinship system. More important, says Tonkinson, traditional religious life still flourishes and helps to promote self-esteem and ethnic pride—attributes that, in turn, help aborigines to maintain the belief that they alone control their destinies.

The crucial element in Jigalong resistance to potentially destructive forces of change is their continued adherence to the Law, a body of precepts concerning customary behavior patterns said to have originated during the Dreamtime, a creative period in the distant past (ibid.:5, 7, 69). That they should continue to be guided by the Law, in a manner matched by few other aboriginal communities in Australia, is attributed by Tonkinson (ibid.:135, 139–140) to a fortuitous combination of relative isolation, sedentarization in a large social grouping, and the unintended side effects of missionization. Whatever the reasons, the Jigalong aborigines have themselves come to associate their well-being with continued adherence to the Law, and they are correspondingly wary of any activities or changes they perceive as threatening to it (ibid.:147).

> From the outsider's viewpoint, the judgment of the Aborigines in this matter seems entirely correct, because their self-esteem lies in their possession and pursuit of a distinctive set of beliefs and practices. Abandonment of the Law would

inevitably bring about a loss of the self-esteem necessary for survival as a viable cultural minority. The Aborigines have seen no examples of their fellows succeeding in wider society, and nothing in their past experience and present situation suggests that this could even be a future possibility. In other words, they see no good alternatives to the Law, only the certainty of a numbing preoccupation with drinking, fighting, and gambling. (Ibid.)

Cases such as this appear to be consistent with the (previously criticized) victims-of-progress model of detribalization. It is said that Westernization and other pressures that threaten tribal societies with destruction have already overcome most aborigines. Those who have not yet become victims of these pressures must, like the Jigalong aborigines, have somehow successfully *resisted* change. But our remaining cases of success are more troublesome, for they all involve tribal peoples said to have successfully accommodated extensive change, or even to have actively sought such change, in their traditional cultures—although all escaped deculturation, as it occurred among the Batak. Two of the three cases are from Southeast Asia; they are similar also in the apparent importance of certain crucial, traditional personality traits or cultural orientations for explaining the success.

The Toba Batak are an Indonesian ethnic group inhabiting the interior mountain region of North Sumatra. They are irrigated rice agriculturalists with patrilineal descent and a segmentary lineage system. According to Bruner (1976:236), the Toba Batak have experienced "rapid and extensive culture change" and today occupy an "important position in contemporary Indonesian society," with many of their numbers enjoying the material advantages of Western civilization. Further, their's is a "relatively successful adaptation thus far," for traditional family, kinship, and ritual life remains intact, and individual Toba Batak appear to experience little psychological distress in reconciling the old and the new (ibid.: 236, 242, 250). Bruner attributes these circumstances in part to societal context but primarily to their indigenous belief system, which enabled them to change rapidly and extensively without destroying their sense of continuity with the past and without forcing them to renounce their own identity in order to become modern (ibid.: 243, 247).

The Iban of Sarawak appear similar in many ways to the Toba Batak. Traditionally shifting cultivators in the hills of Borneo, they are today active participants in the national Malaysian economy. Iban have become doctors, lawyers, and civil servants. Sutlive (1978) argues that the Iban have been "remarkably successful" in coming to terms with contact with other peoples and incorporation into a modern state. They have maintained, he says, a "fierce pride" in their ethnic identity and have suffered neither social disorganization nor cultural disorientation (ibid.: 2–3). Sutlive believes that Iban success is owed, in part, to the circumstance that they have not been *forced* into new economic niches. Rather, they have kept much of their traditional autonomy and feeling of self-direction.

Sutlive's primary explanatory emphasis, however, is on a bundle of seemingly adaptive personality traits—optimism, self-confidence, venturesomeness, achievement orientation—and an overall cultural orientation that accepts ambiguity and ambivalence. The latter serves to immunize the Iban from much of the stress and strain that normally arises as traditional cultural institutions undergo change and loss (ibid.). Their "amazing ability to adjust to new environments" is not to be dismissed merely as the adaptability common to all human beings, for they have maintained considerable continuity with the past even as their "positive inclination toward change" has "predisposed them to seek new experiences and to think new thoughts" (ibid.: 3).

The final illustration of successful adaptation, the Apa Tani of Arunachal Pradesh, in the Himalayan region of India, is a different situation. While they, like the Toba Batak and the Iban, have actively embraced social and economic change, von Fürer-Haimendorf (1982) sees their behavior as the result of unusually enlightened government policies in the region, rather than as a reflection of any unique Apa Tani personal or cultural attributes. Certainly, the evidence of Apa Tani success is impressive, even "spectacular," given their "rapid material, social, and educational development" without loss of ethnic identity (ibid.: 287, 311). As recently as thirty years ago, Apa Tani were isolated subsistence agriculturalists who lacked money and did not use their cattle for traction or carriage. Yet today, Apa Tani have eagerly taken to commercial fish and fruit farming, they have come to own shops and otherwise engage in commerce, and they occupy many government posts (ibid.: 286–295).

In von Fürer-Haimendorf's analysis, the Apa Tani's "harmonious integration into the economic and political structure of the wider Indian society," which stands in marked contrast to the "gloomy picture" in the rest of tribal India, owes in large part to their continued "freedom from oppression and exploitation" by outside peoples (ibid.: 286, 295). That they are still "masters of their own house" reflects a self-conscious government policy to integrate them into a wider political system without disrupting the traditional social order. This goal was achieved by promoting education and by granting the Apa Tani considerable autonomy to run their own affairs while protecting them, with legal measures, from land alienation and economic exploitation by nontribal settlers (ibid.: 295–298).

As diverse as these cases are, they share some important commonalities. First, despite any changes that occurred in "traditional culture," all of these peoples somehow managed to preserve their own identity, a condition typically cited as both evidence for and cause of successful adaptation. In other words, these peoples know who they are and, accordingly, preserve their dignity and self-esteem (e.g., Tonkinson 1974:147; Bruner 1976:243). Second, all of the peoples considered here are active participants, not victimized bystanders, in a changing world: the still-traditional Jigalong aborigines feel they have responsibility for their lives (Tonkinson

1974:5, 8), and the much-changed Toba Batak and Iban remain vigorous and active peoples (Bruner 1976:242) who continue to find "new areas in which to expand and new meanings for their lives" (Sutlive 1978:190). These peoples know who they are and what they are living for. Finally, with the apparent exception of the Apa Tani, continued sentiments of ethnic identity and self-direction have been promoted not merely by societal context but by some crucial aspect of the traditional culture of the tribal people themselves, which enabled them to either successfully resist change or accommodate it in a nondestructive manner.

I will return to these issues shortly. First, an important caveat is that these and other allegations of tribal adaptive success tend *not* to be accompanied by the kinds of evidence singled out in this study to assess Batak adaptive success. Tonkinson does not inform us whether the Jigalong Mob are physically healthier or more successful reproductively than other Australian aborigines, only that the former escaped the "cultural collapse" that Western contact precipitated among most of the latter (1974:5). It is inferred by me, rather than demonstrated by Tonkinson, that persistence of cultural integrity and ethnic identity has positive consequences for adaptive well-being, in the sense used here (see chaps. 4 and 5). (A partial exception to this difficulty is von Fürer-Haimendorf's account of the Apa Tani, which emphasizes economic, educational, and other standard-of-living improvements. Of course, the persistence of tribal cultural integrity and ethnic identity can be seen as a positive value in its own right. This seems to be how Tonkinson views such persistence in the Jigalong case.)

Ethnic Identity, Societal Health, and Tribal Survival

I turn now to the ways in which persistence of ethnic identity (despite the absence of hard evidence in the cases just examined) might foster adaptive well-being. There is a recent, decidedly anthropological approach in medicine wherein *health* is regarded as something more than the mere absence of disease or infirmity. Audy (1971:142), for example, defines health as "a continuing property, potentially measurable by an individual's ability to rally from insults, whether chemical, infectious, psychological, or social." The basic notion is that health is not merely the opposite of disease but has to do with one's *capacity* to cope with the stresses, demands, or "insults" of everyday life. Such a perspective clearly has much in common with my approach to adaptive well-being. For example, Dubos (1961:xvii) regards states of health and disease as "the expression of the success or failure experienced by the organism in its efforts to respond adaptively to environmental challenges." Similarly, ill health has been said to occur when "an individual exists in a life situation which places demands on him that are excessive in terms of his ability to meet them" (Wolf and Goodell 1968:204–205).

I find such approaches to health attractive because of their explicit concern with societal context. Audy (1971:141), for example, cites with approval a World Health Organization definition of health that emphasizes social, as well as physical and mental, health. He admits that many would take exception to applying the concept of health to an entire society, but in his view, "we cannot comprehend the social health of an individual without postulating *societal health* of a group taken as a system" (ibid.:154–155; emphasis in original).

My purpose is not to argue about whether groups, as well as individuals, can be healthy (or can adapt) but to focus attention on the importance of group memberships (such as tribal group memberships) to *individual* health. Then we may ask the question, Why do individuals who are members of certain groups tend to remain healthy? This novel way of asking about adaptive well-being and adaptive capacity leads us to an important and growing medical literature that treats continued health in the face of adversity as something to be *explained* in its own right. Audy (ibid.:143) speaks of the "series of physical, physiological, psychological, and social cocoons" that helps to protect an individual's health over his lifetime. Antonovsky (1979:98–112) examines a similar range of "generalized resistance resources," or GRRs, with the same function. Reminding us not to overlook the obvious, he emphasizes that wealth is an important resource for coping with the stress of life. Money, adequate shelter, and other material resources contribute to keeping people healthy just as surely as immunological resistance, social support, and the like (ibid.:106–107). In the particular case of tribal societies, ancestral lands and other indigenous forms of wealth clearly are important generalized resistance resources for maintaining health.

Of greater interest, for our purposes, is that "remarkable protective capsule," human culture (Audy 1971:143). According to Antonovsky (1979:119), whose research interests include the health of such severely disadvantaged individuals as concentration camp survivors and the very poor, one's culture and the social relationships it fosters are "probably the most powerful GRR[s] of all." In my view, to say that one is protected by the "cocoon" of a culture or a set of social relationships is to say that one has a meaningful *social identity*, or, in the case of many tribal societies, *ethnic identity*. Certainly, a strong sense of identity, such as ethnic pride, was a recurring theme in the examples of successful adaptation.

But *why* is a meaningful social identity so important to health? We encountered part of the answer in chapter 7. We saw, for the Batak, how ethnic group membership gives individuals access to a traditional cultural inventory whose separate elements help them to cope with particular physiological and social stresses. It was in this sense that I argued that deculturation, by eroding such traditional cultural institutions as curing ceremonies, threatened individual adaptive well-being.

There is more, however, to explaining the concept of culture as protective capsule. Peoples like the Iban and the Toba Batak have a strong sense of ethnic identity whose instrumental significance for health apparently transcends the survival (or disappearance) of particular traditional cultural forms. This significance has to do with the vital and more general role that social identity plays in helping individuals to know who they are and what they are living for. The key to understanding such issues, according to Antonovsky (ibid.: 118–119), and much conventional anthropological wisdom, normally arises from an individual's sociocultural milieu. Thus, life's purposes are "learned and consolidated through a lifetime's experience, becoming embodied in the relationships which sustain them" (Marris 1974 : 33). In this vein, Antonovsky (1979 : 116) speaks of "commitment" (to others in a social group) as "the process through which individual interests become attached to the carrying out of socially organized patterns of behavior which are seen as expressing the nature and needs of the person." One reason the more profound forms of sociocultural change are so threatening to health is that they can destroy the "sense of coherence," or way of looking at the world, that is the vital connection between health and one's particular set of GRRs (ibid.: 8, 123–159; see also Kaplan 1983 : 220–221). Since our ability to cope with life's exigencies depends on making sense out of what happens to us, on finding meaning in experience, anything that "invalidates our conceptual structures of interpretation," such as deculturation, thus threatens adaptive well-being (Marris 1974 : 10, 11, 147).

The Batak in Perspective

This brings us back to the Batak and their difficulties. Briefly, I argued that the essential difference between the turn-of-the-century subsistence economy described in chapter 2 and the contemporary subsistence economy described in chapter 3 was that the former was adequate to keep the Batak healthy, but the latter was not. Demographic and physiological evidence for the assertion that the Batak collectively and individually were suffering from chronic ill health, broadly understood, were the subjects of chapters 4 and 5. To *account* for such "adaptive difficulties," as I called them, I relied in part on the material in chapter 3, which concerned factors such as land alienation and dependency relations. I was not convinced, however, that such factors *fully* accounted for the data presented in chapters 4 and 5. This concern led me to explore, in chapters 6 and 7, the notion that new sorts of social stresses, coupled with erosion of traditional means of coping with stress, caused the Batak to behave in ways that were, at times, at variance with their adaptive well-being.

In focusing on the notions of stress and stress coping, it was also my intention to bring the Batak themselves more clearly into my analysis. I wanted to show that the Batak were more than bystanders, victimized by incorporation into a wider social system. Rather, the Batak were actively and responsibly trying to make sense out of, and come to terms with, their changing environment. I also sought to heed Belshaw's (1976) eloquent warning to eschew "scholarly ethnocentrisms" about the alleged predispositions of this or that indigenous people. Belshaw writes:

> I have lived among people who were described in all the official literature, *without any exception*, as having a leisure preference, being happy-go-lucky and lazy, being uninterested in material progress, deriving satisfaction and prestige from ceremonial and ritual, turning beggary into a destructive institution, being at one with nature. But as I came to know them, I learned what should have been obvious: that smiling hid pain, that people were capable of long and sustained physical labor in conditions that no European would have tolerated, that they were always concerned with the real-world future for themselves and their children, that daily life was a round of stress and battle that no concern with the hereafter could possibly remove or counterbalance except in the lives of the saintly and that there were flexibilities and payoffs in the ceremonial, charitable, and religious world that

had distinct importance for the genesis of material benefit. (P. 186)

But I was also aware that as the Batak went about their daily lives of stress and battle, their resources for the endeavor—whether ancestral lands or curing ceremonies— were seriously compromised. Not only were the separate resources eroded but ethnic identity had been eroded as well, thereby disrupting the overall "sense of coherence" (to use Antonovsky's term) *underlaying* these resources.

First, Batak ethnic identity has been sapped by the near-complete erosion of the more visible sorts of cultural forms. Besides the curing and umbay ceremonies, whose demise has been discussed (see chap. 7), other kinds of rituals have virtually disappeared also in recent decades. The *lambay kat taro*, a seven-day period of singing and dancing at the start of each honey season whose purpose is to appeal to the guardian spirit of the bees for success in honey collection, was last celebrated at Langogan in April 1978. Only the Tanabag Batak are likely ever to perform this ritual again. Traditional musical instruments are rarely seen in use; only a few women still make baskets employing traditional designs; only a few men still use bows and arrows; and so on.

As we saw in chapter 4, ethnic identity has not faded uniformly across the various Batak local groups, in part because the erosion of traditional cultural practices and institutions has occurred on different timetables in different locales. Bark cloth is a case in point. Turn-of-the-century photographs of the Batak show men and women wearing bark cloth breechclouts and skirts. Women soon discarded such garments in favor of manufactured clothing. Bark cloth skirts disappeared entirely by 1940, perhaps even earlier. Men wore bark cloth much longer—in some local groups, it is still worn today—but at least by 1950, some men were turning to manufactured clothing for daily wear. At Babuyan, Tagnipa, Caramay, and Buayan, all local groups long in intensive contact with lowlanders, bark cloth was uncommon after about 1960. The principal decade of change at Langogan appears to have been 1970–1980. When I visited there in 1968, most men still regularly wore bark cloth. By 1980, only one man regularly did, and some of the younger men had never worn bark cloth.

A second factor that has undermined Batak ethnic identity is language loss. Some subdialects of Batak have virtually disappeared: there are no surviving native speakers of *kiatratnanen*, once spoken by Batak of the Rizal River area, and there are today less than ten speakers of *buayanen*, a subdialect of the Buayan River area. Further, younger Batak have generally not learned how to speak the "deeper" Batak that is still known to some of their elders. Most obvious is a strong trend everywhere toward substitution of Cuyonon words for their traditional Batak counterparts. I have no hard data on how far word loss and linguistic acculturation have progressed. But the Batak themselves say that such change is extensive and that the "real" Batak language survives in anything near its (presumed) aboriginal form only in several centrally located river valleys. The Batak also recognize the relationship between the loss of their language and the demise of their oral literature on religion and world view. Some spoke urgently to me about the importance of language retention for preservation of their ethnic identity. Given these observations, it may not be impertinent to ask, If the Batak themselves think that preservation of their culture and language is important to the retention of their ethnic identity, why have they not preserved them? Or, looking to the future, could the Batak perhaps still do what the Jigalong Mob, the Apa Tani, and others like them have done? Stated in other terms, the issue is, What circumstances make the Batak so vulnerable to erosion of ethnic identity and the attendant marginalization and, apparently, militate against a more positive and participatory developmental outcome?

Part of the answer, I believe, lies with the characteristic features of aboriginal Batak demography: small population size and scattered settlement pattern. At least in retrospect, such demographic circumstances provided a relatively fragile socioterritorial basis for cultural transmission and continuity. They made the Batak particularly vulnerable to the culturally corrosive effects of depopulation and territorial penetration by outsiders, two important forces of change that will necessarily be experienced more severely by small populations than by such demographically robust tribal peoples as the Iban and Toba Batak. As I showed in chapter 3, furthermore, territorial penetration by outsiders may exacerbate the effects of depopulation by isolating local groups from one another. Today, each local group of Batak is in closer spatial and social contact with a lowland settler community than it is with any other local group of Batak. As many local groups of Batak only number around a dozen households, it is not surprising that many traditional cultural forms survive only in a few larger groups. In short, the simple realities of Batak demography are not congenial to cultural survival and the persistence of ethnic identity.

Much of the rest of the answer lies with the precise *terms* whereby the Batak have been incorporated into a wider economy—terms that entail land tenure insecurity accompanied by extensive (and, for the Batak, vital) relations of trade and clientage with lowland Filipinos. First, as I argued in chapter 3, exchange in forest products appears to contribute to the fragmentation in settlement pattern. Second, as economic life comes increasingly to revolve around exchange and other relationships with outsiders, elements of traditional culture that are irrelevant to such relationships fall by the wayside. It is not unreasonable to state that an individual Batak's economic well-being today depends as much on securing the cooperation of a lowland patron or trading partner as on securing the cooperation of other Batak. That, in such circumstances, individual Batak should not appear highly motivated to invest time and energy in traditional social and cultural life is again unsurprising.

Indeed, the cultural identity of the Batak has come to be defined increasingly in terms of those practices and values related to collection and sale of forest resources and wage labor on lowland farms. In this setting, the ethnic boundaries separating the Batak from the Tagbanua and even from impoverished lowlanders become blurred, for the latter peoples, after all, also sell forest resources and work for better-off settlers.

The terms of incorporation into a wider economy appear to have favored the creation of a generic tribal identity rather than the persistence of a parochial Batak identity and hence of distinctively Batak cultural institutions. (If only in a small way, Philippine government policy has also contributed to the formation of a wider tribal identity through its long-standing tendency to aggregate tribal peoples in a common category, "cultural minorities." In analogous fashion, the activities of the Department of Orang Asli Affairs have helped to foster a common identity among the tribes of peninsular Malaysia; see Carey 1976.)

At least for the Batak, however, any wider tribal identity would be a fragile basis on which to place any hopes for some future ethnic revival or "revitalization movement" (see Wallace 1967). Such movements themselves represent a sort of coping response (Aberle 1966), and, as I showed in chapter 7, Batak coping resources are already seriously depleted. Further, successful revitalization movements (e.g., Worsley 1957; Wallace 1970) require substantial numbers of people, relatively strong traditional leadership, close proximity of social groups, and frequent social interaction among potential members—all of which are lacking in the case of the Batak and their tribal neighbors. In their circumstances, there appears to be relatively little margin for outside intervention (e.g., evangelical missionizing) to shore up ethnic identity and stimulate a more positive developmental outcome.

To be a "Batak," then, will continue to mean less and less. As we saw in chapter 4, there is today genuine confusion among both lowlanders and the Batak about what ethnic designations are most appropriate for many individuals. The Batak have paid dearly for the erosion of their ethnic identity. I believe a direct, causal relationship exists between the erosion of Batak ethnic identity (and the sense of coherence it provided in their lives) and the desultory nature of Batak material life. With respect to their work habits, for example, the Batak at times seem overcome by a great lethargy, reluctant to work beyond the minimum necessary for the moment or even reluctant to work at all. While this behavior in part reflects poor nutrition, if not outright hunger, it also reflects motivational consequences of the blurring of social identity. (Chance [1968] and Savishinsky [1974] offer similar interpretations of the low levels of motivation observable among members of certain native American groups.)

The sad story of the Batak has been repeated again and again throughout the tribal world. There is a sense in which they, and others like them, really have been victims of progress, or at least victims of a process of history. But what has been remarkable in this process is not the inability of tribal peoples to adapt to change but their *ability* to do so in the face of such daunting circumstances. Indeed, it seems that they have already made an enormous effort to adapt, while the "civilized" ones have yet to learn to adjust to the presence and needs of those tribal peoples who remain in their midst. This task will require better recognition of the adaptive significance of ethnic identity and of those personal traits, both virtues and vices, that tribal peoples have in common with all people.

Notes

1: Introduction

1. I use "tribal" not to refer to a form of social organization but, in the more general sense, to refer to a class of societies also known as aboriginal, indigenous, or native. I thus mean the term to include such peoples as the Adivasis ("Tribals") of India, the Australian aborigines, the Orang Asli of Malaysia, the Hill Tribes of Thailand, the Pygmies of Zaire, the Indians in Brazil, and the native Americans in the United States (Hitchcock 1985:458). In the Philippines, comparable people have long been called "cultural minorities" (and, more recently, "cultural communities"), but "Tribal Filipinos" has become popular as well. According to the World Bank, tribal peoples exhibit most or all of the following characteristics: they have low-energy, sustained-yield subsistence systems, such as hunting and gathering, nomadic pastoralism, or shifting cultivation; their economies are nonmonetized or only partially monetized; they are ethnically and linguistically distinct from the national society; and they possess a common territory and traditional political leadership but limited national representation and political rights (Goodland 1982:6).

The notion of tribal society is a thorny one (see, e.g., Fried 1975), but the above alternatives (indigenous, aboriginal) pose difficulties of their own (Swift 1978). Since it is not my intention to talk about *all* peoples, some term to delimit the kinds of peoples in question is essential, and "tribal" remains in common use, particularly in Asia. Within the wider category of tribal societies just described, I am particularly interested here in those of a smaller and more vulnerable sort, recently termed "marginal societies" by Swift (ibid.:4). This term does have the advantage of calling attention to the process by which such societies, small-scale and once relatively isolated and self-sufficient, become marginal to larger and more powerful societies. I will, in fact, address the process of marginalization in the conclusion. But to do so usefully, I do not restrict my comparative analysis of the future of tribal societies only to the smaller and more isolated cases.

2. Many early missionaries and colonial administrators reported that indigenous peoples seemed to be apathetic or to be suffering from some psychological malaise. Often, such conditions were a simple reflection of the devastating impact of introduced diseases. But political oppression, social stress, and cultural disruption sap human motivation as well. When I visited a number of tribal assistance projects in the Philippines during 1984–85, I was often told that such factors as "poor motivation" or "mental health" were major obstacles to even the best-designed community organizing and self-help programs.

2: The Batak as They Were

1. There is some disagreement about whether the Batak are actually "Negrito" or at least about the degree to which they display the "classic" Southeast Asian Negrito racial features. Beyer (1917), Schebesta (1952–1957), and Garvan (1963) all excluded the Batak from their considerations of Philippine Negritos. Cole (1945) and Kroeber (1943) both regarded the Batak as Negritos, however, and they were included in a recent compendium of such peoples by Fox and Flory (1974). The question, in part, concerns the significance of the Batak's relatively wavy (as opposed to consistently woolly or kinky) hair form; see the discussion in LeBar (1975:24). Philippine Negritos today may number as few as fifteen thousand persons (Headland 1984:29).

2. It has long been thought that millet preceded rice as a staple crop throughout Southeast Asia, and there seem to be a number of cases where it has been displaced by rice only within historic times (see Hutterer 1983:183).

3: The Batak as They Are Today

1. Peterson's is an intriguing but one-sided analysis whose intellectual roots may be found in the highly functionalist "cultural ecology" of

the 1960s. She never addresses the question of possible game depletion by Agta specializing in the production of wild meat for exchange. She does briefly suggest that "population interdependence" might have implications for the notion of carrying capacity, but after adducing no relevant data on the subject she curiously concludes that "Agta-Palanan relations certainly appear to be 'ecologically sound'" (1978:346). Peterson also explains that there are other dimensions to the Agta-Palanan relationship than food exchange. Palanan regularly hire Agta to perform farming chores (ibid.:342), but although she notes that other observers have called attention to the potential for abuse in such relationships (p. 336), she makes no mention of such problems in the Agta-Palanan case. Finally, she does acknowledge the presence of a certain amount of conflict between Agta and Palanan over land, arising from the latter's interest in permanently acquiring and improving agricultural land, rather than merely using it for a time for swidden making, as the Agta do. Thus we are told that Palanans acquire the fallow swidden land of Agta "by two means, purchase and land grabbing" (p. 340), and that "the politically and legally more sophisticated peasants encounter few obstacles when they choose to usurp Agta land without compensation" (p. 342). But Peterson's overwhelming emphasis is on the *mutually beneficial* nature of the *exchange* relationships between Agta and Palanan.

4: Demographic Evidence of Adaptive Difficulty

1. The census schedule involved collection of the following information on a household basis:
a. Name, sex, date of birth, ethnolinguistic group, village of birth, and previous places of residence for all members of the household.
b. The genealogical relationships between all members and the date and manner by which each joined the household (e.g., by marriage, birth, or adoption).
c. A mating history for each member, including both legitimate and illegitimate unions, dates and methods of initiation and termination of these unions, numbers of offspring, and places of residence prior to, at the time of, and after marriage, including temporary postmarital residence, if any.
d. The parents and sibling set of each member, including name, sex, order of birth, marital history, and place of residence at time of census or, if deceased, place of death.
Procedures for this and comparable social-anthropological censuses are discussed in detail in Appell (1969) and Eder and Pagayona (1971).

2. While figure 6 shows many more males than females in the 0–4 age cohort, no meaningful inferences about sex ratios may be drawn from such a small sample. But in any case, the Batak say they do not practice infanticide, and infanticide as a cultural institution has never been reported in the Philippines.

3. Many observers have claimed that various Philippine Negrito groups have experienced long-term or short-term population declines, but quantitative data are few. The Casiguran Agta, numbering 609 persons in 1984 and still largely endogamous, experienced 184 births and 193 deaths between 6/15/77 and 6/14/84 and may have numbered as many as 1,000 persons in 1936 (Headland 1986:381, 510).

4. Whether the Batak were in fact once entirely endogamous is a moot point, but claims, by natives or by anthropologists, of complete endogamy are always suspect. Recent research suggests that 100 percent endogamous groups are rare ethnographically, except in very large populations. For allegedly endogamous groups numbering several hundred to several thousand, the actual rate of endogamy is usually between 70 and 90 percent (Adams and Kasakoff 1976). In any case, my larger point here is not that the Batak were once entirely endogamous but that any out-group marriage that occurred in the past did not threaten the demographic or cultural integrity of the population.

5. In the interest of making this initial sample of women as large as possible, I in fact included several who were recently deceased at the time of my study but for whom a close relative (e.g., a sister) survived to provide the desired data. I also included several who were actually less than 40 years old but who were still married and had not had a pregnancy for more than ten years.

6. The ages of the seven mothers in table 14 with zero live births are irrelevant to the calculation in table 15, and it is problematic how many to include. I have arbitrarily included three such women in table 15, to keep them represented in approximately the same proportion (10% of all women) as in the larger sample in table 14. If women with zero live births are excluded entirely from table 15, the total fertility rate rises to 4.20.

5: Physiological Evidence of Adaptive Difficulty

1. Following Lee (1979:285–289).

2. Local standards are, in theory, more desirable, but those available

are of uncertain meaning. A number of anthropometric studies of lowland Philippine populations have been conducted, however, and the results of these studies do provide another basis for comparison. Batak men and women average 91 percent and 89 percent, respectively, of the standard weights for Filipino men and women of their height as reported by Cordero et al. (1956:429, 435). More recently, the Food and Nutrition Research Center (FNRC 1975) has issued a table showing weight for height for Filipinos aged 25–65 years. For each height, a range of weights is shown which is 90 to 110 percent of the mean weight of all individuals measured of that height level. This table cannot be taken as a set of standards, however, as it is not based on a medically, physiologically, and socially "healthy" reference group. Rather, it appears to be the distillation of the results of a large-scale nutrition survey of a socioeconomically heterogeneous sample, which probably included many individuals who were not themselves well nourished. Nevertheless, Batak weight-for-height figures may be compared with these data, with the following results: of the 44 Batak men, 10 fall below the 90–110 percent weight range and the rest fall within; of the 40 women, 13 fall below and the rest fall within. These data simply show that, on the average, the Batak are somewhat worse off nutritionally than are lowland Filipinos.

3. Other observers of San hunter-gatherers have reported seasonal weight fluctuations on the order of 6 percent (Truswell and Hansen 1976:172; Wilmsen 1978). Lee (1979:440–441) argues, however, that such findings reflect the impact of San involvement in a wider commercial economy rather than any shortcomings in the hunting and gathering subsistence economy.

4. If settlement-dwelling Batak enjoyed a full-fledged "grain-based diet," the question of supplemental animal or vegetable protein would have less significance. Rice, the favored staple, is high in protein, and rice protein has high NPU. Although rice protein, like other grain proteins, is deficient in isoleucine and lysine, such deficiencies are easily compensated for by supplementary consumption of legumes (for example). Thus, in theory, Batak could get most of the protein they need from rice itself in a judiciously supplemented rice-based diet—as numerous Asian farming people in fact do. In practice, however, the Batak do not consume legumes, nor do they exert much effort to obtain any kind of supplemental vegetable foods when they are eating rice. Further, it is doubtful whether over time the Batak consume enough rice to meet their caloric requirements, much less their protein requirements (see below).

5. The Food and Nutrition Research Institute (FNRI 1981) recom-

mends 2,500 kcal per day for a 25-year-old Filipino male and 1,900 kcal per for a 25-year-old Filipino female. I did not attempt to adjust these recommendations downward to take account of smaller Batak body size. While the Batak are, on the average, smaller than lowlanders, they may also have a more vigorous activity regimen.

6: Increased Stress Levels as the Cause of Adaptive Difficulty

1. I deliberately write, for purposes of my wider argument, in a way that calls attention to the inadequate health care that the Batak receive and to the stresses that I believe surrounded this particular visit of health care personnel. For their part, city health officials frankly acknowledge that they fail to provide adequate health services for the Batak. They attribute this failure, correctly, in my view, to a woeful lack of funding for such services and to jurisdictional differences with PANAMIN about who in fact should provide them. Given budgetary realities and a large service area, it is not surprising that the City Health Office can only dispatch medical teams infrequently to distant locations. I should also add that another city health team *did* walk in and visit the Langogan Batak at their own settlement once during my stay, successfully treating one seriously ill child. Also, I found those city health workers I came to know personally to be competent and dedicated individuals, genuinely concerned about Batak welfare.

7: Decreased Stress-Coping Ability as the Cause of Adaptive Difficulty

1. There is an unresolved debate, which does not affect my analysis here, about whether social support *buffers* the effects of stress (e.g., through the facilitation of coping resources, the position taken here) or whether it operates more directly to minimize physical and mental illness. The prevailing opinion seems to be that both "buffering effects" and "main effects" are important (see, e.g., Lin et al. 1982; Turner 1983:138–142).

2. The frequent visits that many Batak make to their lowland employers and patrons can be viewed as a contemporary form of support seeking. As I showed in chapter 3, however, the opportunity costs associated with such visits make them costly to welfare.

3. Landor, another turn-of-the-century visitor to the Batak, either observed or was told of a "curious ceremony," apparently the umbay ceremony, that Batak practiced when children reached "the age of puberty." Here is his account: "A boy and a girl who are in love with each other are made to lie down by each other's side, while tree bark and grass are piled upon them, the girl using her own arm as a pillow. They remain thus, absolutely motionless, for some time, no immorality being suspected, much less being committed, after which they rise and give each other some present, such as a shell bracelet or glass beads" (1904:146).

4. Based, apparently, on his 1907 visit to the Batak, Cole cites the following incident to illustrate their negative feelings about "marriage of relatives": "A boy and a girl in the district back of Tinitian insisted upon marriage. They came from distant camps but were cousins. All attempts to dissuade them were unavailing and the elders finally consented, but not until they had caused the couple to sit beside a small basket of rice mixed with filth. A dog was brought and the couple was forced to eat with it from the dish—"since they are like dogs and do not observe relationship" (1945:61).

5. The question of local endogamy and exogamy is complicated by classificatory difficulties (see also Eder and Pagayona 1971:64–65). The local group for marriage purposes (and hence for umbay pairings) was traditionally not the small, bandlike group but the collectivity of such groups associated with a particular river and its watershed. Later, each such collectivity came together in the milieu of a reservation. Present-day local groups, or settlements, are essentially the much-depleted remnants of these aboriginal collectivities. Members of these remnant groups desire to be endogamous but there is today much marriage between them.

References

Aberle, David
1966 *The Peyote Religion among the Navajo*. Chicago: Aldine.
Adams, Richard N.
1974 "Harnessing Technological Development." *In* John J. Poggie and Robert M. Lynch, eds., *Rethinking Modernization*, pp. 37–68. Westport: Greenwood Press.
Adams, John W., and Alice Bee Kasakoff
1976 "Factors Underlying Endogamous Group Size." *In* Carol A. Smith, ed., *Regional Analysis*, vol. 2, *Social Systems*, pp. 149–173. New York: Academic Press.
Antonovsky, Aaron
1979 *Health, Stress, and Coping*. San Francisco: Jossey-Bass.
Appell, George N.
1969 "Social Anthropological Census for Cognatic Societies and Its Application to the Rungus of Northern Borneo," *Bijdragen tot de Taal-, Land- en Volkenkunde* 125:80–93.
1982 "The Health Consequences of Social Change: A Set of Postulates for Developing General Adaptation Theory." Paper presented at the National Conference on Social Stress Research, University of New Hampshire, October 11–12.
Audy, J. Ralph
1971 "Measurement and Diagnosis of Health." *In* Paul Shepard and Daniel McKinley, eds., *Environ/Mental: Essays on the Planet as Home*, pp. 140–162. Boston: Houghton Mifflin.

Bailey, Robert C., and Nadine R. Peacock
n.d.   "Efe Pygmies of Northeast Zaire: Subsistence Strategies in the
        Ituri Forest." *In* I. de Garine and G. A. Harrison, eds., *Un-
        certainty in the Food Supply*. New York: Cambridge University
        Press. In press.
Baker, Paul T.
1984   "The Adaptive Limits of Human Populations," *Man* 19:1–14.
Bayliss-Smith, Tim P.
1975   "Ontong Java: Depopulation and Repopulation." *In* Vern
        Carroll, ed., *Pacific Atoll Populations*, pp. 417–484. Honolulu:
        University of Hawaii Press.
Belshaw, Cyril S.
1976   *The Sorcerer's Apprentice*. New York: Pergamon.
Berkman, Lisa F.
1981   "Physical Health and the Social Environment: A Social
        Epidemiological Perspective." *In* Leon Eisenberg and Arthur
        Kleinman, eds., *The Relevance of Social Science for Medicine*, pp.
        51–75. Dordrecht, Holland: D. Reidel.
Berlin, Elois Ann, and Edward K. Markel
1977   "An Assessment of the Nutritional and Health Status of an
        Aguaruna Jivaro Community, Amazonas, Peru," *Ecology of
        Food and Nutrition* 6:69–81.
Berry, John W.
1980   "Acculturation as Varieties of Adaptation." *In* Amado M.
        Padilla, ed., *Acculturation: Theory, Models, and Some New
        Findings*, pp. 9–25. AAAS Selected Symposium 39. Boulder:
        Westview Press.
Beyer, H. Otley
1917   *Population of the Philippine Islands in 1916*. Manila: Philippine
        Education Company.
Bieliauskas, Linas A.
1982   *Stress and Its Relationship to Health and Illness*. Boulder:
        Westview.
Binford, Lewis R., and W. J. Chasko, Jr.
1976   "Nunamiut Demographic History: A Provocative Case."
        In Ezra Zubrow, ed., *Demographic Anthropology*, pp. 63–143.
        Albuquerque: University of New Mexico Press.
Birdsell, Joseph B.
1968   "Some Predictions for the Pleistocene Based on Equilibrium
        Systems among Recent Hunter-Gatherers." *In* Richard B. Lee
        and Irven DeVore, eds., *Man the Hunter*, pp. 229–240.
        Chicago: Aldine.

Blair, E. H., and A. J. Robertson
  1903–1909 *The Philippine Islands 1493–1898.* 55 vols. Cleveland: A. H. Clark Co.
Bodley, John H.
  1982 *Victims of Progress.* 2d ed. Palo Alto: Mayfield.
Bongaarts, John
  1980 "Does Malnutrition Affect Fecundity? A Summary of Evidence," *Science* 208:564–569.
Bossen, Laurel
  1983 "Sexual Stratification in Mesoamerica." *In* Carl Kendall, John Hawkins, and Laurel Bossen, eds., *Heritage of Conquest: Thirty Years Later,* pp. 35–71. Albuquerque: University of New Mexico Press.
Brain, Robert
  1972 *Into the Primitive Environment.* Englewood Cliffs: Prentice-Hall.
Bruner, Edward M.
  1976 "Tradition and Modernization in Batak Society." *In* George A. DeVos, ed., *Responses to Change: Society, Culture, and Personality,* pp. 234–252. New York: D. Van Nostrand.
Buchbinder, Georgeda
  1977 "Nutritional Stress and Postcontact Population Decline among the Maring of New Guinea." *In* Lawrence S. Greene, ed., *Malnutrition, Behavior, and Social Organization,* pp. 109–142. New York: Academic Press.
Cadeliña, Rowe V.
  1982 "Batak Interhousehold Food Sharing: A Systemic Analysis of Food Management of Marginal Agriculturalists in the Philippines." Ph.D. diss., Department of Anthropology, University of Hawaii.
Caplan, G.
  1974 *Support Systems and Community Mental Health: Lectures on Concept Development.* New York: Behavioral Publications.
Carey, Iskandar
  1976 *Orang Asli: The Aboriginal Tribes of Peninsular Malaysia.* Kuala Lumpur: Oxford University Press.
Cavalli-Sforza, L. L.
  1977 "Biological Research on African Pygmies." *In* G. A. Harrison, ed., *Population Structure and Human Variation,* pp. 273–284. New York: Cambridge University Press.
Chance, Norman A.
  1968 "Implications of Environmental Stress: Strategies of Develop-

mental Change in the North," *Archives of Environmental Health* 17:571–577.

Chen, E., and S. Cobb
1960 "Family Structure in Relation to Health and Disease," *Journal of Chronic Diseases* 12:544–567.

Cipriani, Lidio
1966 *The Andaman Islanders*. New York: Praeger.

Cobb, Sidney
1976 "Social Support as a Moderator of Life Stress," *Psychosomatic Medicine* 38:300–314.

Coelho, George V., and Paul I. Ahmed, eds.
1980 *Uprooting and Development: Dilemmas of Coping with Modernization*. New York: Plenum.

Cole, Fay-Cooper
1945 *The Peoples of Malaysia*. New York: D. Van Nostrand.

Commission of the Census
1939 *Census of the Philippines*. Philippine Commonwealth, Commission of the Census, Manila.

Conelly, W. Thomas
1983 "Upland Development in the Tropics: Alternative Economic Strategies in a Philippine Frontier Community." Ph.D. diss., University of California, Santa Barbara.
1985 "Copal and Rattan Collecting in the Philippines," *Economic Botany* 39:39–48.

Conklin, Harold C.
1949 "Preliminary Report on Field Work on the Islands of Mindoro and Palawan, Philippines," *American Anthropologist* 51:268–273.

Cooper, John M.
1940 "Andamanese-Semang-Eta Cultural Relations," *Primitive Man* 13:29–47.

Cordero, Narciso et al.
1956 "Philippine Physiological Standards: Body Weight in Relation to Height and Age for Adults," *Acta Medica Philipina* 13:417–440.
1981 *Woman the Gatherer*. New Haven: Yale University Press.

Dahlberg, Francis
1981 "Introduction." In Francis Dahlberg, ed., *Woman the Gatherer*, pp. 1–33. New Haven: Yale University Press.

Davis, Shelton H.
1977 *Victims of the Miracle*. New York: Cambridge University Press.

Deci, Edward L.
1980 *The Psychology of Self-Determination.* Lexington, Mass.: D. C. Heath and Co.

Dobyns, Henry F.
1966 "Estimating Aboriginal American Population: An Appraisal of Techniques with a New Hemispheric Estimate," *Current Anthropology* 7 : 395–449.

Dobzhansky, Theodosius
1974 "Chance and Creativity in Evolution." *In* F. J. Ayala and Theodosius Dobzhansky, eds., *Studies in the Philosophy of Biology,* pp. 309–339. Berkeley and Los Angeles: University of California Press.

Dohrenwend, Barbara S., and Bruce P. Dohrenwend, eds.
1974 *Stressful Life Events: Their Nature and Effects.* New York: Wiley.

Dole, Gertrude E.
1961 "The Influence of Population Density on the Development of Social Organization among the Amahuaca of Eastern Peru." Paper presented at the Annual Meeting of the American Anthropological Association, Philadelphia.

Draper, Patricia
1975 "!Kung Women: Contrasts in Sexual Egalitarianism in Foraging and Sedentary Contexts." *In* Rayna R. Reiter, ed., *Toward an Anthropology of Women,* pp. 77–109. New York: Monthly Review Press.

Dressler, William
1982 *Hypertension and Culture Change: Acculturation and Disease in the West Indies.* South Salem, Mass.: Redgrave.

Driver, Harold E.
1969 *Indians of North America.* 2d ed. Chicago: University of Chicago Press.

Dubos, René
1961 *Man Adapting.* New Haven: Yale University Press.

Dubos, René, and Jean Dubos
1952 *The White Plague.* Boston: Little, Brown.

Dunn, Fred L.
1972 "Intestinal Parasitism in Malayan Aborigines (Orang Asli)," *Bulletin of the World Health Organization* 46 : 99–113.

Durham, William H.
1979 "Toward a Coevolutionary Theory in Human Biology and Culture." *In* Napoleon A. Chagnon and William Irons, eds., *Evolutionary Biology and Human Social Behavior: An Anthropo-*

logical Perspective, pp. 39–59. North Scituate, Mass.: Duxbury Press.

Eder, James F.

1975   "Naming Practices and the Definition of Affines among the Batak of the Philippines," *Ethnology* 14:59–70.

1978   "The Caloric Returns to Food Collecting: Disruption and Change among the Batak of the Philippine Tropical Forest," *Human Ecology* 6:55–69.

1982   *Who Shall Succeed? Agricultural Development and Social Inequality on a Philippine Frontier.* New York: Cambridge University Press.

Eder, James F., and Ben Pagayona

1971   "Applications of a Social-Anthropological Census among the Batak of Palawan," *Philippine Sociological Review* 19:57–66.

Endicott, Karen Lampell

1979   "Batek Negrito Sex Roles." M.A. thesis, Australian National University, Canberra.

Endicott, Kirk M.

1974   "Batek Negrito Economy and Social Organization." Ph.D. diss., Harvard University, Cambridge.

1979a   "The Impact of Economic Modernization on the *Orang Asli* (Aborigines) of Northern Peninsular Malaysia." *In* J. J. Jackson and M. Rudner, eds., *Issues on Malaysian Development,* pp. 167–204. Singapore: Heinemann Educational Books.

1979b   *Batek Negrito Religion.* Oxford: Clarendon Press.

1984   "The Economy of the Batek of Malaysia: Annual and Historical Perspective," *Research in Economic Anthropology* 6:29–52.

Endicott, Kirk, and Karen Lampell Endicott

1983   "The Sociology of Land Use among the Batek of Malaysia." Paper presented at the Third International Conference on Hunting and Gathering Societies, Bad Homburg, West Germany, June 13–16.

Epstein, T. Scarlett

1968   *Capitalism, Primitive and Modern: Some Aspects of Tolai Economic Growth.* Manchester: Manchester University Press.

Erasmus, Charles J.

1977   *In Search of the Common Good.* New York: Free Press.

Estioko-Griffin, Agnes, and P. Bion Griffin

1981   "Woman the Hunter." *In* Frances Dahlberg, ed., *Woman the Gatherer,* pp. 121–152. New Haven: Yale University Press.

Farrington, Keith
  1982   "The General Stress Model: An Alternative to the Life Events
          Approach to the Study of Social Stress." Paper presented at
          the National Conference on Social Stress Research, University
          of New Hampshire, October 11–12.
Feeney, Griffith
  1975   "Demographic Concepts and Techniques for the Study of
          Small Populations." In Vern Carroll, ed., *Pacific Atoll Popula-*
          tions, pp. 20–63. Honolulu: University of Hawaii Press.
Fernandez, Carlos A., II, and Frank Lynch, S. J.
  1972   "The Tasaday: Cave-Dwelling Food Gatherers of South
          Cotabato, Mindanao," *Philippine Sociological Review* 20:279–
          313.
Field Museum
  1983   "The Batak of the Philippines" (museum display). Robert F.
          Cummings Expedition. Field Museum of Natural History,
          Chicago.
Finney, Ben R.
  1973   *Big Men and Business: Entrepreneurship and Economic Growth*
          in the New Guinea Highlands. Canberra: Australian National
          University Press.
Fix, Alan
  1982   "Genetic Structure of the Semai." In Michael H. Crawford and
          James H. Mielke, eds., *Current Developments in Anthropological*
          Genetics. Vol. 2, *Ecology and Population Structure*, pp. 179–204.
          New York: Plenum.
Flannery, Kent V.
  1968   "Archaeological Systems Theory and Early Mesoamerica." In
          Betty Meggers, ed., *Anthropological Archaeology in the Amer-*
          icas, pp. 67–87. Washington, D.C.: Anthropological Society of
          Washington.
Fleuret, Patrick, and Anne Fleuret
  1980   "Nutrition, Consumption, and Agricultural Change," *Human*
          Organization 39:250–260.
FNRC
  1974   *Food Composition Table, Handbook I.* 4th rev. Manila: National
          Science Development Board.
  1975   "Weight for Height for Filipinos (25–65 years)." Publication
          No. 159a. Manila: National Science Development Board.

FNRI
  1981   *First Nationwide Nutrition Survey: Philippines 1978.* Manila:
         National Science Development Board.
Fox, Richard G.
  1969   "'Professional Primitives': Hunters and Gatherers of Nuclear
         South Asia," *Man in India* 49:139–160.
Fox, Robert B.
  1952   "The Pinatubo Negritos: Their Useful Plants and Material
         Culture," *Philippine Journal of Science* 81:173–414.
  1967   "The Archaeological Record of Chinese Influences in the Phil-
         ippines," *Philippine Studies* 1:41–62.
  1971   "The Function of Religion in Society: The Christian Worker
         and Social Change." *In* Peter G. Gowing and William Henry
         Scott, eds., *Acculturation in the Philippines: Essays on Changing
         Societies*, pp. 1–8. Quezon City, Philippines: New Day
         Publishers.
  1982   *Religion and Society among the Tagbanua of Palawan Island,
         Philippines.* Monograph No. 9. Manila: National Museum.
Fox, Robert B., and Elizabeth H. Flory
  1974   "The Filipino People" (map). Manila: National Museum.
Freeman, Derek
  1955   *Report on the Iban.* Sarawak: Government Printing Office.
Fried, Morton H.
  1975   *The Notion of Tribe.* Menlo Park, Cal.: Cummings.
Friedlander, Judith
  1975   *Being Indian in Hueyapan: A Study of Forced Identity in Con-
         temporary Mexico.* New York: St. Martin's Press.
Frisch, R. E.
  1978   "Population, Food Intake, and Fertility: Historical Evidence for
         a Direct Effect of Nutrition on Reproductive Ability," *Science*
         199:22–29.
Frisch, R. E., and J. W. McArthur
  1974   "Menstrual Cycles: Fatness as a Determinant of Minimum
         Weight for Their Maintenance or Onset," *Science*
         185:949–951.
Garvan, John M.
  1955   "Pygmy Personality," *Anthropos* 50:769–796.
  1963   *The Negritos of the Philippines.* Horn-Wien: Verlag Ferdinand
         Berger.

Glass, D. C., and J. E. Singer
  1972 *Urban Stress: Experiments on Noise and Social Stressors.* New York: Academic Press.

Gold, P. W., W. T. Gwirtsman, P. C. Avgerinos, L. K. Nieman, W. T. Gallucci, W. Kaye, D. Jimerson, M. Ebert, R. Rittmaster, L. Loriaux, and G. Chrousos
  1986 "Abnormal Hypothalamic-Pituitary-Adrenal Function in Anorexia Nervosa," *New England Journal of Medicine* 314:1335–1342.

Gomes, Alberto G.
  1982 "Ecological Adaptation and Population Change: Semang Foragers and Temuan Horticulturalists in West Malaysia." Research Report No. 12, East-West Environment and Policy Institute. Honolulu: East-West Center.

Goodland, Robert
  1982 *Tribal Peoples and Economic Development: Human Ecologic Considerations.* Washington, D.C.: World Bank.

Gould, Richard A., Don D. Fowler, and Catherine S. Fowler
  1972 "Diggers and Doggers: Parallel Failures in Economic Acculturation," *Southwestern Journal of Anthropology* 283:265–281.

Gould, Stephen Jay, and Richard Lewontin
  1979 "The Spandrels of San Marco and the Panglossian Paradigm: A Critique of the Adaptationist Programme," *Proceedings of the Royal Society of London* B205:581–598.

Greenwood, Davydd J.
  1984 *The Taming of Evolution: The Persistence of Nonevolutionary Views in the Study of Humans.* Ithaca: Cornell University Press.

Griffin, P. Bion
  1981 "Northern Luzon Agta Subsistence and Settlement," *Pilipinas* 2:26–42.
  1984 "Agta Forager Women of the Philippines," *Cultural Survival Quarterly* 8:21–23.

Hammel, E. A., C. K. McDaniel, and K. W. Wachter
  1979 "Demographic Consequences of Incest Tabus: A Microsimulation Analysis," *Science* 205:972–977.

Hansen, Art, and Anthony Oliver-Smith, eds.
  1982 *Involuntary Migration and Resettlement: The Problems and Responses of Dislocated People.* Boulder: Westview.

Harpending, Henry, and LuAnn Wandsnider
1982   "Population Structures of Ghanzi and Ngamiland !Kung." *In*
        Michael Crawford and James Mielke, eds., *Current Develop-
        ments in Anthropological Genetics*, pp. 29–50. New York:
        Plenum Press.

Harrell, Barbara B.
1981   "Lactation and Menstruation in Cultural Perspective," *Amer-
        ican Anthropologist* 83:796–824.

Hart, John A.
1978   "From Subsistence to Market: A Case Study of Mbuti Net
        Hunters," *Human Ecology* 6:325–353.

Headland, Thomas N.
1975   "The Casiguran Dumagats Today and in 1936," *Philippine
        Quarterly of Culture and Society* 3:245–257.
1984   "Agta Negritos of the Philippines," *Cultural Survival* 8:29–31.
1985   "Imposed Values and Aid Rejection among Casiguran Agta."
        In P. Bion Griffin and Agnes Estioko-Griffin, eds., *The Agta of
        Northeastern Luzon: Recent Studies*, pp. 102–118. Cebu City,
        Philippines: University of San Carlos.
1986   "Why Foragers Do Not Become Farmers: A Historical Study
        of a Changing Ecosystem and Its Effect on a Negrito Hunter-
        Gatherer Group in the Philippines." Ph.D. diss., University of
        Hawaii, Honolulu.

Hitchcock, Robert K.
1982   "Patterns of Sedentism among the Basarwa of Eastern
        Botswana." *In* Eleanor Leacock and Richard Lee, eds.,
        Politics and History in Band Societies, pp. 223–267. New York:
        Cambridge University Press.
1985   "The Plight of Indigenous Peoples," *Social Education*
        49:457–462.

Hoffman, Carl L.
1984   "Punan Foragers in the Trade Networks of Southeast Asia." *In*
        Carmel Schrire, ed., *Past and Present in Hunter-Gatherer Studies*,
        pp. 123–149. Orlando: Academic Press.

Hogbin, H. Ian
1930   "The Problem of Depopulation in Melanesia as Applied to
        Ongtong Java (Solomon Islands)," *Journal of Polynesian Society*
        39:43–66.

Holmes, Thomas H.
1956   "Multidiscipline Studies in Tuberculosis." *In* Phineas J. Sparer,

ed., *Personality, Stress, and Tuberculosis*, pp. 65–152. New York: International Universities Press.

Holmes, Thomas H., and Richard H. Rahe

1967 "The Social Readjustment Rating Scale," *Journal of Psychosomatic Research* 11:213–218.

Houston, B. Kent

1972 "Control over Stress, Locus of Control, and Response to Stress," *Journal of Personality and Social Psychology* 21:249–255.

Howell, Nancy

1973 "The Feasibility of Demographic Studies in 'Anthropological' Populations." *In* M. H. Crawford and P. L. Workman, eds., *Methods and Theories of Anthropological Genetics*, pp. 249–262. Albuquerque: University of New Mexico Press.

1979 *Demography of the Dobe !Kung.* New York: Academic Press.

Howell, Signe

1983 "Chewong Women in Transition: The Effects of Monitisation on a Hunter-Gatherer Society in Malaysia." University of Kent Centre of South-East Asian Studies, Occasional Paper 1, Women and Development in Southeast Asia, pp. 46–80.

1984 *Society and Cosmos: Chewong of Peninsular Malaysia.* New York: Oxford University Press.

Huffman, S. L., A. K. M. Chowdhury, and W. H. Mosley

1978 "Postpartum Amenorrhea: How Is It Affected by Maternal Nutritional Status?" *Science* 200:1155–1157.

Huss-Ashmore, Rebecca

1980 "Fat and Fertility: Demographic Implications of Differential Fat Storage," *Yearbook of Physical Anthropology* 23:65–91.

Hutterer, Karl L.

1977 "Prehistoric Trade and the Evolution of Philippine Societies: A Reconsideration." *In* Karl L. Hutterer, ed., *Economic Exchange and Social Interaction in Southeast Asia: Perspectives from Prehistory, History, and Ethnography*, pp. 177–196. Michigan Papers on South and Southeast Asia, No. 13. Ann Arbor: Center for South and Southeast Asia Studies, University of Michigan.

1983 "The Natural and Cultural History of Southeast Asian Agriculture: Ecological and Evolutionary Considerations," *Anthropos* 78:169–212.

Isaac, Barry L.

1977 "The Siriono of Eastern Bolivia: A Reexamination," *Human*

Ecology 5:137—154.

Jackson, Joan K.
1954 "The Problem of Alcoholic Tuberculosis Patients." *In* P. F. Sparer, ed., *Personality, Stress, and Tuberculosis*, pp. 504—538. New York: International Universities Press.

Jelliffe, D. B.
1966 *The Assessment of the Nutritional Status of the Community.* WHO Monograph Series, No. 54. Geneva: World Health Organization.

Jochim, Michael A.
1981 *Strategies for Survival.* New York: Academic Press.

Johnson, Alan W.
1975 "Time Allocation in a Machiguenga Community," *Ethnology* 14:301—310.

Johnson, Alan W., and Orna R. Johnson
1975 "Male/Female Relations and the Organization of Work in a Machiguenga Community," *American Ethnologist* 2:634—648.

Johnson, James H., and Irwin G. Sarason
1979 "Moderator Variables in Life Stress Research." *In* I. G. Sarason and C. D. Spielberger, eds., *Stress and Anxiety*, vol. 6, pp. 151—167. New York: Hemisphere.

Kaplan, Howard B.
1983 "Psychosocial Distress in Sociological Context: Toward A General Theory of Psychosocial Stress." *In* Howard B. Kaplan, ed., *Psychosocial Stress*, pp. 195—264. New York: Academic Press.

Kaplan, B. H., J. Cassel, and S. Gore
1977 "Social Support and Health," *Medical Care* (Supplement) 15:47—58.

Kelly, Robert L.
1983 "Hunter-Gatherer Mobility Strategies," *Journal of Anthropological Research* 39:277—306.

Kessler, Ronald C., Richard H. Price, and Camille B. Wortman
1985 "Social Factors in Psychopathology: Stress, Social Support, and Coping Processes," *Annual Review of Psychology* 36:531—572.

Kress, Jonathan H.
1977 "Contemporary and Prehistoric Subsistence Patterns on Palawan." *In* William Wood, ed., *Cultural-Ecological Perspectives on Southeast .Asia*, pp. 29—47. Ohio University, Center for International Studies, Southeast Asia Series No. 41.

Kroeber, Alfred L.
  1943 "Peoples of the Philippines." American Museum of Natural History, Handbook Series 8, rev. ed., pp. 1–244.
Landor, A. Henry Savage
  1904 *The Gems of the East.* New York: Harper and Brothers Publishers.
Larkin, John A.
  1972 *The Pampangans.* Berkeley, Los Angeles, London: University of California Press.
Lazarus, Richard S.
  1966 *Psychological Stress and the Coping Process.* New York: McGraw-Hill.
Leacock, Eleanor
  1978 "Women's Status in Egalitarian Society: Implications for Social Evolution," *Current Anthropology* 19:247–255.
LeBar, Frank M., ed.
  1975 *Ethnic Groups of Insular Southeast Asia.* Vol. 2, *Philippines and Formosa.* New Haven: HRAF Press.
Lee, Richard B.
  1972 "Population Growth and the Beginnings of Sedentary Life among the !Kung Bushmen." *In* Brian Spooner, ed., *Population Growth: Anthropological Implications,* pp. 329–342. Cambridge: Massachusetts Institute of Technology Press.
  1979 *The !Kung San: Men, Women, and Work in a Foraging Society.* New York: Cambridge University Press.
Lee, Richard B., and Irven DeVore, eds.
  1968 *Man the Hunter.* Chicago: Aldine.
Levine, Sol, and Norman A. Scotch
  1970 "Social Stress." *In* Sol Levine and Norman A. Scotch, eds., *Social Stress,* pp. 1–16. Chicago: Aldine.
Lin, Nan, Stephen C. Light, and Mary Woelfel
  1982 "The Buffering Effects of Social Support: A Theoretical Framework and an Empirical Investigation." Paper presented at the National Conference on Social Stress Research, University of New Hampshire, October 11–12.
Linsky, Arnold S., and Murray A. Straus
  1982 "Measuring Stress in Social Systems." Paper presented at the National Conference on Social Stress Research, University of New Hampshire, October 11–12.
Livi, L.
  1949 "Considerations Theoriques et Practiques sur le Concept de

'Minimum de population,'" *Population* 4 : 754–756.

Loucks, A. B., and S. M. Horvath
  1985 "Athletic Amenorrhea: A Review," *Medicine and Science in Sports and Exercise* 17 : 56–72.

Love, Thomas
  1983 "To What are Humans Adapting?" *Reviews in Anthropology* 10 : 1–8.

Lumsden, Paul D.
  1975 "Toward a Systems Model of Stress Feedback from an Anthropological Study of the Impact of Ghana's Volta River Project." *In* Irwin G. Sarason and Charles D. Speilberger, eds., *Stress and Anxiety*, vol. 2, pp. 191–228. Washington, D.C.: Hemisphere/Wiley.

MacArthur, Norma
  1968 *Island Populations of the Pacific.* Honolulu: University of Hawaii Press.

MacCluer, Jean Walters, and Bennett Dyke
  1976 "On the Minimum Size of Endogamous Populations," *Social Biology* 23 : 1–12.

McDonagh, Sean
  1983 "Modernization, Multinationals, and the Tribal Filipino," *Solidarity* 4 : 73–82.

McFalls, Joseph A., and Marguerite Harvey McFalls
  1984 *Disease and Fertility.* Orlando: Academic Press.

McFarland, David D.
  1970 "Effects of Group Size on the Availability of Marriage Partners," *Demography* 7 : 411–415.

McGrath, Joseph E.
  1970 "A Conceptual Formulation for Research on Stress." *In* J. E. McGrath, ed., *Social and Psychological Factors in Stress*, pp. 10–15. New York: Holt, Rinehart, and Winston.

Malina, R. M., and J. M. Himes
  1977 "Seasonality of Births in a Rural Zapotec Municipio, 1945–1970," *Human Biology* 49 : 125–137.

Marche, Alfred
  1970 *Luzon and Palawan.* First published 1883. Translated from the French by Carmen Ojeda and Jovita Castro. Manila: Filipiniana Book Guild.

Marris, Peter
  1974 *Loss and Change.* New York: Pantheon Books.

Menkin, J., J. Trussell, and S. Watkins
1981 "The Nutrition-Fertility Link: An Evaluation of the Evidence," *Journal of Interdisciplinary History* 9:425–441.
Miller, E. Y.
1905 "The Bataks of Palawan." Philippines Department of the Interior, Ethnological Survey Publications 2:179–189.
Moran, Emilio F.
1979 *Human Adaptability: An Introduction to Ecological Anthropology.* North Scituate: Duxbury.
Morris, Brian
1982 "The Family, Group Structuring, and Trade among South Indian Hunter-Gatherers." *In* Eleanor Leacock and Richard Lee, eds., *Politics and History in Band Societies*, pp. 171–188. New York: Cambridge University Press.
Mosher, Steven W.
1979 "Birth Seasonality among Peasant Cultivators: The Interrelationship of Workload, Diet, and Fertility," *Human Ecology* 7:151–181.
Murphy, Richard F.
1958 "Mundurucu Religion," *University of California Publications in Archaeology and Ethnology* 49:1–154.
1960 *Headhunter's Heritage: Social and Economic Change among the Mundurucu Indians.* Berkeley and Los Angeles: University of California Press.
National Census and Statistics Office
1970 Census of the Philippines. Manila: Bureau of Printing.
1980 Census of the Philippines. Manila: Bureau of Printing.
National Economic and Development Authority (NEDA)
1980 *Philippine Statistical Yearbook.* Manila: National Economic and Development Authority.
Neel, James V., and Kenneth M. Weiss
1975 "The Genetic Structure of a Tribal Population, the Yanomama Indians," XII Biodemographic Studies, *American Journal of Physical Anthropology* 42:25–52.
Pearlin, Leonard I.
1983 "Role Strains and Personal Stress." *In* Howard B. Kaplan, ed., *Psychosocial Stress*, pp. 3–32. New York: Academic Press.
Pentony, B.
1953 "Psychological Causes of Depopulation in Primitive Groups," *Oceania* 24:142–145.

Peterson, Jean T.
  1976   "Folk Traditions and Inter-ethnic Relations." *In* A. Kaeppler and H. Arlo Nimmo, eds., *Directions in Pacific Oral Literature*, pp. 319–330. Honolulu: Bishop Museum Press.
  1978   "Hunter-Gatherer/Farmer Exchange," *American Anthropologist* 80:335–351.

Rahman, Rodolf
  1963   "The Negritos of the Philippines and the Early Spanish Missionaries." *In* Festschrift Paul J. Schebesta, *Studia Instituti Anthropos* 18:137–157.

Rai, Navin Kumar
  1982   "From Forest to Field: A Study of Philippine Negrito Foragers in Transition." Ph.D. diss., University of Hawaii, Honolulu.

Rambo, A. Terry
  1982   "Orang Asli Adaptive Strategies: Implications for Malaysian Natural Resource Development Planning." *In* Colin McAndrews and Chia Lin Sien, eds., *Too Rapid Rural Development: Perceptions and Perspectives from Southeast Asia*, pp. 251–299. Athens: Ohio University Press.
  1984   "Why Are the Semang? Ecology and Ethnogenesis in Peninsular Malaysia." Paper presented at the Conference on Ethnicity and the Control of Natural Resources in Southeast Asia, Ann Arbor, Michigan, August 22–24.

Reed, William A.
  1904   "Negritos of Zambales." Department of the Interior, Ethnological Survey Publications, vol. 2, part 1, pp. 1–90. Manila: Bureau of Printing.

Rice, Delbert, and Rufino Tima
  1973   *A Pattern for Development*. Quezon City, Philippines: Christian Institute for Ethnic Studies in Asia.

Rivers, W. H. R.
  1922   "The Psychological Factor." *In* W. H. R. Rivers, ed., *Essays on the Depopulation of Melanesia*, pp. 84–113. London: Cambridge University Press.

Rocamora, Joel
  1979   "The Political Uses of PANAMIN," *Southeast Asia Chronicle* 67:11–21.

Saffirio, John, and Raymond Hames
  1983   "The Forest and the Highway." *In* Report No. 11, *The Impact of Contact: Two Yanomamo Case Studies*, pp. 1–52. Cambridge, Mass.: Cultural Survival, Inc.

Saleeby, Najeeb M.
1908   "The History of Sulu." Division of Ethnological Publications,
       vol. 4, part 2. Manila: Bureau of Printing.
Salisbury, Richard F.
1970   *Vunamami*. Berkeley, Los Angeles, London: University of
       California Press.
Savishinsky, Joel S.
1974   *The Trail of the Hare: Life and Stress in an Arctic Community*.
       New York: Gordon and Breach.
Schebesta, Paul
1952–1957   *Die Negrito Asiens*. 3 vols. Vienna-Modling: St. Gabriel
       Verlag.
Schrire, Carmel
1980   "An Inquiry into the Evolutionary Status and Apparent Iden-
       tity of San Hunter-Gatherers," *Human Ecology* 8:9–32.
Scott, Alan, and Robert Howard
1970   "Models of Stress." *In* Sol Levine and Norman A. Scotch, eds.,
       Social Stress, pp. 259–278. Chicago: Aldine.
Scrimshaw, N. S., C. E. Taylor, and J. E. Gordon
1968   *Interactions of Nutrition and Infection*. Geneva: WHO.
Scudder, Thayer
1975   "Resettlement." *In* N. F. Stanley and M. P. Alpers, eds., *Man-
       made Lakes and Human Health*, pp. 453–471. London:
       Academic Press for the Institute of Biology.
Scudder, Thayer, and Elizabeth Colson
1982   "From Welfare to Development: A Conceptual Framework for
       the Analysis of Dislocated People." *In* Art Hansen and
       Anthony Oliver Smith, eds., *Involuntary Migration and Resettle-
       ment*, pp. 267–287. Boulder: Westview.
Seligman, M. E. P.
1975   *Helplessness: On Depression, Development, and Death*. San Fran-
       cisco: Freeman.
Shangold, M. M.
1984   "Effects of Exercise on Reproductive Function," *Advances in
       Clinical Obstetrics and Gynecology* 2:146–157.
Shimizu, Hiromu
1983   "Communicating with Spirits: A Study of the *Manganito*
       Seance among the Southwestern Pinatubo Negritos," *East
       Asian Cultural Studies* 22:129–167.
Shkilnyk, Anastasia M.
1985   *A Poison Stronger than Love: The Destruction of an Ojibwa Com-*

munity. New Haven: Yale University Press.

Solheim, Wilhelm G., II
  1981   "Philippine Prehistory." *In* G. Casal et al., eds., *The People and Art of the Philippines*, pp. 17–83. Museum of Cultural History, University of California.

Spencer, J. E.
  1966   *Shifting Cultivation in Southeast Asia*. Berkeley and Los Angeles: University of California Press.

Spurr, G. B.
  1983   "Nutritional Status and Physical Work Capacity," *Yearbook of Physical Anthropology* 26:1–35.

Stearman, Allyn MacLean
  1984   "The Yuqui Connection: Another Look at Siriono Deculturation," *American Anthropologist* 86:630–650.

Stone, A. A., and J. M. Neale
  1982   "Development of a Methodology for Assessing Daily Experiences." *In* A. Baum and J. Singer, eds., *Advances in Environmental Psychology*. Vol. 4, *Environment and Health*, pp. 49–89. New York: Erlbaum.

Sutlive, Vinson H., Jr.
  1978   *The Iban of Sarawak*. Arlington Heights, Ill.: AHM Publishing Corporation.

Swedlund, Alan C.
  1978   "Historical Demography as Population Ecology," *Annual Review of Anthropology* 7:137–173.

Swift, Jeremy
  1978   "Marginal Societies at the Modern Frontier in Asia and the Arctic," *Development and Change* 9:3–19.

Taylor, John R.
  1977   "Diet, Health, and Economy: Some Consequences of Planned Social Change in an Aboriginal Community." *In* R. M. Bernt, ed., *Aborigines and Change*, pp. 147–158. Atlantic Highlands, N.J.: Humanities Press.

Thomas, Elizabeth Marshall
  1965   *The Harmless People*. New York: Random House.

Tobias, P. V.
  1964   "Bushman Hunter-Gatherers: A Study in Human Ecology." *In* D. H. S. Davis, ed., *Ecological Studies in Southern Africa*, pp. 69–86. The Hague: Mouton.

Tonkinson, Robert
  1974   *The Jigalong Mob: Aboriginal Victors of the Desert Crusade.*

Menlo Park, Cal.: Cummings Publishing Co.

Trimble, Joseph E.

1980 "Forced Migration: Its Impact on Shaping Coping Strategies." *In* George V. Coelho and Paul I. Ahmed, eds., *Uprooting and Development: Dilemmas of Coping with Modernization,* pp. 449–478. New York: Plenum.

Trusell, James

1978 "Menarche and Fatness: Reexamination of the Critical Body Composition Hypothesis," *Science* 200:1506–1509.

Truswell, A. Stewart, and John D. L. Hansen

1968 "Medical and Nutritional Studies of !Kung Bushmen in Northwest Botswana: A Preliminary Report," *South African Medical Journal* 42:1338–1339.

1976 "Medical Research among the !Kung." *In* Richard B. Lee and Irven DeVore, eds., *Kalahari Hunter-Gatherers,* pp. 166–194. Chicago: Aldine.

Turnbull, Colin M.

1965 "The Mbuti Pygmies: An Ethnographic Survey," *Anthropological Papers of the American Museum of Natural History* 501:139–282.

1972 *The Mountain People.* New York: Simon and Schuster.

1983 *The Mbuti Pygmies: Change and Adaptation.* New York: Holt, Rinehart, and Winston.

Turner, R. Jay

1983 "Direct, Indirect, and Moderating Effects of Social Support on Psychological Distress and Associated Conditions." *In* Howard B. Kaplan, ed., *Psychosocial Stress,* pp. 105–155. New York: Academic Press.

Van Arkadie, Brian

1978 "The Future of Vulnerable Societies," *Development and Change* 9:161–174.

Van Arsdale, Peter W.

1978 "Population Dynamics among Asmat Hunter-Gatherers of New Guinea: Data, Methods, Comparisons," *Human Ecology* 6:435–467.

1981 "The Elderly Asmat of New Guinea." *In* Pamela T. Amcee and Stevan Harrell, eds., *Other Ways of Growing Old,* pp. 111–123. Stanford: Stanford University Press.

Vanoverbergh, Morice

1937–1938 "Negritos of Eastern Luzon," *Anthropos* 32:905–928, 33:119–164.

Venturello, Manuel H.
1907   "Manners and Customs of the Tagbanuas and Other Tribes of the Island of Palawan, Philippines." Mrs. Edward Y. Miller, trans. *Smithsonian Miscellaneous Collections* 48:514–558.

Von Fürer-Haimendorf, Christoph
1982   *Tribes of India: The Struggle for Survival.* Berkeley, Los Angeles, London: University of California Press.

Wagley, Charles
1977   *A Welcome of Tears.* New York: Oxford University Press.

Wallace, Anthony F. C.
1967   "Revitalization Movements in Development." *In* Richard J. Ward, ed., *The Challenge of Development: Theory and Practice,* pp. 448–454. Chicago: Aldine.
1970   *The Death and Rebirth of the Seneca.* New York: Alfred A. Knopf.

Warner, Katherine
1979   "Walking on Two Feet: Tagbanwa Adaptation to Philippine Society." Ph.D. diss., University of California, Santa Barbara.

Warren, Charles P.
1959   "A Vocabulary of the Batak of Palawan." Transcript No. 7, Philippine Studies Program, University of Chicago.
1961   "The Batak of Palawan: A Culture in Transition." M.A. thesis, Department of Anthropology, University of Chicago.
1964   "The Batak of Palawan: A Culture in Transition." Research Series No. 3, Philippine Studies Program, University of Chicago.
1975   "Batak." *In* Frank M. LeBar, ed., *Ethnic Groups of Insular Southeast Asia.* Vol. 2, *Philippines and Formosa,* pp. 68–70. New Haven: HRAF Press.

Warren, James Francis
1981   *The Sulu Zone, 1768–1898.* Singapore: Singapore University Press.

Waterlow, J. C., R. Buzina, J. M. Lane, M. Z. Nichaman, and J. M. Tanner
1977   "The Presentation and Use of Height and Weight Data for Comparing the Nutritional Status of Groups of Children Under the Age of Ten Years," *Bulletin of the World Health Organization* 55:489–498.

Weiss, Kenneth M.
1976   "Demographic Theory and Anthropological Inference," *Annual Review of Anthropology* 5:351–381.

Wentz, A. C.
1977 "Psychogenic Amenorrhea and Anorexia Nervosa. *In* R. Givens, ed., *Endocrine Causes of Menstrual Disorders*, pp. 87–113. Chicago: Year Book Medical Publishers.

Wernstedt, Frederik L., and J. E. Spencer
1967 *The Philippine Island World: A Physical, Cultural, and Regional Geography.* Berkeley and Los Angeles: University of California Press.

White, Isobel M.
1977 "From Camp to Village: Some Problems in Adaptation." *In* R. M. Berndt, ed., *Aborigines and Change*, pp. 100–105. Atlantic Highlands, N.J.: Humanities Press.

Wilmsen, Edwin N.
1978 "Seasonal Effects of Dietary Intake on Kalahari San," *Federation Proceedings of American Societies for Experimental Biology* 37:65–72.

Wirsing, Rolf L.
1985 "The Health of Traditional Societies and the Effects of Acculturation," *Current Anthropology* 26:303–322.

Wobst, H. Martin
1975 "The Demography of Finite Populations and the Origins of the Incest Taboo." *In* Alan Swedlund, ed., *Population Studies in Archaeology and Biological Anthropology: A Symposium*, pp. 75–81. Special Supplement to *American Antiquity* 40(2), part 2, memoir 30.

Wolf, S., and H. Goodell
1968 *Harold G. Wolff's Stress and Disease.* 2d ed. Springfield, Ill.: Thomas.

Wood, Corinne Shear
1979 *Human Sickness and Health.* Palo Alto: Mayfield.

Worsley, Peter
1957 *The Trumpet Shall Sound: A Study of "Cargo Cults" in Melanesia.* London: Macgibbon and Kee.

Index

Designer: U.C. Press Staff
Compositor: Asco Trade Typesetting Limited
Text: 12/13 Palatino
Display: Palatino
Printer: McNaughton & Gunn, Inc.
Binder: John H. Dekker & Sons